Smaller C
Lean Code for Small Machines

Marc Loy

Beijing · Boston · Farnham · Sebastopol · Tokyo

Smaller C

by Marc Loy

Published by O'Reilly Media, Inc., 1005 Gravenstein Highway North, Sebastopol, CA 95472.

O'Reilly books may be purchased for educational, business, or sales promotional use. Online editions are also available for most titles (*http://oreilly.com*). For more information, contact our corporate/institutional sales department: 800-998-9938 or *corporate@oreilly.com*.

Acquisitions Editor: Amanda Quinn	**Indexer:** nSight, Inc.
Development Editor: Amelia Blevins	**Interior Designer:** David Futato
Production Editor: Daniel Elfanbaum	**Cover Designer:** Karen Montgomery
Copyeditor: nSight, Inc.	**Illustrator:** Kate Dullea
Proofreader: Piper Editorial Consulting, LLC	

June 2021:   First Edition

Revision History for the First Edition
2021-05-27:   First Release

See *http://oreilly.com/catalog/errata.csp?isbn=9781098100339* for release details.

978-1-098-10033-9

[LSI]

Table of Contents

Preface

In a world where new JavaScript frameworks come and go almost daily, why would you dive into an aging, bare-bones language like C? Well, for one, if you hope to keep up with all those framework fads (ouch, opinion alert), you might want a background in just such aging, bare-bones technologies that provide a foundation for so many "modern" languages. Did you look up popular programming languages on a site like TIOBE (*https://oreil.ly/ZTdwN*) and find C consistently at the top? Maybe you're interested in the amazingly advanced video cards and want to see how the software that drives them works. Or perhaps you're exploring newer—and much smaller—gadgets like Arduinos and heard that C is the right tool for the job.

No matter the reason, it's great to have you here. All of those reasons are valid ones, by the way. C is a foundational language and understanding its syntax and quirks will give you a very long-lived computer language literacy that will help you pick up new languages and styles more easily. C (and its cousin C++) are still widely used when writing low-level code for device drivers or operating systems. And the Internet of Things is breathing new life into microcontrollers with limited resources. C is a great fit for wringing the most of those tiny environments.

While I'll be focusing on that last idea of writing clean, tight code for tiny, limited machines, I'll still start with the basics of computer programming and cover a variety of rules and patterns that apply to C anywhere you might find it.

How to Use This Book

This book aims to cover all the basics of good C programming for any of the situations mentioned above. We'll look at control structures, operators, functions, and other elements of C's syntax along with examples of alternate patterns that can shave a few bytes off the size of your compiled program. We'll also be looking at the Arduino environment as a great application for lean C code. To best enjoy the Arduino section, you should have some basic experience with building simple circuits and using components like LEDs and resistors.

Here's a preview of the chapters:

Chapter 1, The ABCs of C
A brief look at the history of the C language and steps to set up your development environment.

Chapter 2, Storing and Stating
An introduction to statements in C, including basic I/O, variables, and operators.

Chapter 3, Flow of Control
Here I cover branching and looping statements and go a little deeper on variables and their scope.

Chapter 4, Bits and (Many) Bytes
A quick return to storing data. I show you C's facilities for manipulating individual bits and storing lots of bigger things in arrays.

Chapter 5, Functions
I'll look at how to break up your code into manageable chunks.

Chapter 6, Pointers and References
Getting a little more advanced, I create more complex data structures and learn how to pass them to, and return them from, functions.

Chapter 7, Libraries
Learn how to find and use popular bits of code that can help you with common or intricate tasks.

Chapter 8, Real-World C With Arduino
The real fun begins! We'll set up the Arduino development environment and make some LEDs blink.

Chapter 9, Smaller Systems
Try out several electronic peripherals including sensors, buttons, and LCD displays with complete Arduino projects.

Chapter 10, Faster Code
Learn some tricks for writing code especially designed to help small processors get the most out of their resources.

Chapter 11, Custom Libraries
Build on your C library skills with tips and tricks for writing friendly, well-documented libraries compatible with the Arduino IDE.

Chapter 12, Next Next Steps
Try a quick Internet of Things project with a few parting thoughts and some ideas for what to try next as you continue to improve your lean coding skills.

The appendices include a handy collection of links to the hardware and software I use, as well as information on downloading and configuring the C and Arduino examples shown throughout the book.

Conventions Used in This Book

The following typographical conventions are used in this book:

Italic
> Indicates new terms, URLs, email addresses, filenames, and file extensions.

`Constant width`
> Used for program listings, as well as within paragraphs to refer to program elements such as variable or function names, databases, data types, environment variables, statements, and keywords.

`Constant width bold`
> Shows commands or other text that should be typed literally by the user.

`Constant width italic`
> Shows text that should be replaced with user-supplied values or by values determined by context.

 This element signifies a tip or suggestion.

 This element signifies a general note.

 This element indicates a warning or caution.

Using Code Examples

Many of the code examples in this book are quite succinct, and you'll often benefit from typing them in by hand. But that isn't always fun and sometimes you want to start with a known, working copy and modify stuff. You can grab the source for all of the examples from GitHub at *https://github.com/l0y/smallerc*. Appendix A has detailed instructions on downloading the code and setting up the files for use with your development environment.

If you have a technical question or a problem using the code examples, please send an email to *bookquestions@oreilly.com*.

This book is here to help you get your job done. In general, you may use the example code offered with this book in your programs and documentation. You do not need to contact us for permission unless you're reproducing a significant portion of the code. For example, writing a program that uses several chunks of code from this book does not require permission. Selling or distributing examples from O'Reilly books does require permission. Answering a question by citing this book and quoting example code does not require permission. Incorporating a significant amount of example code from this book into your product's documentation does require permission.

We appreciate, but generally do not require, attribution. An attribution usually includes the title, author, publisher, and ISBN. For example: "*Smaller C* by Marc Loy (O'Reilly). Copyright 2021 Marc Loy, 978-1-098-10033-9."

If you feel your use of code examples falls outside fair use or the permission given above, feel free to contact us at *permissions@oreilly.com*.

O'Reilly Online Learning

 For more than 40 years, *O'Reilly Media* has provided technology and business training, knowledge, and insight to help companies succeed.

Our unique network of experts and innovators share their knowledge and expertise through books, articles, and our online learning platform. O'Reilly's online learning platform gives you on-demand access to live training courses, in-depth learning paths, interactive coding environments, and a vast collection of text and video from O'Reilly and 200+ other publishers. For more information, visit *http://oreilly.com*.

How to Contact Us

Please address comments and questions concerning this book to the publisher:

O'Reilly Media, Inc.
1005 Gravenstein Highway North
Sebastopol, CA 95472

800-998-9938 (in the United States or Canada)
707-829-0515 (international or local)
707-829-0104 (fax)

We have a web page for this book, where we list errata, examples, and any additional information. You can access this page at *https://oreil.ly/smaller-c*.

Email *bookquestions@oreilly.com* to comment or ask technical questions about this book.

For news and information about our books and courses, visit *http://oreilly.com*.

Find us on Facebook: *http://facebook.com/oreilly*.

Follow us on Twitter: *http://twitter.com/oreillymedia*.

Watch us on YouTube: *http://youtube.com/oreillymedia*.

Acknowledgments

I would like to thank Amelia Blevins for shepherding another book for me through the publication process. Her project management skills are surpassed only by her ability to improve my writing through her artful suggestions. Thanks also go to Amanda Quinn and Suzanne McQuade for helping me get the project off the ground in the first place, and Danny Elfanbaum for his superb tech support. The entire crew at O'Reilly are peerless.

Our technical reviewers brought a wide range of expertise to the table, and I could not have asked for better feedback. Tony Crawford tightened up my C code discussions, and I heartily recommend you read his book: *C in a Nutshell*. Alex Faber ran every example in the book on multiple platforms and made sure I kept new programmers in mind. Eric Van Hoose made my writing clearer and helped focus the flow of the book overall. Chaim Krause filled in at the last minute and highlighted a few gaps that have been duly filled in turn.

Personal thanks to my husband Ron for wordsmithing advice and general moral support. Reg Dyck also provided some welcome encouragement. If you ever want to really learn a topic, explain it to friends and family like Reg and Ron. Neither gent has much interest in programming or electronics, but their friendly questions helped me suss out the core of what I wanted to say on many difficult topics.

CHAPTER 1

The ABCs of C

C is a powerful language. It is procedural (meaning you do a lot of your coding work with procedures) and compiled (meaning the code you write must be translated for use by a computer using a compiler). You can write your procedures anywhere you can edit a text file, and you can compile those procedures to run on anything from supercomputers to the tiniest of embedded controllers. It's a fantastic, mature language—I'm glad you're here learning about it!

C has been around for quite some time: it was developed in the early 1970s by Dennis Ritchie at Bell Labs. You might have heard of him as one of the authors of the canonical C programming book, *The C Programming Language* with Brian Kernighan (Pearson). (If you see or hear or read about the phrase "K&R" in the programming world, that's a reference to the book.) As a general purpose, procedural language built with an eye toward keeping programmers connected to the hardware their programs would run on, C caught on with both academic and industrial institutions outside Bell Labs to run a growing array of computers and remains a viable systems programming language.

Like all languages, C is not static. And with nearly 50 years under its belt, C has undergone many changes and spawned a great number of other languages. You can see its influence in the syntax of languages as disparate as Java and Perl. Indeed, some of C's elements are so universal that you see it show up in pseudocode examples meant to represent "any" language.

As C grew in popularity, it became necessary to organize and standardize its syntax and features. The first part of this book will focus on Standard C (*https://oreil.ly/9MDKn*) as defined by the International Organization for Standardization (ISO) and the code we write will be portable to any C compiler on any platform. The latter part of this book will focus on using C with specific hardware such as the Arduino microcontroller.

Strengths and Weaknesses

When you think about solving actual problems with a computer these days, using a high-level language is a must. C provides a great balance between code you can think about and code that performs well when compiled for actual hardware. C has straightforward code structures and a wealth of useful operators. (These are the features that have spread into so many subsequent languages and makes it such a good option for lean code on microcontrollers.) C also gives you room to break problems up into smaller subproblems. You can reason about the code (and its inevitable bugs) as a human—quite a handy thing.

C does have its downsides, though. C does not have some of the fancier features available today in other languages such as Java's automatic memory garbage collection. Many modern languages hide most of those details from the programmer at the expense of a little performance. C requires you to be more deliberate in how you allocate and manage resources like memory. Sometimes that requirement can feel tedious.

C also lets you write some pretty impressive bugs. It has no type safety or really any safety checks at all. Again, as a programmer, this hands-off approach means you can write clever, efficient code that really hums on the hardware. It also means that if you get something wrong, it's up to you to find and fix the problem. (Tools like linters and debuggers help; we'll definitely be looking at those along the way.)

Getting Started

So how do we get started? As with any compiled language, we'll first need a file containing some valid C instructions. We'll then need a compiler that can translate those instructions. With the right contents in the file and a compiler for your own computer's hardware, you can have a C program running in just a few minutes.

If you have spent any time learning any computer language at all, you're likely familiar with the idea of a "Hello, World" program. It's an admirably simple idea: create a tiny program that proves several things in one go. It proves you can write valid code in the language. It proves your compiler or interpreter works. It also proves you can produce visible output, which comes in very handy for humans, as it turns out. Let's get started!

Tools Required

Folks use computers today for a vast array of tasks. Entertainment such as games and streaming video takes up as many (if not more) CPU cycles as business productivity work or even application development. And because computers are used as much for consuming as they are for producing, very few systems come with the tools required to do stuff like application development. Happily, those tools are freely available, but you do have to go get them yourself and then set them up to work on your system.

As I've noted before, this book focuses on writing clean, efficient C code. I take care in our examples to avoid overly clever patterns. I also work hard to ensure the examples do not rely on a particular compiler or a particular development platform. To that end, I'll be working with the minimum setup required for any software development: a good editor and a good compiler.[1]

If you're comfortable hunting down software online and want to dive right in, we'll be installing Visual Studio Code (*https://oreil.ly/kXf3h*) (often just "VS Code") from Microsoft as our editor and the GNU developer tools (*https://oreil.ly/xclHh*) from the GNU Foundation to handle compiling. More links and details follow, but feel free to jump to "Creating a C 'Hello, World'" on page 15 after installing these tools on your own or if you already have an editor and a compiler you're comfortable using.

Windows

Microsoft Windows owns the lion's share of the desktop market. If you only write programs for one system, Windows gets you the most bang for your buck. But that means that you'll find a lot more competition in the software that helps you write those programs. There are more commerical developer applications for Windows than any other platform. Fortunately, many of those applications have a free or "community" version that will suffice for our purposes. (When we get to the Arduino focus in the second part of this book, we'll be looking at some Arduino-specific tools that include compilers.)

You can't talk about Windows and software development without mentioning the Visual Studio IDE (Integrated Development Environment) from Microsoft. If you want to build applications for Windows itself, it's hard to beat Visual Studio. They even offer a community edition for students and individual developers. While I won't be discussing either edition for the examples in this book, Visual Studio is a great IDE for Windows users and will easily handle our code. (I will, however, be using a close cousin called Visual Studio Code as our editor on all three of the major platforms.)

 Another popular commerical IDE is CLion (*https://oreil.ly/E1Oxh*) from Jetbrains. CLion is also cross-platform so you can easily move between different operating systems and still feel productive. If you have experience with any of the other quality applications from Jetbrains, CLion can be a familiar way to get started writing and debugging C code.

---

1 Well, "any" is awfully expansive; if your language is an interpreted language, then of course you would need a good interpreter rather than a good compiler!

There are myriad other text editors, each with some pros and cons. You can even use tools like the built-in Notepad application, although programming-specific editors will have some handy features that can make reading and debugging your code easier.

GNU tools on Windows.   On Windows, installing the GCC tool from GNU can be a bit tedious. There's no quick, friendly installer.[2] You can find a variety of binary packages (*https://oreil.ly/atDoI*) that provide most of what we need, but you still have to take care to download the GNU compiler subpackages and then configure your Windows environment.

We will install the Cygwin environment to get our Windows version of GCC. Cygwin is a much larger collection of tools and utilities that provides Windows users with a nice Unix shell environment. But "nice" is pretty subjective, and if you don't know Unix or its derivatives such as Linux or modern macOS, you probably won't use much else of the collection.

Grab the Cygwin setup (*https://oreil.ly/Loj7l*) executable. Once it's done downloading, go ahead and launch it. You may need to "allow this app from an unknown publisher to make changes to your device." You can try the "Install from Internet" option, but if you have any trouble, go back and use the "Download Without Installing" option. You'll still want to follow the package selection step, but after the download completes, you can run this installer program a second time and choose the "Install from Local Directory" option and use the folder where you downloaded all of the packages.

Go ahead and accept the defaults for any questions the installer asks. When you get to the mirror selection page, use one physically close to you if you can identify a university or business you know. Otherwise, any mirror should do—but it's OK to come back and pick a different one if you have any troubles with the download.

On the "Select Package" screen, you do need to make an extra selection as gcc is not included by default. Switch the View dropdown to "Full" and then enter "gcc" as a search term. You want the "gcc-core" package as highlighted in Figure 1-1. Any of the versions available are sufficient for our needs. At the time of this writing, we selected the most recent gcc-core version, which was 10.2.0-1.

---

2 J. M. Eubank, however, has done the legwork on a single-file installer that you might want to check out if the general steps for a more complete setup look overwhelming: tdm-gcc (*https://oreil.ly/RWJcB*).

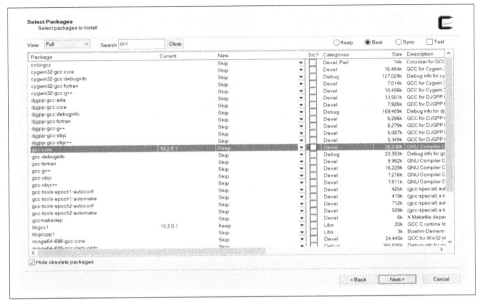

Figure 1-1. Selecting the Cygwin GCC package

Confirm your selections on the Review page and start the download! It may take a little time to download and install everything, but you should eventually hit the Finish screen. You can add the desktop icon if you want to play around with a Unix-like command prompt, but it is not required for the work we'll be doing. What is required, though, is an extra step to add the Cygwin tools to Microsoft's command prompt.

You may wish to search online for a guided tour of creating and editing Windows environment variables, but here are the basics. (If you've done this type of thing before, feel free to skip to the Cygwin folder selection and just put that in your path.)

From the Start menu, search for "env" and you should quickly see an option to edit the system environment variables at the top, as shown in Figure 1-2.

The System Properties dialog should open, and you want to click the "Environment Variables…" button near the bottom right corner, as shown in Figure 1-3.

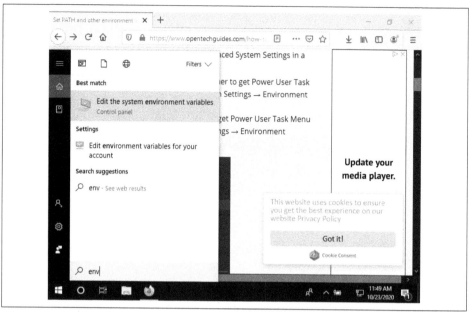

Figure 1-2. Finding the environment variable editor in Windows

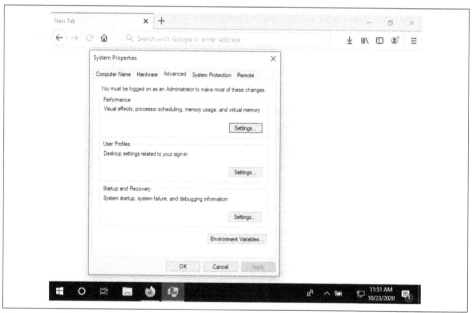

Figure 1-3. The System Properties dialog in Windows

You can set just your path or set it system wide. Highlight the PATH entry you want to update and then click Edit. Next, click the New button on the "Edit environment variables" dialog and then click the Browse button to navigate to the Cygwin *bin* folder, as shown in Figure 1-4. (If you recall the root folder you chose for the Cygwin installer to put everything in, you can also just type that in, of course.)

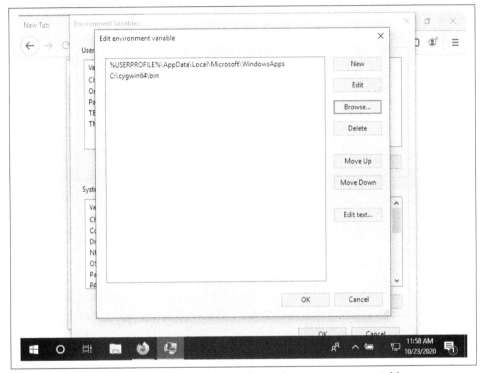

Figure 1-4. Adding the Cygwin bin folder to the Path environment variable

Select the OK button to close each of the dialogs and you should be set!

For the editor, you can find VS Code (*https://oreil.ly/27eCl*) at the Visual Studio site. Depending on your system, you will most likely want either the 64-bit or 32-bit user installer version.[3]

Use the Extensions view shown in Figure 1-5 to grab the C/C++ extension. You can search for the simple letter "c," but you might also see the extension right away on the "Popular" list. Go ahead and click the small green Install button for the extension.

---

3 If you're unsure whether you have a 64-bit or 32-bit version of Windows, check out the Microsoft FAQ (*https://oreil.ly/kyR5d*).

Figure 1-5. The C extension in VS Code

Let's test the GCC tool from those Cygwin utilities. (You may need to restart Visual Studio Code for it to recognize your Cygwin tools.) From the View menu, select the Terminal option. The Terminal tab should open at the bottom. You may need to hit the Enter key to get a prompt. Run **gcc --version** at the prompt. Hopefully, you'll see output similar to that in Figure 1-6.

You should see the version number matching the package you selected as you were installing Cygwin. If you do, hooray! Jump down to "Creating a C 'Hello, World'" on page 15 and get started with your first C program. If you don't see any output or get a "not recognized" error, review the steps to set up Windows environment variables. And as always, searching online for particular errors you see can help you solve most installation and setup issues.

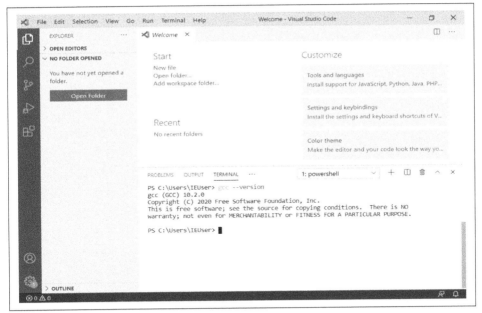

Figure 1-6. Testing GCC in the Terminal tab

macOS

If you live mostly with graphical applications and tools, you might not be aware of the Unix underpinnings of macOS. While you can mostly remain blissfully ignorant of those underpinnings, it is useful to know a bit about navigating the world from a command prompt. We'll be using the Terminal app to download and install GCC, but as with Windows, it is worth noting that Apple's official developer tool, Xcode, can be used to write and compile C code. Fortunately we don't need all of Xcode to get going with C, so we'll stick to the minimum.

The Terminal app is in the Application → Utilities folder. Go ahead and start it. You should see something like Figure 1-7.

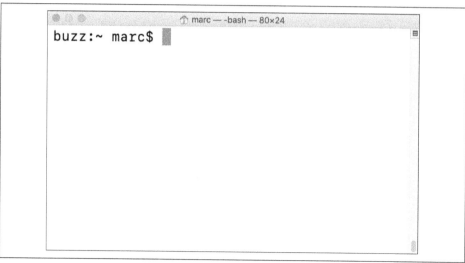

Figure 1-7. A basic macOS Terminal window

If you already have the main Apple programming application, Xcode, you can quickly check to see if GCC is also available. Try running **gcc -v**:

```
$ gcc -v
Configured with: --prefix=/Library/Developer/CommandLineTools/usr --with...
Apple clang version 11.0.3 (clang-1103.0.32.62)
Target: x86_64-apple-darwin19.6.0
Thread model: posix
InstalledDir: /Library/Developer/CommandLineTools/usr/bin
```

The exact versions aren't that important; we just want to make sure GCC is in fact available. If not, you'll need to install the xcode-select command-line tool, which will bring GCC along for the ride. Type in **xcode-select --install** and follow the prompts. A dialog will ask if you want to install the command-line tools; say yes and you're on your way.

After the installation completes, go ahead and run that **gcc -v** command to make sure you have the compiler. If you don't get a good response, you may need to visit Apple's Developer Support site (*https://oreil.ly/JyXV8*) and search on "command-line tools."

Installing VS Code on macOS is much simpler. Visit the same VS Code downloads (*https://oreil.ly/kUgwI*) page at the Visual Studio site. Select the macOS download. You should receive a ZIP file in your standard download folder. Double-click that file to unzip it, and then drag the resulting *Visual Studio Code.app* file to your *Applications* folder. If you are prompted for your password to move the app to *Applications*, go ahead and provide it now.

Once relocated, go ahead and open VS Code. We want to add the C/C++ extension and then check that we can access GCC from the Terminal tab.

Pull up the Extensions panel in VS Code by clicking the "boxes" icon shown in Figure 1-8. You can search for the simple letter "C" and likely find the correct extension at the top of the results.

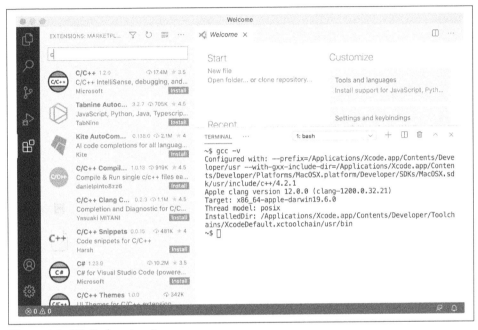

Figure 1-8. VS Code extensions

To try out the Terminal tab, open it from the View → Terminal menu item. You should see a new section at the bottom of your editor space. Go ahead and try running our GCC check command (**gcc -v**) in that new area. You should see results similar to Figure 1-9.

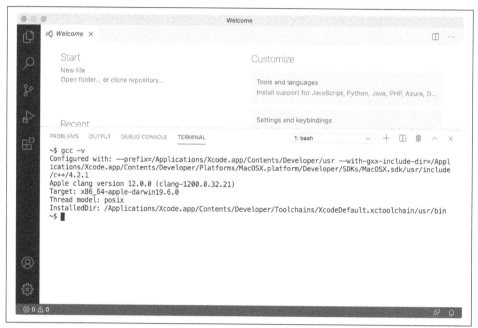

Figure 1-9. Trying GCC in VS Code on macOS

Again, if you don't get the expected results from running the gcc command, check Apple's developer site. You can also find several video tutorials online that may help you with your particular setup.

Linux

Many Linux systems are geared toward folks who tinker. You might already have GCC available. You can check quickly by starting the Terminal app and running the same check used on other operating systems. If **gcc -v** returns an answer—other than "Command not found," of course—then you are good to go and can download VS Code. If you need to install GCC, you can use the package manager on your platform. You might have a nifty graphical application for such things; look for "developer tools" or "software development" and then read the description to see if GCC or GNU utilities are included.

For Debian/Ubuntu systems, you can grab the build-essential metapackage that will include GCC along with lots of other useful (or required) libraries and tools:

```
$ sudo apt install build-essential
```

For Redhat/Fedora/CentOS systems, the Dandified Yum (dnf) tool can be used. We only need GCC for our work in this book:

```
$ su -
# dnf install gcc
```

Although if you're curious about software development in general, you might want to grab the "Development Tools" group package, which includes GCC along with lots of other nifty things:

```
$ su -
# dnf groupinstall "Development Tools"
```

Manjaro is another popular Linux distribution based on Arch Linux. You can use the pacman tool here:

```
$ su -
# pacman -S gcc
```

If you have some other flavor of Linux that doesn't use apt, dnf, or pacman, you can easily search for "install gcc **my-linux**" or use the search option with your system's package manager to look for "gcc" or "gnu."

As a Linux user, you may already have some experience with text editors for writing shell scripts or other languages. If you're already comfortable with your editor and the terminal, you can skip forward. But if you are new to coding or don't have a favorite editor, go ahead and install VS Code. Visit the same VS Code downloads (*https://oreil.ly/ptJFA*) page at the Visual Studio site as mentioned for the other operating systems. Get the appropriate bundle for your system. (If your flavor of Linux doesn't use *.deb* or *.rpm* files, you can get the *.tar.gz* version.)

Double-click the downloaded file and you should be prompted to go through a standard installation. You may be asked for an administrative password if you are installing VS Code for all users. Different distributions will put VS Code in different spots, and different desktops have different app launchers. You can also launch VS Code from the command line using the code command.

As with the other operating systems, we want to add the C/C++ extension and then check that we can access GCC from the Terminal tab.

Pull up the Extensions panel in VS Code by clicking the "boxes" icon shown in Figure 1-10. You can search for the simple letter "C" and likely find the correct extension at the top of the results.

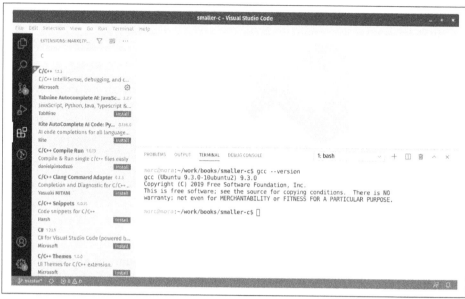

Figure 1-10. VS Code extensions on Linux

To try out the Terminal tab, open it from the View → Terminal menu item. You should see a new section at the bottom of your editor space. Go ahead and try running our GCC check command (**gcc -v**) in that new area. You should see (verbose and slightly messy) results similar to Figure 1-11.

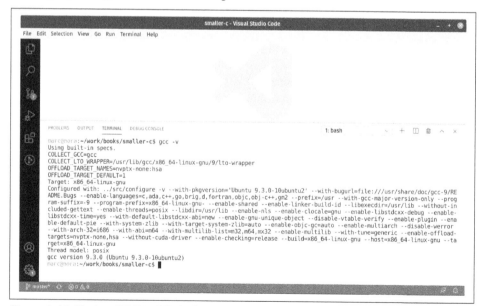

Figure 1-11. Trying GCC in VS Code on Linux

Hooray, hooray. Hopefully, you have a simple C development environment up and running. Let's go write some code!

Creating a C "Hello, World"

With your editor and compiler in place, we can try out the acclaimed first program many developers write in any new language: the "Hello, World" program. It is meant to show you can write valid code in the new language and that you can output information.

C, as a language, can be terse. We'll be getting into all the nitty-gritty of semicolons, curly braces, backslashes, and other strange symbols in this first program, but for now, copy this small bit of code verbatim. You can create a new file in VS Code using a right-click in the Explorer on the left, or using the File → New File menu item, or by pressing Ctrl+N.

```
#include <stdio.h>

int main() {
    printf("Hello, world\n");
}
```

Go ahead and save the file and name it *hello.c*. We'll also go ahead and open the Terminal in VS Code (View → Terminal menu item or Ctrl+`). You should see something similar to Figure 1-12.

Figure 1-12. "Hello, World" and our Terminal tab

If you know other languages already then you can probably guess what's happening. Either way, let's take a quick moment to review each line. But don't worry if some of these explanations feel opaque. Learning to program requires a lot of practice and a lot of patience. Later chapters will help you reinforce both skills.

```
#include <stdio.h>
```

This line loads the *header file* for the "standard input/output" *library*. Libraries (roughly speaking) are external pieces of code that can be attached to your own code when you run gcc. Header files are succinct descriptions of these external entities. It's a very common line for a very popular part of a very common library. Among other things, this header includes the definition of the printf() function we use to get our actual output. Almost every C program you write will use it. This line is always at the top of the file, although as we'll see in Chapter 6 you will often use several libraries, each with their own header file #include line.

```
int main() {
```

Complex programs can have dozens (even hundreds or thousands) of separate C files. Separating big problems into tinier parts is a fundamental part of being a good programmer. These smaller "bites" are easier to debug and maintain. They also tend to help you find moments of repeated tasks where you can reuse code you have already written. But whether you have a big, complex program, or a tiny, simple one, you need some place to start. This line is that starting place. The main() function is always required, though it occasionally looks a little different. We'll tackle *types* like the int you see at the beginning of the line in Chapter 2 and look more closely at functions in Chapter 5. But pay attention to that { at the end of the line. That character opens a *block* of code.

```
    printf("Hello, world\n");
```

This statement is the heart of our program. Less romantically speaking, it represents the *body* of our main() function block. Blocks contain one or more lines of code bounded (in C) by curly braces, and we often refer to the content of any block as its body. This particular body does one thing: it uses the printf() function (again, defined in *stdio.h*) to produce a friendly, global greeting. We'll be going through printf() and things like the "Hello, world\n" snippet in much more detail in "printf() and scanf()" on page 34.

I also want to quickly highlight the semicolon at the end of the line. That bit of punctuation tells the C compiler when you have finished a statement. That marker doesn't mean much here with only one statement in our block, but it will help down the road when we have more statements and statements that are messy enough to span several lines.

And last but certainly not least, here is the "closing" curly brace to match up with the "opening" curly brace two lines up:

```
}
```

Every block will have these open/close braces. One of the most common mistakes in programming is having one too many open or close braces. Happily, most modern editors have fancy syntax highlighting that can help you match up any pair of braces (and thus identify any braces that don't have a partner as well).

Compiling Your Code

Now we finally get to put all that software installation headache to use! In the Terminal tab, run the following command:

```
gcc hello.c
```

If all goes well, you won't see any output, just a new command prompt. If something *did* go wrong, you'll get an error message (or many messages) that hopefully point you to what needs fixing. We'll see debugging tricks as we encounter more examples, but for now, look back at your code and the example above to see if you can spot any differences.

 If you are still having trouble with this first file, don't give up! Check out Appendix A on downloading the sample code for this book from GitHub. You can compile and run the code as is, or use our examples as a starting point for your own tweaks and modifications.

Running Your Code

After successfully compiling our first C program, how do we test it? If you list the files in your directory, you'll notice a new file named *a.out* on Linux and macOS systems, and *a.exe* on Windows systems. To run it, just type its name. On many Linux and macOS systems, your executable path may not include your working directory. In that case, use the local path prefix "./". (The period means the current directory; the slash is just the standard path separator character.) Figure 1-13 shows the output.

Figure 1-13. Saying hello on macOS and Linux

Figure 1-14 shows the output on Windows.

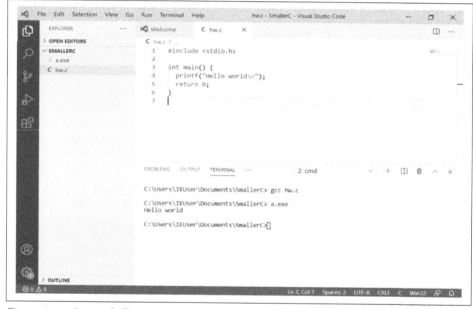

Figure 1-14. Saying hello on Windows

 On Windows, the *.exe* suffix marks a file as executable. However, you do not need to include the suffix when you run the program. You can just type **a**. Depending on the command prompt application used (cmd or PowerShell, for example), you may also need to use the local directory prefix similar to macOS or Linux (.\).

As a name, though, "a" is pretty boring and definitely doesn't tell us what the program does. You can use the -o (output) option to the gcc command to specify a better name for your program if you like.

On Linux and macOS:

```
$ gcc hello.c -o hello
```

On Windows:

```
C:\> gcc hello.c -o hello.exe
```

Try that command and then look at the files in your folder. You should have a newly minted *hello* (or *hello.exe*) file that you can run. Much nicer.

Distributing Your Code

You have a fully functioning C program compiled and ready to take over the world! How do you let someone else run your code? That question is unfortunately messy. If you want to share your *a.out* or *hello.exe* file with someone running the same operating system as you on similar hardware, you can just copy the program to their machine and it will work. But if you compiled your *hello.exe* on a Windows box and want to share it with a macOS user, you're out of luck. We have compiled a native application. Native applications can get the best performance out of your hardware, but that comes at the expense of needing a different compiled version (sometimes called a "binary") for every platform you want to support.

You can certainly share your source code, though! If you email your *hello.c* file from Windows to Linux, or from macOS to Windows, or from an Ubuntu distro to Arch, the recipient can set up their own development environment and compile your code.

Next Steps

Whew…that's a lot of effort to get your computer to say hi! If it helps, it took humanity eons to get the first computer to do what you just did. :) But now that we have a working development environment, the next chapters will explore the details of the C language and show you how to write, debug, and maintain much more interesting programs. And with our microcontrollers, the popular term for smaller computers typically used for dedicated tasks like reporting the current temperature or counting the number of boxes waiting on a conveyor belt, we'll turn those interesting programs into interesting, physical creations!

CHAPTER 2

Storing and Stating

The essence of programming is the manipulation of data. A programming language provides humans an interface for telling the computer what that data is and what you want to do to that data. Languages designed for powerful machines may hide (or infer) a lot of the details about storing data, but C remains fairly simple in this regard. Perhaps simple is the wrong word, but its approach to data storage is straightforward while still allowing for complex manipulation. As we'll see in Chapter 6, C also provides the programmer with a window into the low-level aspects of where the data is stored in the computer's memory. When we start working directly with microcontrollers in the latter half of this book, that access will become more important.

For now though, I want to tackle some of the basics of C's syntax so that we can start composing original programs rather than just copying lines of code from a book. This chapter has plenty of those lines, and you are heartily encouraged to copy them as you read! But hopefully, we'll get to the point where you can create novel answers to your own programming challenges.

 If you already feel comfortable with programming from your experience in another language, feel free to skim this chapter. You should read "printf() and scanf()" on page 34 on the printf() and scanf() functions, but other sections will likely be familiar.

Statements in C

Another concept you hear about as a fundamental element of programming is the notion of an *algorithm*. Algorithms are sets of instructions that process data and generally get things done on computers. One classic analogy for an algorithm is a kitchen recipe. Given a set of ingredients, here are the individual steps you take to turn those ingredients into something like a cake. In programming, those "individual steps" are statements.

In C, statements come in a variety of flavors. In this chapter, I'll be looking at declaration statements, initialization statements, function calls, and comments. Later chapters will tackle control statements and not-quite statements like creating your own functions and preprocessor commands.

Statement Separators

Statements are separated from each other using a semicolon. Semicolons in C work a lot like periods do in English. Long sentences in English might span multiple lines, but you know to keep going until you see a period. Likewise, you might have several short sentences bunched up together on a single line, but you can easily distinguish them based on those periods. It can be easy to forget the semicolon at the end of a statement. If each statement fits on its own line, it becomes tempting to assume the compiler "sees" the same structure that humans can so easily pick out. Unfortunately, the compiler cannot. Even with our first, very simple program from "Creating a C 'Hello, World'" on page 15, the statement we used to print out some text in our terminal window needs to end with a semicolon. If you're curious, try deleting that semicolon, save your file, and then recompile it. You'll end up with something like this:

```
$ gcc hello.c
hello.c:4:27: error: expected ';' after expression
  printf("Hello, world\n")
                         ^
                         ;
1 error generated.
```

Yuck. An error. But at least the error message is useful. It tells us two critical things: *what* went wrong ("expected ';' after expression") and *where* the compiler had trouble ("hello.c:4:27", or the *hello.c* file, line 4, column 27). I don't want to scare you off with an error message so early in your exploration of C, but you will definitely run into them. A lot. Happily, it just means you need to look at your source code a little closer and then try again.

Statement Flow

The separators tell the compiler where one statement ends and where the next begins. That order matters, too. The flow of statements is top to bottom, or left to right if multiple statements are on the same line. And multiple statements are definitely allowed! We can quickly expand our simple "Hello, World" program to be a little more verbose.

When you have the time and energy, I highly recommend transcribing the source code by hand. This will give you a little more practice with C's syntax. You'll often make a mistake or two, as well. Spotting and fixing those mistakes is a great way to learn! Even if those mistakes can be a little frustrating from time to time.

Consider the following program, *ch02/verbose.c* (*https://oreil.ly/wqnYC*):

```
#include <stdio.h>

int main() {
  printf("Ahem!\n");                                  ❶
  printf("May I have your attention, please?\n");     ❷
  printf("I would like to extend the warmest of\n");  ❸
  printf("greetings to the world.\n");
  printf("Thank you.\n");
}
```

❶ We start with a very similar statement to the one we used in *hello.c*. The only real difference is the text we print. Note that we end the line with our semicolon separator.

❷ We have a second `printf()` statement similar to the first. It will indeed be executed second.

❸ And just to drive the point home, this third statement will be called after the first two. And the last two calls will come after this one.

Here's the output of our simple multiline upgrade:

```
$ gcc verbose.c
$ ./a.out
Ahem!
May I have your attention, please?
I would like to extend the warmest of
greetings to the world.
Thank you.
```

Nice. You can see how the output precisely follows the order of the statements in our program. Try switching them around and confirm for yourself that the flow of the program goes top to bottom. Or try putting two `printf()` calls on the same line. This isn't meant to be tricky. I just want you to practice writing, running, and compiling code as often as possible. The more examples you try, the better you'll get at avoiding the simple mistakes and the easier it will be to follow along with new code examples.

Variables and Types

We can do much more than just print text, of course. We can also store and manipulate data as we work to implement an algorithm or perform a task. In C (and in most languages), you store data in *variables*, which are powerful tools in problem solving. Those variables have *types*, which dictate what kinds of data you can store. Both of these concepts figure heavily in two of the statement flavors I mentioned: declarations and initializations.

A variable is a placeholder for a value. A variable can hold simple values like numbers (how many students are in the class? what's the total cost of the items in my shopping cart?) or more complex things (what's the name of this particular student? what are each student's grades? or even an actual complex value like the square root of −1). Variables can store data received from users, and they allow you to write programs that can solve general problems without rewriting the program itself.

Getting User Input

We'll be exploring the details of defining and initializing variables shortly, but let's first run with that idea of getting some input for the user to create dynamic output without recompiling our program every time. We'll return to our "Hello, World" program and upgrade it a little. We can ask the user to give us their name and then greet them personally!

You've seen one output statement so far, our `printf()` function call we used to greet the planet. There is a counterpart, input function, too: `scanf()`. You can use print/scan pairs to prompt the user and then wait for them to type in an answer. We'll store that answer in a variable. If you have done some programming in other languages, this next program should look familiar. If you're new to programming and to C, the listing may be a little dense or weird—and that's OK! Typing in these programs and getting them to run after fixing any typos you make is a useful way to learn.

 A lot of programming is just thoughtful plagiarism. That's a bit of a joke, but only a bit. You start out much the way humans start out with spoken language: repeating something you see (or hear) without necessarily understanding everything about it. If you perform that repetition enough, you discover the patterns inherent in the language and learn where you can make useful changes. Make enough of those useful changes, and you discover how to create new, meaningful things from scratch. That is our goal.

This *ch02/hello2.c* (*https://oreil.ly/OrUqu*) program is simply another bit of code you can copy as you start down the path of programming discovery:

```c
#include <stdio.h>

int main() {
  char name[20];

  printf("Enter your name: ");
  scanf("%s", name);
  printf("Well hello, %s!\n", name);
}
```

Hopefully, the structure of this program looks familiar. We include our standard I/O library, we have a `main()` function, and that function has a body with multiple statements inside a pair of curly braces. That body, though, contains several new items. Let's go through each line.

```c
char name[20];
```

Here is our first example of the declaration of a variable. The variable's name is, well, "name". Its type is `char`, which is what C uses to refer to a single (ASCII) character.[1] It is also an *array*, meaning it stores multiple `char` values in sequence. In our case, 20 such values can be stored. More on arrays in Chapter 4. For now, just note that this variable can keep a person's name as long as it is less than 20 characters long.

```c
printf("Enter your name: ");
```

This is a fairly standard `printf()` call—very similar to the one we used in our first program back in "Creating a C 'Hello, World'" on page 15. The only meaningful difference is the last characters inside the set of double quote marks. If you look at *hello.c* or *verbose.c*, you'll notice the last two characters are a backslash and the letter "n". The combination of those two characters (`\n`) represents a single "newline" character. If you add `\n` at the end, you are printing one line and any subsequent call to `printf()` will go on the next line. Conversely, if you omit the `\n`, the cursor in the terminal stays on the current line. This can be handy if you want to do things like print out a table but do so one table cell at a time. Or, in our case, if you want to prompt the user for some input, and then allow them to enter their response on the same line as the question.

```c
scanf("%s", name);
```

---

[1] While some support for wide characters was added to C in the1990s, C generally does not deal well with the more popular UTF character encodings such as UTF-8, UTF-16, etc. Those encodings allow for multibyte characters, and C's char type was built with single bytes in mind. (More on types in "Strings and Characters" on page 27.) If you work with international or localized text, you'll want to research some libraries to help. While I won't cover localization in detail, I do go into more depth on libraries in general in Chapter 7.

Here is that new function I mentioned at the beginning of this section. The `scanf()` function "scans in" characters and can convert them into C data types like numbers, or in this case, an array of characters. Once converted, `scanf()` expects to store each "thing" in a variable. In this line, then, we're scanning for a bunch of characters and we'll store them in our `name` variable. We'll look at the very strange syntax of the stuff inside the parentheses in "printf() and scanf()" on page 34.

```
printf("Well hello, %s!\n", name);
```

And lastly, we want to print our greeting. Again, this should look familiar, but now we have more strange syntax. If the `%s` jumps out at you as the same weird thing that was in the call to `scanf()`, congrats! You just spotted a very useful pattern. That pair of characters is exactly what C uses when printing or scanning an array of characters. An array of characters is such a common type in C that it has a simpler name: string. Hence the use of an "s" in this pair.

So what's happening with `name`? The `scanf()` call took whatever name you typed in (not including the Return key[2] you pressed) and stored it in memory. Our `name` variable contains the memory location of those characters. When we come along with our `printf()` call, our first argument (the `"Well hello, %s!\n"` part) contains a few literal characters such as those in the word "Well" and a placeholder for a string (the `%s` part). Variables are great for filling placeholders. Whatever name you typed in will now be displayed back to you!

Also notice that we do include the special `\n` newline here on our greeting. That means we'll print the greeting and then "hit the Return key" so that anything else to be shown in the terminal will go on the next line.

Let's go ahead and run the program to see how things work. You can use the Terminal tab at the bottom of VS Code, or the Terminal or Command app for your platform. You'll need to compile it first with `gcc` then run either `a.out` or whatever name you chose using the `-o` option. You should get something similar to Figure 2-1.

Notice that when you type in a name, it appears on the same line as the prompt asking you to enter it. That is exactly what we wanted when we left off the newline (`\n`) character. But try running it again and type in a different name. Did you get the results you expected? Try a third time. This dynamic behavior of responding to user input makes variables invaluable in computer programming. The same program can produce different output based on different input without being recompiled. That ability, in turn, has helped make computer programs invaluable to our everyday lives.

---

2 You might still see discussions online about including or excluding a "carriage return," which is just old coder jargon for an end-of-line marker. It is a term inherited from early typewriters which had a literal mechanism to return the paper carriage to a starting position so you could begin the next line of text.

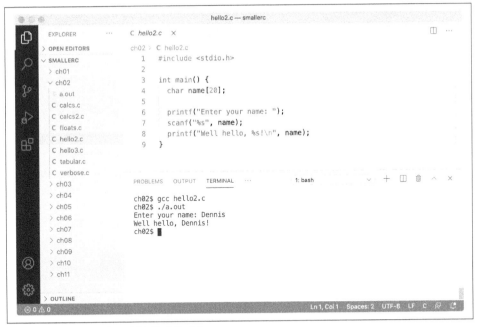

Figure 2-1. Our tailored Hello World output

Strings and Characters

Let's look a little closer at the char type as well as its close cousin, the array of characters—char[]—better known as a string. When you declare a variable in C, you give it
both a name and a type. The simplest declaration looks something like this:

```
char response;
```

Here we create a variable named response with a type of char. The char type holds
one character. We could store a "y" or an "n", for example. Chapter 5 will go through
the memory address and reference details, but for now, just remember that a variable
declaration sets aside a spot in memory with enough space to store one of whatever
type you specified. If we had a series of questions to ask, then we could create a series
of variables:

```
char response1;
char response2;
char finalanswer;
```

Each of these variables can hold one character. But again, when you use a variable,
you don't have to predict or decide what that character will be in advance. The contents can vary. (Vary…variable…get it? :)

C compilers determine which encoding your source characters use. Older compilers use the older ASCII[3] format while more recent compilers typically use UTF-8. Both encodings include lower- and uppercase letters, numbers, and most of the symbols you see on your keyboard. To talk about a specific character rather than a variable of type char, you use single quotes to delimit it. For example, 'a', 'A', '8', and '@' are all valid.

Special characters

A character can also be special. C supports things like tabs and newlines. We've seen the newline character (\n), but there are also a few other special characters listed in Table 2-1. These special characters are coded using "escape sequences," and the backslash is known as the "escape character".

Table 2-1. Escape sequences in C

Char	ASCII	Name	Description
\a	7	BEL	Make the terminal "beep" when printed
\n	10	LF	Line Feed (standard line ending on Mac and Linux)
\r	13	CR	Carriage Return (when used with \n, common line ending on Windows)
\t	15	HT	(Horizontal) Tab
\\	92		Used to place a literal backslash in a string or char
\'	39		Used to place a literal single quote in a char (no escape required in a string)
\"	34		Used to place a literal double quote in a string (no escape required in a char)

This is not an exhaustive list, but covers the characters we will use in this book.

These named shortcuts only cover the most popular characters. If you have to use other special characters, say an end of transmission (EOT, ASCII value 4) signal from a modem, you can give the character's ASCII value in octal with the backslash. Our EOT character, then, would be '\4', or sometimes you see three digits: '\004'. (Since ASCII is a 7-bit encoding, three octal digits cover the highest ASCII character. Which, if you're curious, is delete (DEL, ASCII 127) or '\177' as an octal escape sequence. Some folks prefer the consistency of always seeing three digits.)

You might not need many of these shortcuts, but since Windows path names use the backslash character, it's important to remember that some characters require this special prefix. And, of course, the newline character will continue to show up in many of our print statements. As you may have noticed with the octal escape sequences, the

---

3 American Standard Code for Information Interchange, originally a 7-bit encoding built for Teletype machines. Now with 8-bit variants, it is still based on English. Other, more extensible encodings such as Unicode and its UTF-8 option have become the norm.

prefixing backslash is included inside the single quotes. So a tab is `'\t'` and the backslash is `'\\'`.

Strings

Strings are a series of chars, but a very formalized series. Many programming languages support such series, called arrays. Chapter 4 introduces arrays in much more detail, but the array of char type—char[] in C syntax—is so common that I want to mention it separately.

We've been working with strings without being very explicit about them. In our very first hello program, we called printf() with a string argument. A string in C is a collection of zero or more chars with a special, final "null" character, \0 (with the ASCII value of 0). You typically include the characters in your code between double quotes, such as our "Hello, world!\n" argument. Happily, when you use those double quotes, you don't have to add the \0 yourself. It is implicit in the definition of a string literal.

Declaring string variables is as simple as declaring char variables:

```
char firstname[20];
char lastname[20];
char jobtitle[50];
```

Each of these variables could store simple things like a name, or more complex things like a multipart title, e.g., "Senior Code and Tasty Pie Developer." A string can also be empty: "". That may seem silly, but think about forms where you are entering things like names. If you happen to be a wildly successful pop star with just one name, the lastname variable above could be given the valid value "" (i.e., just the terminating '\0') to indicate that Drake and Cher are doing just fine without a surname.

Numbers

Not surprisingly, C also has types that can store numeric values. Or more precisely, C has types for storing numbers larger than what typically fits in variable of type char. (Even though the examples in this chapter so far have used char for storing actual characters, it's still a numeric type and is good for storing small numbers that have nothing to do with a character encoding.) C breaks these numeric types into two subcategories: integers and floating point numbers (i.e., decimals).

Integer types

The integer types store simple numbers. The main type is called int, but there are many variations. The main difference in the variations is the size of the biggest number that can be stored in a variable of the given type. Table 2-2 summarizes the types and their storage capacities.

Table 2-2. Integer types and their typical sizes

Type	Bytes	Range	Notes
char	1	−127 to +127 or 0 to 255	Normally for letters; can also store small numbers
short	2	−32,767 to +32,767	
int	2 or 4	−32,767 to +32,767 or −2,147,483,647 to +2,147,483,647	Varies by implementation
long	4	−2,147,483,647 to +2,147,483,647	
long long	8	−9,223,372,036,854,775,807 to +9,223,372,036,854,775,807	Introduced in C99

While char *is defined as one byte, the other sizes are system dependent.*

Most of the types above are *signed* types,[4] which means that they can store values less than zero. All five types also have an explicit *unsigned* variation (e.g., unsigned int or unsigned char) that is the same size in bits/bytes but does not store negative values. Their ranges start at zero and end at roughly double the top of the signed range, as shown in Table 2-3.

Table 2-3. Unsigned integer types and their typical sizes

Type	Bytes	Range
unsigned char	1	0 to 255
unsigned short	2	0 to 65535
unsigned int	2 or 4	0 to 65535 or 0 to 4,294,967,295
unsigned long	4	0 to 4,294,967,295
unsigned long long	8	0 to 18,446,744,073,709,551,615

Here are some sample integer type declarations. Note the declaration of the x and y variables. You often see coordinates on a grid or graph discussed in terms of "x and y." C allows you to declare multipe variable names with the same type using a comma to separate them. There's nothing special about this format, but if you ever have some short, related variable names, this might be a nice option.

```
int studentcount;
long total;
int x, y;
short volume, chapter, page;
unsigned long long nationaldebt;
```

If you have small values to store, say "up to one dozen" or "top 100," remember that you can use the char type. It is only 1 byte in length and the compiler doesn't care if you ever print the value as an actual character or as a simple number.

---

4 The char type can actually be either signed or unsigned depending on your compiler.

Floating point types

If you are storing fractional or financial numbers, you can use the `float` or `double` types. These are both floating point types where the decimal point is not fixed (e.g., it can float), capable of storing values like 999.9 or 3.14. But because we are talking about computers that think in discrete chunks, the floating point types store an approximation of the value encoded in 1s and 0s like an `int`. The `float` type is a 32-bit encoding that can store a wide range of values from very small fractions to very large exponentials. But `float` is most accurate in a narrow band between roughly –32k to 32k and six significant places after the decimal point.

The `double` type has "double" the precision of a `float`.[5] This means roughly 15 decimal digits will be accurately represented. We'll see a few places where this approximation can cause problems, but for general purposes like a receipt total or a reading from a temperature sensor, these types are sufficient.

As with the other types, you place the type before the name:

```
float balance;
float average;
double microns;
```

 Since normal decimal numbers can also store integral values like 6 (as 6.0), it might be tempting to use `float` for your default numeric type. But manipulating numbers encoded with decimal points can be expensive on tiny CPUs like an Arduino. And even on big chips, it is still more expensive than working with simple integers. For performance and accuracy reasons, most C programmers stick with `int` unless they have an explicit reason not to.

Variable Names

Regardless of what type a variable is, it has a name. For the most part, you are free to use any name you want, but there are a few rules you have to follow.

In C, variable names can start with any letter or the underscore character ("_"). After that initial character, a name can have more letters, more underscores, or numbers. Variable names are case sensitive (`total` and `Total` are not the same variable) and are (usually) limited to 31 characters long,[6] although convention keeps them shorter.

---

5 These formats were specified by the IEEE (Institute of Electrical and Electronics Engineers). The 32-bit version is called "single precision," and the 64-bit version is "double." Higher precisions exist, and the spec (IEEE 754 (*https://oreil.ly/rxm00*)) continues to be developed.

6 The GNU C compiler, for example, does not impose any limit. But for compatibility and conformity, sticking to much less than 31 characters is still advisable.

C also has several *keywords* that are reserved for use by the C language itself. Because the keywords in Table 2-4 already mean something to C, they cannot be used as variable names. Some implementations may reserve other words (such as `asm`, `typeof`, and `inline`), but most alternate keywords begin with one or two underscores to help make conflicts with your own variable names unlikely.

Table 2-4. C keywords

Reserved words			
_Bool	default	if	static
_Complex	do	int	struct
_Imaginary	double	long	switch
auto	else	register	typedef
break	enum	restrict	union
case	extern	return	unsigned
char	float	short	void
const	for	signed	volatile
continue	goto	sizeof	while

If you do stumble upon a conflict with a keyword when declaring your variables, you'll see an error similar to the error you get if you use an invalid variable name, such as one starting with a number:

```
badname.c: In function 'main':
badname.c:4:9: error: expected identifier or '(' before 'do'
    4 |    float do;
      |          ^~
badname.c:5:7: error: expected identifier or '(' before numeric constant
    5 |    int 5r;
      |        ^~
```

That phrase "expected identifier" is a strong indicator your variable is the cause of the error. The compiler was expecting a variable name but found a keyword instead.

Variable Assignments

In our *hello2.c* example, we relied on a rather implicit assignment to our `name` variable. As an argument to the `scanf()` function, whatever the user types is stored in that variable. But we can (and often do) make direct assignments to variables. You use the equal sign ("=") to indicate an assignment like so:

```
int total;
total = 7;
```

You have now successfully stored the value 7 in the variable `total`. Congratulations!

You can overwrite that value at any time, too:

```
int total;
total = 7;
total = 42;
```

While back-to-back assignments is a bit wasteful, there is nothing wrong with this snippet of C. The variable total will only retain one integer value, though, so the most recent assignment is the winner, 42 in this case.

You often see variables defined and assigned an initial value (*initialized* in programmer-speak) at the same time:

```
int total = 7;
char answer = 'y';
```

Both total and answer now have values you can use, but both can still be changed as needed. That's exactly what variables do.

Literals

Those simple values we are plugging into variables in these examples are called *literals*. A literal is just a value that needs no interpretation. Numbers, characters inside single quotes, or strings inside double quotes all count as literals:

```
int count = 12;
char suffix = 's';
char label[] = "Description";
```

Hopefully, those first two variable definitions look familiar. But notice when we initialized our string called label, we did not give the array a length. The C compiler infers the size from the literal we use in the initialization. In this case, then, label is 12 characters long; 11 for the letters in the word "Description" and one more for the terminating '\0'. You can give string variables more room if you know you'll need it later in your code, but you should not specify too little room.

```
char automatic[] = "A string variable with just the right length";
char jobtitle[50] = "Chief Acceptable Length Officer";
char warning[5] = "This is a bad idea.";
```

If you do try to assign a string literal that is too long for its char[] variable, you'll likely see a warning from the compiler:

```
toolong.c: In function 'main':
toolong.c:6:21: warning: initializer-string for array of chars is too long
    6 |    char warning[5] = "This is a bad idea.";
      |                      ^~~~~~~~~~~~~~~~~~~~~
```

That's a fairly specific error, so hopefully you'll find it easy to fix. Your program will still run, by the way. Notice that the compiler gave you a *warning* rather than an *error* as we've seen in some previous examples with compiler problems. Warnings typically mean the compiler thinks you are making a mistake, but you get the benefit of the doubt. It's usually best to address warnings anyway, but it is not required.

printf() and scanf()

We have already seen how to print out information using `printf()` and how to accept user input with `scanf()`, but I glossed over many of the details of both functions. Let's look at some of those details now.

printf() Formats

The `printf()` function is C's primary output function. We have already used it for printing simple strings like `"Hello, world\n"`. We also peeked at using it to print a variable in "Getting User Input" on page 24. It can print all variable types, you just need to supply the correct *format string*.

When we call `printf()`, the first thing we supply is usually a string literal. That first argument is known as the format string. You can have simple strings that are echoed "as is" to the terminal, or you can print (and format) the values of variables. You use the format string to let `printf()` know what's coming. You do that by including *format specifiers* such as our `%s` from *ch02/hello2.c* (*https://oreil.ly/DcU5k*). Let's print a few of those variables we have been creating while discussing declarations and assignments. Consider *ch02/hello3.c* (*https://oreil.ly/qhIIT*):

```
#include <stdio.h>

int main() {
  int count = 12;
  int total = 7;
  char answer = 'y';
  char jobtitle[50] = "Chief Acceptable Length Officer";
  // char warning[5] = "This is a bad idea.";

  printf("You can have %d, you currently have %d.\n", count, total);
  printf("You answered: %c\n", answer);
  printf("Please welcome our newest %s!\n", jobtitle);
}
```

And here's the result:

```
ch02$ gcc hello3.c
ch02$ ./a.out
You can have 12, you currently have 7.
You answered: y
Please welcome our newest Chief Acceptable Length Officer!
```

Compare the output to the source code. You can see that we mostly print out the characters in our format string as is. But when we encounter a format specifier, we substitute the value of one of the arguments that follow the format string. Look closely at our first call to `printf()`. We have two format specifiers in the format string. After that string, we supply two variables. The variables fill in the format specifiers in order, left to right. If you check the output, you can see that first line of output does indeed include the value of `count` first, followed by the value of `total`. Neat. And we got the output of our `char` and string variables, too.

If you noticed that each type uses a different specifier, congratulations! You're finding the important differences in these statements. (And if it all still looks a little like gibberish, don't give up! The patterns—and the things that don't fit the patterns—will start to stand out as you read and practice more.) In fact, `printf()` has quite a range of format specifiers, as shown in Table 2-5. Some are obvious and are clearly associated with a particular type. Others are a little more esoteric, but that's what books are for. You'll memorize the few specifiers you use most often and can always look up the less popular ones when you need them.

Table 2-5. Common format specifier types for `printf()`

Specifier	Type(s)	Description
%c	char	Print out a single character
%d	int, short, long	Print integer values in base 10 ("decimal")
%f	float, double	Print floating point values
%i	int, short	Print integer values in base 10
%li, %lli	long, long long	Print long integer values in base 10
%s	char[] (string)	Print array of char as text

There are other formats as well, but I'll leave those for later where we need to print out odd or special bits of data. These formats will cover the vast majority of what you need day-to-day. Appendix B includes a more detailed discussion of all the formats used in this book.

Tailored Output

But what about formatting those values? After all, C uses the phrases "format string" and "format specifier." You add information to the format specifier to achieve this goal. One of the most common examples of this is printing floating point numbers like bank account balances or analog sensor readings. Let's give ourselves some interesting decimals and try printing them out.

```c
#include <stdio.h>

int main() {
  float one_half = 0.5;
  double two_thirds = 0.666666667;
```

```
    double pi = 3.14159265358979323846426433;

    printf("1/2: %f\n", one_half);
    printf("2/3: %f\n", two_thirds);
    printf("pi:  %f\n", pi);
}
```

We declare three variables, one `float` and two `double` types. We use the `%f` format specifier in our `printf()` statements. Great! Here's what we get after compiling and running the program:

```
1/2: 0.500000
2/3: 0.666667
pi:  3.141593
```

Hmm, they all had six decimal places, even though we didn't specify how many we wanted and none of our variables have exactly six decimal places. To get just the right amount of information, you give the format specifier some extra details. All specifiers can accept both width and precision arguments. Both are optional, and you can supply either or both. The extra details look like a decimal number: *width.precision* and these details go between the percent sign and the type character, as shown in Figure 2-2.

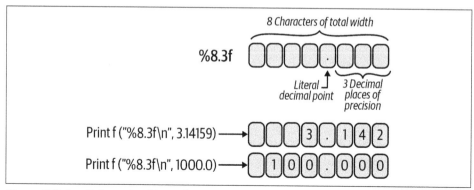

Figure 2-2. Implicit casting hierarchy

Using both of these options makes a lot of sense for floating point numbers. We can now ask for more or less digits. Try changing the three `printf()` calls in *ch02/floats.c* (*https://oreil.ly/Os37q*) like so:

```
    printf("1/2: |%5.2f|\n", one_half);
    printf("2/3: |%12f|\n", two_thirds);
    printf("pi:  |%12.10f|\n", pi);
```

I added the vertical bar or pipe character (|) just before and after the expanded format specifiers so that you can see just how the width element affects the output. Take a look at the new results:

```
1/2: | 0.50|        ❶
2/3: |   0.666667|  ❷
pi:  |3.1415926536|  ❸
```

❶ Our value, `0.5`, is displayed with two decimal places of precision in a total field width of five characters. Because we don't need all five spots, one space character is added at the beginning.

❷ A longer decimal number is printed within 12 spots. Notice that we get the same six decimal places as we did without specifying any width or precision.

❸ An even longer decimal number is shown within 12 spots but includes 10 places of precision. Notice here that 12 is the *total* width—including the spots occupied by the numbers after the decimal point.

> For `printf()`, the precision you request and the actual value you are printing take precedence over the width if given. You regularly see floating point formats like "`%0.2f`" or "`%.1f`" that give you the right number of decimal places within the exact number of spots required. Applying these two example formats to π, for example, would result in `3.14` and `3.1`, respectively.

With other types such as strings or ints, the width option is fairly straightforward. For example, you can print tabular data quite easily, as shown in *ch02/tabular.c* (*https://oreil.ly/nQC7x*), by using the same widths regardless of the value being printed like so:

```
float root2 = 1.4142;
float phi = 1.618034;
float pi = 3.1415926;
printf("      %10s%10s%10s\n", "Root 2", "phi", "pi");
printf(" 1x  %10.4f%10.4f%10.4f\n", root2, phi, pi);
printf(" 2x  %10.4f%10.4f%10.4f\n", 2 * root2, 2 * phi, 2 * pi);
```

With wonderful columnar results:

```
         Root 2      phi        pi
   1x     1.4142    1.6180    3.1416
   2x     2.8284    3.2361    6.2832
```

Very nice. And notice how I tackled the column labels. I used format specifiers and string literals rather than a single string with the labels manually spaced apart. I did it this way to highlight the use of output widths, even though doing it manually wouldn't be difficult. In fact, it would be easier to center the labels over these few columns manually. If you're up for a little exercise, open the *tabular.c* file and try adjusting that first `printf()` to see if you can get the labels centered.

While the width option is straightforward for all types, for nonfloating point formats, the effect of adding the precision option may not be as intuitive. For strings, specifying a precision results in truncating text to fit the given field width. (For int and char types, it typically has no effect, but your compiler may warn you not to rely on such "typical" behavior.)

scanf() and Parsing Inputs

On the flip side of output is input. We took a peek at using the scanf() function to do this at the beginning of this chapter in "Getting User Input" on page 24. By now you might recognize the %s we used in that simple program as a format specifier. That familiarity goes deeper: you can use all of the format specifiers listed in Table 2-5 with scanf() to get those types of values from user input.

There is one important point I need to make about the variables you use with scanf(). We got a little lucky scanning for a string in our first example. Strings in C, if you recall, are really just arrays of type char. We'll see more on this topic in Chapters 4 and 6, but for our purpose here, I'll just note that arrays are a special case of *pointers* in C. Pointers are special values that refer to the *address* (location) of things in memory. The scanf() function uses the address of a variable, not its value. Indeed, the point of scanf() is to put a value into a variable. Since arrays are really pointers, you can use a char array variable directly. But to use numeric and individual char variables with scanf(), you have to use a special prefix on the variable name, the ampersand (&).

I'll go into the & prefix in a lot more detail in Chapter 6, but it tells the compiler to use the address of the variable—perfect for scanf(). Take a look at this small snippet:

```
char name[20];
int  age;

printf("Please enter your first name and age, separated by a space: ");
scanf("%s %d", name, &age);
```

Notice the difference in the use of the name variable in the scanf() line and the use of the &age variable. That is solely down to name being an array and age being a simple integer. This is regrettably one of those things that is easy to forget. Not regrettably, it is easy to fix and the compiler will remind you if you forget:

```
warning: format '%d' expects argument of type 'int *',
         but argument 3 has type 'int' [-Wformat=]
   15 |   scanf("%s %d", name, age);
      |                      ~^       ~~~
      |                       |         |
      |                       |         int
      |                  int *
```

When you see this "expects type" error, just remember that int, float, char, and similar nonarray variables always need the & prefix when used with scanf().

Operators and Expressions

With variables and I/O statements, we now have some really powerful building blocks in our programming toolbox. But storing and printing values is pretty boring as coding goes. We want to start doing some work with the contents of those variables. One of the first rungs up the code complexity ladder is the ability to calculate new values. In C (and many other languages), you can perform calculations with the help of *operators*, symbols that allow you to do things like add, subtract, multiply, or compare (i.e., perform an "operation") on two or more values.

C includes several predefined operators for doing basic mathematic and logic work. (Advanced math and logic can be done by writing your own functions, which we'll look at in Chapter 5.) With the exception of a special ternary operator (?:, discussed in "The Ternary Operator and Conditional Assignment" on page 63), C's operators work with either one or two values. Figure 2-3 shows how these unary and binary operators fit with values and expressions.

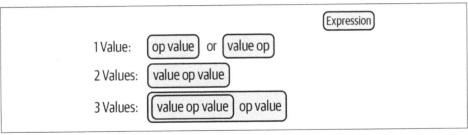

Figure 2-3. Binary operator syntax

Notice that you can use operators on more than two values in a sequence, but under the hood, C will be treating that sequence as a series of pairs. In general, operators work with *expressions*. The term "expression" is quite expansive. An expression can be as simple as a literal value or a single variable. It can also be so complex that it requires multiple lines of code to write down. The key thing to remember when you see discussions of expressions is that they have (or will produce) a value.

Arithmetic Operators

Perhaps the most intuitive operators in C are those used for mathematical calculations. Table 2-6 shows the operators built into C.

Table 2-6. Arithmetic Operators

Operator	Operation	Description
+	Addition	Add two values
-	Subtraction	Subtract the second value from the first
*	Multiplication	Multiply two values
/	Division	Divide the first value by the second
%	Remainder	Find the remainder after dividing the first (integer) value by the second

You can do math with literals or variables or expressions, or some combination of those things. Let's try a simple program to ask the user for two integers and then use those values to do some calculations.

```c
#include <stdio.h>

int main() {
  int num1, num2;
  printf("Please enter two numbers, separated by a space: ");
  scanf("%d %d", &num1, &num2);
  printf("%d + %d is %d\n", num1, num2, num1 + num2);
  printf("%d - %d is %d\n", num1, num2, num1 - num2);
  printf("%d * %d is %d\n", num1, num2, num1 * num2);
  printf("%d / %d is %d\n", num1, num2, num1 / num2);
  printf("%d %% %d is %d\n", num1, num2, num1 % num2);
}
```

Try this short program out yourself. You can type it in or open up the *ch02/calcs.c* (*https://oreil.ly/w13kJ*) file. Compile and run and you should get output similar to this:

```
ch02$ gcc calcs.c
ch02$ ./a.out
Please enter two numbers, separated by a space: 233 17
233 + 17 is 250
233 - 17 is 216
233 * 17 is 3961
233 / 17 is 13
233 % 17 is 12
```

Hopefully, most of those answers make sense and fit with your expectations. Some results that seem odd might be our attempt to divide two numbers. Instead of getting a floating point approximation of something like 8.33333, we got a flat-out 8. Remember that the int type does not support fractions. If you divide two ints, you always get another int as the result and any decimal portion is simply dropped. And I do mean dropped, not rounded. A division result of 8.995, for example, would come back as simply 8, and a negative answer, say –7.89, would come back as –7.

Order of Operations

But what if we make a more complex expression with two (or more) operators? We can upgrade our program a little to take three integers and combine them in different ways. Check out *ch02/calcs2.c* (*https://oreil.ly/wznGj*):

```
#include <stdio.h>

int main() {
  int num1, num2, num3;
  printf("Please enter three numbers, separated by a space: ");
  scanf("%d %d %d", &num1, &num2, &num3);
  printf("%d + %d + %d is %d\n", num1, num2, num3, num1 + num2 + num3);
  printf("%d + %d - %d is %d\n", num1, num2, num3, num1 + num2 - num3);
  printf("%d * %d / %d is %d\n", num1, num2, num3, num1 * num2 / num3);
  printf("%d + %d / %d is %d\n", num1, num2, num3, num1 + num2 / num3);
  printf("%d * %d %% %d is %d\n", num1, num2, num3, num1 * num2 % num3);
}
```

Feel free to tweak the code to try other combinations if you like. As it stands, you can compile and run this program to get the following output:

```
ch02$ gcc calcs2.c
ch02$ ./a.out
Please enter three numbers, separated by a space: 36 19 7
36 + 19 + 7 is 62
36 + 19 - 7 is 48
36 * 19 / 7 is 97
36 + 19 / 7 is 38
36 * 19 % 7 is 5
```

Do these answers match what you expected? If not, it's likely due to the *precedence* of different operators. C does not handle large expressions in a simple, left-to-right manner. Some operators are more important than others—they have precedence over lesser operators. C will perform the most important operations first, wherever they are in the expression, before moving on to do the remaining operations. You'll often see the phrase "order of operations" used when talking about evaluating expressions with a mix of operators.

Multiplication, division, and remainder (*, /, %) operations will all be done before addition and subtraction (+, -) operations. Where you have a series of the same or equivalent operators, then those calculations are done left to right. Usually that's fine and we can get the answer we need by being a little careful in how we arrange the parts of our expression. When we can't rely on a simple arrangement, we can use parentheses to create a specific, custom order of operations. Consider this snippet:

```
int average1 = 14 + 20 / 2;    // or 14 + 10 which is 24
int average2 = 14 / 2 + 20;    // or  7 + 20 which is 27
int average3 = (14 + 20) / 2;  // or 34 /  2 which is 17, yay!
```

Here we have three orderings, but only the final one, `average3`, is correct. The parenthetical expression, `14 + 20`, is evaluated first. One way to think about this is that parentheses have a higher order of precedence than arithmetic operations. You are free to use parentheses anywhere you like, by the way, even if it only adds visual clarity to an otherwise correctly ordered expression.

 The notion of "visual clarity" is very subjective. If the parentheses are necessary for calculating the correct answer, then of course you need to use them. If they are not strictly necessary, use them wherever they help you read the expression more easily. It is possible to have too many parentheses, making it more difficult to read your code. Above all, be consistent in your use.

Parentheses can also be nested if you have particularly messy expressions similar to some of these:

```
int messy1 = 6 * 7 / ((4 + 5) / 2);
int messy2 = ((((1 + 2) * 3) + 4) / 5);
```

In expressions like these, the innermost parenthetical expression, `(1 + 2)`, is evaluated first and then you work your way back out.

Type Casting

We've talked about variable types quite a bit in this chapter, but expressions also have a type, and sometimes that leads to surprises for the uninitiated. Consider this following snippet:

```
double one_third = 1 / 3;
int x = 5;
int y = 12;
float average = (x + y) / 2;
```

Any guesses at what will show up if we print out `one_third` and `average`? Try creating a small C program to test your theory. Your results should look like this:

```
One third: 0.000000
Average: 8.000000
```

But "one third" should be 0.333333 and our average of 12 and 5 should be 8.5. What happened? Well, the compiler saw a bunch of integers and performed integer math. If you think back to grade school, you may have learned to do long division with remainders, i.e., "3 goes into 1 zero times with a remainder of 3." For C, that means that integer 1 divided by integer 3 is integer 0. (Recall that the `%` operator will give you the remainder value if you need it.)

Is there any way to get the floating point answer we want? Yes! In fact, there are a number of ways to get the right answer. Perhaps the simplest way to do this in our made-up examples is to use floating point literals in the initialization expressions:

```
double one_third = 1.0 / 3.0;
int x = 5;
int y = 12;
float average = (x + y) / 2.0;
```

Try changing your program, and hopefully you'll get new, correct output:

```
One third: 0.333333
Average: 8.500000
```

But what about cases where we are not using literals? What if we change our average calculation in the snippet to use a third, int variable?

```
int x = 5;
int y = 12;
int count = 2;
float average = x + y / count;
```

How could we get the average to come out correctly in this case? C supports *type casting*, which allows you to tell the compiler to treat a value as if it had some other type. Very handy for just this type of situation. We can *cast* our count variable as a float like so:

```
float average = x + y / (float)count;
```

You put the type you want in parentheses before the value or expression that you want to convert. And now that we have a floating point value in our calculation, the rest of the calculation will be "upgraded" to a floating point expression and we'll get the correct answer. That process of upgrading is not just a happy accident. The compiler does this on purpose and the process even has a name, *implicit type casting*.[7] Figure 2-4 shows you the upgrade path for many of the numeric types we have discussed.

In any expression with different types involved, the "biggest" type wins and everyone else will be promoted to that type. Notice that you can occasionally lose some important information in such conversions. A negative number will lose its sign if it gets promoted to an unsigned type. Or a long integer might be approximated rather poorly if it gets promoted to float or even to a double.

---

7 Sometimes you may hear the terms "type promotion" or "automatic type conversion" as well.

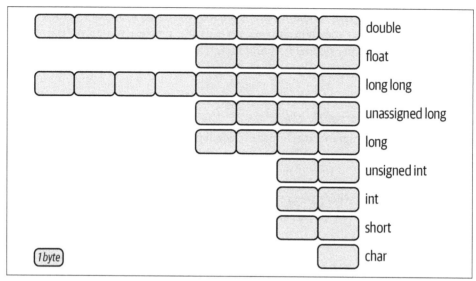

Figure 2-4. Implicit casting hierarchy

As with parentheses that add clarity without changing the calculation, you can always use an explicit cast if it helps you understand what your expression is doing. But note that the order of operations is still in effect. For example, the following statements are *not* all the same:

```
float average1 = (x + y) / (float)count;
float average2 = (float)(x + y) / count;
float average3 = (float)((x + y)/ count);
```

If you add those lines to your testing program and then print out the three averages, you'll notice that the first two work fine, but the third does not. Do you see why? The parentheses in the third calculation cause the original, wrong average with all integer types to be performed *before* that wrong answer is promoted to a `float`.

I should also point out that any time you want to move down the promotion ladder to a "smaller" type, you must use an explicit cast. Luckily, the compiler can usually catch these situations and warn you.

Next Steps

Statements comprise the core of any computer language and we've seen the basic syntax for how C uses them to assign values, perform calculations, and print results. You may have to get used to including that semicolon at the end of statements, but that'll start to feel natural before long. Typing in the examples and running them is your best route to that happy feeling.

If you did try any of the calculating demo programs, you may have been tempted to enter a zero for one of the divisors. (If you weren't tempted, go try it now!) However, C cannot divide by zero and gives up. You will get an error like "Floating point exception (core dumped)" or a result like "NaN" for "not a number." How could we prevent such a crash? The next chapter will look at comparison operations and control statements that grant us exactly this ability.

CHAPTER 3

Flow of Control

Now that you have seen the basic format of a statement in C, it's time to start branching out...pun intended. In code, the idea of making decisions and then selecting a particular bit of code to run instead of some other bit of code is often referred to as *branching* or *conditional branching*. And repetition is often discussed in terms of *looping* or *iterating*. Collectively, branching and looping statements comprise the *flow of control* in a language.

Some problems can be solved with a simple series of linear steps. Many programs that automate various computer tasks work just this way, taking a tedious routine and reducing that to a single app you can run whenever you need it. But programs can do much more than just process a batch of commands. They can make decisions based on the values in a variable or the state of a sensor. They can repeat tasks like turn on every LED in a string of lights or process every line in a log file. And they can combine the decision-making and repetition in complex, nested ways that allow you as the programmer to solve just about any problem you can think of. In this chapter we'll look at how C implements these concepts.

Boolean Values

To ask a question in C, you typically compare two (or more) things. C has several operators meant for just this task. You can check to see if two things are the same. You can check to see if two things are not the same. You can see if some value is less than or greater than some other value.

When you ask questions like "is x the same as y," you get a yes or no, true or false answer. In computer science, these are called Boolean values, after George Boole, who worked to formalize a system of logical operations and outcomes. Some languages have an actual type for Boolean values and variables, but C mostly uses integers: 0 is false/no and 1 is true/yes.[1]

 Technically, any value in C that is not 0 is true. So 1 is true, 2 is true, –18 is true, etc. I'll point out anytime I perform a check that relies on this fact. It can be convenient, and you will definitely see it used in the real world, but I'll be concentrating on performing explicit comparisons wherever I can.

Comparison Operators

Math, of course, is not the only thing computers are good at. When we get into writing more complex programs, we'll need the ability to make decisions about the state of our system. We'll need to compare variables against desired values and safeguard against error conditions. We'll need to detect the end of lists and other data structures. Happily, all of these requirements can be accommodated with C's comparison operators.

C defines six operators (shown in Table 3-1) that can be used to compare values. We use these operators much like we used the mathematical operators from Table 2-6. You have a variable or value or expression on the left, the operator, and a variable or value or expression on the right. The difference here is that the result of using a comparison operator is always a Boolean int, meaning it is always a 1 or a 0.

Table 3-1. Comparison operators

Operator	Comparison
==	Is equal to
!=	Is not equal to
<	Is less than
>	Is greater than
<=	Is less than or equal to
>=	Is greater than or equal to

In C, the comparison operators work on characters, integers, and floating point numbers. Some languages support operators that work on more complex bits of data like arrays (I'll cover these in Chapter 4), records, or objects, but C uses functions (covered in Chapter 5) to do that type of work.

---

1 C99 introduced a new type, _Bool, but we won't be using this in our lean code. If you find yourself working with Boolean logic in your own coding, though, be sure to check out the *stdbool.h* header. You can find more details on just about everything C in Prinz and Crawford's *C in a Nutshell* (O'Reilly).

When comparing two expressions of the same type, you can use the operators in Table 3-1 without really thinking about it. If you compare expressions of different types, say a `float` variable and an `int` value, the same notion of implicit casting (see Figure 2-4) applies and the value with the "lower" type will be promoted before being compared.

We'll put these comparison operators to use shortly in "Branching" on page 52 and "Loop Statements" on page 65, but we can take a quick detour and show the 0-or-1 results with some simple print statements. Consider *ch03/booleans.c* (*https://oreil.ly/2dSZx*):

```
#include <stdio.h>

int main() {
  printf(" 1 == 1  : %d\n", 1 == 1);
  printf(" 1 != 1  : %d\n", 1 != 1);
  printf(" 5 < 10  : %d\n", 5 < 10);
  printf(" 5 > 10  : %d\n", 5 > 10);
  printf("12 <= 10 : %d\n", 12 <= 10);
  printf("12 >= 10 : %d\n", 12 >= 10);
}
```

Go ahead and compile that file and run it. You should see output similar to this:

```
ch03$ gcc booleans.c
ch03$ ./a.out
 1 == 1  : 1
 1 != 1  : 0
 5 < 10  : 1
 5 > 10  : 0
12 <= 10 : 0
12 >= 10 : 1
```

You can see here that a "true" comparison results in a 1, as I noted before. Conversely, "false" is a 0 behind the scenes.

Logical Operators

Some questions we want to ask in our code cannot be reduced to a single comparison. A very popular question, for example, is to ask if a variable is within a range of values. We need to know if the variable in question is *both* greater than some minimum value *and* also less than some maximum. C does not have the kinds of operators that create ranges or that test for membership in such ranges. But C does support logical operators (sometimes you'll hear about Boolean operators) to help you build up logic expressions that can be quite complex.

To get started, look at the operators in Table 3-2.

Table 3-2. Boolean operators

Operator	Operation	Notes
!	Not	Unary operator that produces the logical opposite of its operand
&&	And	Conjunction; both operands must be true to yield true
||	Or	Disjunction; true if at least one operand is true

These operators probably look a little strange and you may not be familiar with logical operations, so give yourself some time to play with these symbols. Don't worry if they aren't comfortable yet. Boolean algebra is not a common grade school topic! But you will definitely encounter these operators in code you find online, so let's make sure you understand how they work.

Calling it "logic" or "boolean algebra" is useful when discussing programming languages, but you probably do have experience with these concepts from human languages (like the English I'm using here): these operators form *conjunctions*. The classic "and," "but," and "or" from grammar lessons are roughly equivalent to the &&, !, and || in C. Putting these Boolean expressions into English can even help you grasp their intent. Consider "x > 0 && x < 100." Go ahead and read that expression out loud: "x is greater than zero and x is less than 100." If spelling these expressions out helps, it's an easy trick to pull out when coming across new code.

In logic, these operators can be described best by their outcomes. Those outcomes, in turn, are often shown in *truth tables* that enumerate all possible combinations of inputs and their results. Luckily, with only two possible values, true and false, the combinations are manageable. Each operator gets its own truth table. Table 3-3 lists the inputs and results for the && operator. Let's start there.

Table 3-3. The && (and) operator

a	b	a && b
true	true	true
true	false	false
false	true	false
false	false	false

As the table illustrates, this is a fairly restrictive operator. Both inputs have to be true for the result to be true. Per the previous tip, it can be useful to think in terms of an English conjunction: "We can't go to the party until both Reg *and* Kaori are ready." If Reg isn't ready, we have to wait. If Reg is ready, but Kaori isn't, we have to wait. Of course, if neither are ready, we wait.[2] It's only when both are good to go that we can start our trek. For the record, Reg and Kaori are both quite prompt individuals. Waiting is rarely an issue. ;)

Table 3-4 shows the results when using || for the same combination of inputs.

Table 3-4. The || (or) operator

a	b	a ‖ b
true	true	true
true	false	true
false	true	true
false	false	false

This is a more permissive operator. Back to our party trip metaphor, perhaps it falls on a weeknight and we can't expect both of our friends to drop everything and join. For this variation, if *either* Reg *or* Kaori can join, then we will have a nice time with a good dinner companion. Similar to the && operator, if both can join, then hooray! We still have an enjoyable evening ahead.[3] If both inputs are false, though, the overall answer is still false and we'll be stuck on our own.

The final operator C supports for building logic expressions is !. It is a *unary* operator, meaning it operates on only one thing rather than the two that go into a *binary* operation like the math or comparison operators require. That means its table, Table 3-5, is a little simpler.

Table 3-5. The ! (not) operator

a	!a
true	false
false	true

In coding, this "not" operation is often used to guard against errors before continuing on. Our final party example: we will arrive at the party on time as long as we do *not* run into traffic. This operator creates an opposite result. So "traffic is bad" versus "no traffic is good." The conversion to English is not quite as literal, but hopefully still illustrates the point that you can talk about the logic being performed.

---

2 Many languages, including C, are clever enough to realize that if Reg is not ready, we don't even have to bother checking on Kaori. This behavior is often referred to as "short circuit evaluation." Short circuit comparisons can be very useful when the tests involved are computationally expensive.

3 And like the && operator, the C compiler optimizes the case where Reg can join by not asking Kaori at all.

Branching

Now that we know how to translate logic questions into valid C syntax, how can we put those questions to use? We'll start with the notion of conditional statements, or *branches*. We can ask a question and then execute some group of statements (or not) depending on the answer.

The if Statement

The simplest conditional statement is the `if` statement. It has three forms, with the simplest being a do-it-or-don't configuration. The syntax of this statement is fairly straightforward. You supply the `if` keyword, a test inside parentheses, and then a statement or code *block* (a grouping of one or more statements inside curly braces) like so:

```
// For single statements, like a printf():
if (test)
  printf("Test returned true!\n");

// or for multiple statements:
if (test) {
  // body goes here
}
```

If the Boolean expression we use is true, we will execute the statement or block following the `if` line. If the expression is false, we will skip the statement or block.

Consider a simple program that asks the user for a numeric input. You might want to let the user know about uncommon inputs, in case they made a typo. For example, we could allow negative numbers, but maybe they aren't the usual way to go. We still want the program to run, but we alert the user that they might get a surprising result. The program in *ch03/warnings.c* (*https://oreil.ly/sP2kJ*) is a simple example:

```
#include <stdio.h>

int main() {
  int units = 0;
  printf("Please enter the number of units found: ");
  scanf("%d", &units);
  if (units < 0) { // start of our "if" code block
    printf("  *** Warning: possible lost items ***\n");
  } // end of our "if" code block
  printf("%d units received.\n", units);
}
```

If we run this with a few different inputs, you can see the effect of the `if` statement. Only the final run shows the warning:

```
ch03$ gcc warnings.c
ch03$ ./a.out
```

```
Please enter the number of units found: 12
12 units received.

ch03$ ./a.out
Please enter the number of units found: 7
7 units received.

ch03$ ./a.out
Please enter the number of units found: -4
  *** Warning: possible lost items ***
-4 units received.
```

Try entering the program and then compile and run it yourself. Try changing the test to look for other things like even or odd numbers, or numbers inside or outside a range.

We can also use if statements to get some more human-friendly responses from Boolean values. Instead of printing out simple ones and zeros, we can put the tests into an if statement and then print out any true response. Here's our updated example; we'll call it *ch03/booleans2.c* (*https://oreil.ly/neHcZ*):

```
#include <stdio.h>

int main() {
  if (1 == 1) {
    printf(" 1 == 1\n");
  }
  if (1 != 1) {
    printf(" 1 != 1\n");
  }
  if (5 < 10) {
    printf(" 5 < 10\n");
  }
  if (5 > 10) {
    printf(" 5 > 10\n");
  }
  if (12 <= 10) {
    printf("12 <= 10\n");
  }
  if (12 >= 10) {
    printf("12 >= 10\n");
  }
}
```

Give this new program a try and you should get output similar to this:

```
ch03$ gcc booleans2.c
ch03$ ./a.out
 1 == 1
 5 < 10
12 >= 10
```

Great! Only tests that return true are printing. That is much more readable. This type of `if` combined with `printf()` is a common debugging trick. Anytime you have an interesting (or worrying) condition, print out a warning and maybe include the relevant variables to help you fix the problem.

else

With a simple `if`, we can see nice output for tests that return true. But what if we also want to know when a test is false? That's what the second form of the `if` statement is for; it includes an `else` clause. You always use an `else` in conjunction with an `if`. (An `else` on its own is a syntax error and the program won't compile.) The `if/else` statement ends up with two branches: one executes if the test is true, the other executes if the test is false. Let's build *ch03/booleans3.c (https://oreil.ly/neHcZ)* and get either a thumbs-up or a thumbs-down answer for every test:

```c
#include <stdio.h>

int main() {
  if (1 == 1) {
    printf(" 1 == 1\n");
  } else {
    printf(" *** Yikes! 1 == 1 returned false\n");
  }
  if (1 != 1) {
    printf(" *** Yikes! 1 != 1 returned true\n");
  } else {
    printf(" 1 != 1  is false\n");
  }
  if (5 < 10) {
    printf(" 5 < 10\n");
  } else {
    printf(" *** Yikes! 5 < 10 returned false\n");
  }
  if (5 > 10) {
    printf(" *** Yikes! 5 > 10 returned true\n");
  } else {
    printf(" 5 > 10  is false\n");
  }
  if (12 <= 10) {
    printf(" *** Yikes! 12 <= 10 returned false\n");
  } else {
    printf("12 <= 10 is false\n");
  }
  if (12 >= 10) {
    printf("12 >= 10\n");
  } else {
    printf(" *** Yikes! 12 >= 10 returned false\n");
  }
}
```

And if we run this with the same inputs from before, we'll see a gratifying expansion of answers:

```
ch03$ gcc booleans3.c
ch03$ ./a.out
 1 == 1
 1 != 1  is false
 5 < 10
 5 > 10  is false
12 <= 10 is false
12 >= 10
```

Perfect. We have readable answers for every test. Now we don't have to wonder if a test ran and failed or was somehow skipped altogether. We get a useful response every time. Try upgrading the *warnings.c* file so that you still get the warning if a number is "unusual," but it also gives the user a friendly message indicating their input is in the expected range.

else if chains

We now have some pretty powerful decision statements in our toolkit. We can do something or skip it. We can do one thing or an alternative. What if we need to decide between three statements? Or four? Or more? One possible pattern for this scenario is the third variation of if: the if/else if/else combination.

C allows you to "chain" if/else pairs together to achieve a one-of-many branch selection. Consider game scores that get rated with one, two, or three stars depending on how well you did. You could get that type of answer with this idea of else if blocks. Here is *ch03/stars.c* (*https://oreil.ly/Fe8q9*):

```c
#include <stdio.h>

int main() {
  int score = 0;
  printf("Enter your score (1 - 100): ");
  scanf("%d", &score);
  if (score > 100) {
    printf("Bad score, must be between 1 and 100.\n");
  } else if (score >= 85) {
    printf("Great! 3 stars!\n");
  } else if (score >= 50) {
    printf("Good score! 2 stars.\n");
  } else if (score >= 1) {
    printf("You completed the game. 1 star.\n");
  } else {
    // Only here because we have a negative score
    printf("Impossible score, must be positive.\n");
  }
}
```

Here are some example runs:

```
ch03$ gcc stars.c
ch03$ ./a.out
Enter your score (1 - 100): 72
Good score! 2 stars.

ch03$ ./a.out
Enter your score (1 - 100): 99
Great! 3 stars!

ch03$ ./a.out
Enter your score (1 - 100): 4567
Bad score, must be between 1 and 100.

ch03$ ./a.out
Enter your score (1 - 100): 42
You completed the game. 1 star.

ch03$ ./a.out
Enter your score (1 - 100): -42
Impossible score, must be positive.
```

But maybe our game is special and has four star performances. (Wow!) The file *ch03/ stars2.c* (*https://oreil.ly/uXLDr*) shows how to bring one more else if clause to the rescue!

```c
#include <stdio.h>

int main() {
  int score = 0;
  printf("Enter your score (1 - 100): ");
  scanf("%d", &score);
  if (score > 100) {
    printf("Bad score, must be between 1 and 100.\n");
  } else if (score == 100) {
    printf("Perfect score!! 4 stars!!\n");
  } else if (score >= 85) {
    printf("Great! 3 stars!\n");
  } else if (score >= 50) {
    printf("Good score! 2 stars.\n");
  } else if (score >= 1) {
    printf("You completed the game. 1 star.\n");
  } else {
    // Only here because we have a negative score
    printf("Impossible score, must be positive.\n");
  }
}
```

And a few more examples of the output to verify that our new top score works:

```
ch03$ gcc stars2.c
ch03$ ./a.out
```

```
Enter your score (1 - 100): 100
Perfect score!! 4 stars!!

ch03$ ./a.out
Enter your score (1 - 100): 64
Good score! 2 stars.

ch03$ ./a.out
Enter your score (1 - 100): 101
Bad score, must be between 1 and 100.
```

You could continue those chains ad infinitum. Well, within reason. You'll eventually be limited by memory and beyond a handful of clauses, it becomes difficult to follow the flow of such chains. If it feels like you have too many else/if blocks in one chain, it might be worth spending a little time examining your algorithm to see if there are other ways to break down your tests.

if gotchas

The syntax of those else/if chains hints at a detail of C's syntax I previously mentioned briefly. The if and else chunks do not require the curly braces if you have exactly one statement in the clause. For example, our *booleans3.c* could be written like this (*ch03/booleans3_alt.c* (*https://oreil.ly/FrXzk*)):

```
#include <stdio.h>

int main() {
  if (1 == 1)
    printf(" 1 == 1\n");
  else
    printf(" *** Yikes! 1 == 1 returned false\n");
  if (1 != 1)
    printf(" *** Yikes! 1 != 1 returned true\n");
  else
    printf(" 1 != 1  is false\n");
  // ...
}
```

You will definitely run across code like this online. It saves a little typing and can make for more compact code where the tests and the statements are simple. You *can* use the curly braces to create a block with a single statement just as we did in the original *booleans3.c* code. It works like using extra parentheses in mathematic operations: not necessary but useful for readability. It is mostly just a matter of style when you have only the one thing to do. Since doing two or more things always requires the curly braces, though, I'll stick to using curly braces as a way to future-proof our code. (And as a matter of style, I prefer the consistency of seeing the braces.) If we come back later to update some example and need to add another print statement, say, we won't have to remember to add the braces; they'll be there ready and waiting.

The tests you use in if statements can also cause problems if you aren't careful. Remember the comment about C treating a zero as false and any other number as true? Some programmers rely on that fact to write very compact tests. Consider this snippet:

```
int x;
printf("Please enter an integer: ");
scanf("%i", x);
if (x) {
  printf("Thanks, you gave us a great number!\n");
} else {
  printf("Oh. A zero. Well, thanks for \"nothing\"! ;)\n");
}
```

The if clause will execute for any positive or negative number, as if we had built a real test like x != 0 or even a fancier logical expression like (x < 0 || x > 0). This pattern gets used as a (sometimes lazy) shortcut for asking "does this variable have any value at all" where a zero is assumed to be an invalid possibility. It's a fairly common pattern, although I usually prefer to write explicit tests.

One other big quirk of C using integers as proxies for Boolean values: there is a very subtle typo that can cause real trouble. Take a look at this next snippet:

```
int first_card = 10;
int second_card = 7;
int total = first_card + second_card;

if (total = 21) {
  printf("Blackjack! %d\n", total);
}
```

If you're curious, go ahead and create a program to try this gotcha. When you run it, you'll see that you *always* get the "Blackjack! 21" output. What happened? Look closely at the test in the if statement. What we meant to write was total == 21 using the double equal sign comparison operator. By using the single equal sign, we actually *assigned* the value 21 to our total variable right there inside the if test! Assignments in C are expressions just like our mathematic calculations. The value of an assignment expression is the same as the new value being assigned. The upshot is that this test is akin to if (21) ..., which will always be true since 21 is not 0. It is frustratingly easy to make this mistake. Just watch out for if statements that always seem to execute no matter how you change your inputs. That behavior is a hint to reexamine the test you're using.

The switch Statement

I noted in "else if chains" on page 55 that the if/else if chains can become difficult to follow if you have too many tests chained together. Sometimes, though, you really do have a bunch of specific cases you need to check, say, what shirts are in stock at your favorite online store based on your size. If those cases all involve the same variable and all use simple equality (==) as the test, then you can use the switch statement in C as a nice alternative.

A switch statement takes an expression (the control expression), typically a variable or simple calculation, and then systematically compares the value of that expression to one or more constant values using case labels. If the control expression value matches a case, the code following that value starts executing and continues until the end of the switch statement (which is always a curly brace block) or the program hits a break command. The *ch03/medals.c* (*https://oreil.ly/LVkuZ*) file contains a simple example:

```
#include <stdio.h>

int main() {
  int place;
  printf("Enter your place: ");
  scanf("%i", &place);
  switch (place) {
  case 1:
    printf("1st place! Gold!\n");
    break;
  case 2:
    printf("2nd place! Silver!\n");
    break;
  case 3:
    printf("3rd place! Bronze!\n");
    break;
  }
}
```

If you compile and run the program a few times with the three possible inputs, you should see results like this:

```
ch03$ gcc medals.c
ch03$ ./a.out
Enter your place: 2
2nd place! Silver!

ch03$ ./a.out
Enter your place: 1
1st place! Gold!

ch03$ ./a.out
Enter your place: 3
3rd place! Bronze!
```

Neat! Exactly what we expected. But what if we comment out those break lines? Let's try that now because this illustrates a critical quirk with switch that can trip up new programmers. Here is our altered program, *ch03/medals2.c* (*https://oreil.ly/MluI4*):

```c
#include <stdio.h>

int main() {
  int place;
  printf("Enter your place: ");
  scanf("%i", &place);
  switch (place) {
  case 1:
    printf("1st place! Gold!\n");
  case 2:
    printf("2nd place! Silver!\n");
  case 3:
    printf("3rd place! Bronze!\n");
  }
}
```

And here is the new output using the same series of inputs we used the first time:

```
ch03$ gcc medals2.c
ch03$ ./a.out
Enter your place: 2
2nd place! Silver!
3rd place! Bronze!

ch03$ ./a.out
Enter your place: 1
1st place! Gold!
2nd place! Silver!
3rd place! Bronze!

ch03$ ./a.out
Enter your place: 3
3rd place! Bronze!
```

Huh. That's really strange. Once it gets started, the program just keeps executing statements in the switch even if they are part of separate cases. While that might seem like a bad idea, it is meant to be a feature of switch, not a bug. This design allows you to perform the same action for several values. Consider the following snippet that describes any number between 1 and 10 in terms of even, odd, and prime:

```c
printf("Describing %d:\n", someNumber);
switch(someNumber) {
  case 2:
    printf("  only even prime\n");
    break;
  case 3:
  case 5:
  case 7:
    printf("  prime\n");
  case 1:
  case 9:
```

```
  // 1 isn't often described as prime, so we'll just let it be odd
    printf("  odd\n");
    break;
  case 4:
  case 6:
  case 8:
  case 10:
    printf("  even\n");
    break;
}
```

We can arrange cases in such a way that the `switch` feature of flowing until a `break` gives us exactly the right output. While this feature is most often used to collect a related series of distinct values (such as our even numbers) and then give them the same block to execute, the flow of printing the "prime" qualifier and then continuing on to add the "odd" designation is valid and can be handy sometimes.

Handling defaults

There is one other feature in `switch` that is similar to the `else` clause that can be used with `if` statements. Sometimes you want your `switch` statement to handle every possible input. But listing out a few thousand integers or even just every letter in the alphabet can be very tedious, to say the least. And usually, you don't have unique actions for all those thousands of options. In these situations, you can use the `default` label as your final "case" and it will execute regardless of the control expression value.

> Technically, `default` can appear anywhere in the list of cases, not just as the final option. However, since the `default` case *always* runs when encountered, it doesn't make sense to include subsequent, specific cases.

For example, with our *medals.c* program, what about contestants that didn't make the podium? Try running it again with some number larger than three. What do you get? Nothing. No error, no output, nada. Let's write *ch03/medals3.c* (*https://oreil.ly/l1AHK*) and use the `default` option to print a message and at least prove we saw the input:

```
#include <stdio.h>

int main() {
  int place;
  printf("Enter your place: ");
  scanf("%i", &place);
  switch (place) {
  case 1:
    printf("1st place! Gold!\n");
    break;
```

```
  case 2:
    printf("2nd place! Silver!\n");
    break;
  case 3:
    printf("3rd place! Bronze!\n");
    break;
  default:
    printf("Sorry, you didn't make the podium.\n");
  }
}
```

Compile and run this new program and try some values larger than three:

```
ch03$ gcc medals3.c
ch03$ ./a.out
Enter your place: 8
Sorry, you didn't make the podium.

ch03$ ./a.out
Enter your place: 88
Sorry, you didn't make the podium.

ch03$ ./a.out
Enter your place: 5792384
Sorry, you didn't make the podium.
```

Lovely! No matter what number greater than three we give, we get some feedback to show that we have processed that input. Exactly what we wanted. And we can use `default` even with `switch` statements that include the multiple-cases-per-block arrangement. Let's add a "Top 10" level to our medal description program, *ch03/medals4.c* (*https://oreil.ly/lS1tv*):

```
#include <stdio.h>

int main() {
  int place;
  printf("Enter your place: ");
  scanf("%i", &place);
  switch (place) {
  case 1:
    printf("1st place! Gold!\n");
    break;
  case 2:
    printf("2nd place! Silver!\n");
    break;
  case 3:
    printf("3rd place! Bronze!\n");
    break;
  case 4:
  case 5:
  case 6:
  case 7:
  case 8:
```

```
    case 9:
    case 10:
      printf("Top 10! Congrats!\n");
      break;
    default:
      printf("Sorry, you didn't make the podium.\n");
    }
  }
```

One more compile and then run it with a few inputs:

```
ch03$ gcc medals4.c
ch03$ ./a.out
Enter your place: 4
Top 10! Congrats!

ch03$ ./a.out
Enter your place: 1
1st place! Gold!

ch03$ ./a.out
Enter your place: 20
Sorry, you didn't make the podium.

ch03$ ./a.out
Enter your place: 7
Top 10! Congrats!
```

Great. Here's a quick homework assignment for you. Modify *medals4.c* so that if you get 4th or 5th place, you get labeled a "runner up." Places 6 through 10 should still be listed as top 10. (It's a small change. You can check your answer against mine in *ch03/medals5.c* (*https://oreil.ly/W7uci*).)

The Ternary Operator and Conditional Assignment

One last conditional topic that gets a lot of use in lean code is the notion of conditional assignment. C includes a ternary operator, ?:, that takes three operands. It allows you to use one of two values in a very compact syntax. The result of this ternary expression is indeed a value like any other expression in C, so you can use ?: anywhere a value is legal.

The syntax of ?: uses a Boolean expression as the first operand, then the question mark, then an expression to evaluate if the boolean is true, then the colon, and finally an alternate expression to evaluate if the boolean is false.

A great example of using the ternary operator is grabbing the smaller of two values. Consider a simple program processing two bids for some graphic design work. Budget is sadly the driving factor, so you need to accept the lowest bid.

```
int winner = (bid1 < bid2) ? bid1 : bid2;
```

Very dense! It takes a little practice even just to read these ternary expressions, but once you have the hang of it, I think you'll find it a very handy operator. The alternative is a somewhat drawn out if/else:

```
int winner;
if (bid1 < bid2) {
  winner = bid1;
} else {
  winner = bid2;
}
```

Certainly not an awful alternative, but it is definitely more verbose. Plus there are times where the ternary approach really simplifies things. Remember the first program on Boolean expressions, *booleans.c*, in "Comparison Operators" on page 48? We had to live with interpreting a 1 as "true" and a 0 as "false." We eventually printed nice statements in *booleans3.c*, but we had to use that fairly verbose if/else pattern. With ?:, however, we can make human-friendly output directly in the printf() statements. Try *ch03/booleans4.c* (*https://oreil.ly/Hnumr*) and see what you think:

```
#include <stdio.h>

int main() {
  printf(" 1 == 1  : %s\n", 1 == 1 ? "true" : "false");
  printf(" 1 != 1  : %s\n", 1 != 1 ? "true" : "false");
  printf(" 5 < 10  : %s\n", 5 < 10 ? "true" : "false");
  printf(" 5 > 10  : %s\n", 5 > 10 ? "true" : "false");
  printf("12 <= 10 : %s\n", 12 <= 10 ? "true" : "false");
  printf("12 >= 10 : %s\n", 12 >= 10 ? "true" : "false");
}
```

And here is our updated output:

```
ch03$ gcc booleans4.c
ch03$ ./a.out
 1 == 1  : true
 1 != 1  : false
 5 < 10  : true
 5 > 10  : false
12 <= 10 : false
12 >= 10 : true
```

Much better.

It was a bit of a pain wrapping each of those print calls in an `if`/`else` block in *booleans3.c*. Not just annoying, the shared parts in the printed text can get out of sync if you make any changes. If you found a typo at the beginning of a line, for example, you would have to make sure you fixed the beginning of both the `if` clause `printf()` and again in the `else` clause. It is all too easy to forget one or the other.

Any time you can avoid such duplicated code by using a different conditional statement or operator, it's worth considering. But don't be overzealous; if your `if`/`else` chain feels readable and produces the right output, that is still a fine option.

Loop Statements

You can solve some interesting problems with just variables and the input, output, and branching statements we have covered so far. But one of the spots where computers really shine is when you need to repeat a test or batch of statements. To perform repetitions, you can use one of C's *loop* statements. Your program will execute all of the (optional) statements, and at the end of those statements, "loop" back to the start and execute them all again. Usually you don't want that loop to run forever, so each loop statement has a condition to check and see when the loop should stop.

The for Statement

One type of repetition that crops up in programming is repeating a block for a specific number of times. For example, doing something for each day of the week, or processing the first 5 lines of input, or even just counting to 10. In fact, let's see the `for` loop that counts to 10, shown in Figure 3-1 where I have marked the parts of the loop. (Feel free to type this in or open up the *ch03/ten.c* (*https://oreil.ly/qqDiQ*) file.) It can look a little messy at first, but over time it'll become familiar.

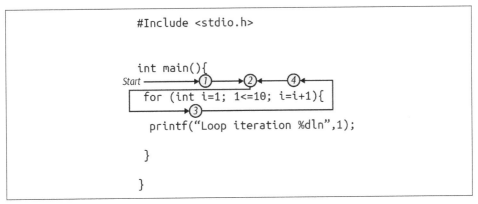

Figure 3-1. An annotated for loop

Before we look at the details of the loop, here's the output:

```
ch03$ gcc ten.c
ch03$ ./a.out
Loop iteration: 1
Loop iteration: 2
Loop iteration: 3
Loop iteration: 4
Loop iteration: 5
Loop iteration: 6
Loop iteration: 7
Loop iteration: 8
Loop iteration: 9
Loop iteration: 10
```

❶ (int i = 1) This is our loop variable. We use the same declaration and initialization syntax as we do for normal variables. This portion of the loop is always executed first, and is only executed once when the loop starts.

❷ (i <= 10) Here is the test to see when the loop should stop. The loop will run as long as this test returns true. If this condition is false—even the first time it is checked—the loop will end.

❸ The body of the loop is executed next, assuming the test in ❷ returned true.

❹ (i = i + 1) After completing the body, this adjustment expression is evaluated. This expression typically increments or decrements our loop variable by one. After this step, control jumps back to ❷ to see if the loop should continue.

The initialization, the check for when to end, and the adjustment are all quite flexible. You can use whatever name you like and can count up or down by any amount. You can even use the char type for a variable if you want sequential characters for any reason.

Let's try a few more simple for loops to practice its syntax and its flow. We'll initialize our loop variable, check to make sure we should start the loop, execute the statements in the body, perform the adjustment, and then check to see if we should continue. Lather. Rinse. Repeat.[4] We'll try some loops with different adjustments including a decrement that can be used to count backward, *ch03/more_for.c* (*https://oreil.ly/ jzGZe*):

```
#include <stdio.h>
```

---

4 Did you know many shampoo bottles come with an algorithm for washing your hair? But don't follow the algorithm too closely: many times the instructions really are as simple as "lather, rinse, repeat," which is an infinite loop! There is no check as to when you have repeated enough.

```
int main() {
  printf("Print only even values from 2 to 10:\n");
  for (int i = 2; i <= 10; i = i + 2) {
    printf("  %i\n", i);
  }
  printf("\nCount down from 5 to 1:\n");
  for (int j = 5; j > 0; j = j - 1) {
    printf("  %i\n", j);
  }
}
```

Here's our output:

```
ch03$ gcc more_for.c
ch03$ ./a.out
Print only even values from 2 to 10:
  2
  4
  6
  8
  10

Count down from 5 to 1:
  5
  4
  3
  2
  1
```

Try tweaking some of the values in the loops and recompile. Can you count backward by twos? Can you count to 100? Can you count from 1 to 1,024 by doubling?

Increment shortcuts

Incrementing or decrementing a variable like we do in those adjustment expressions is such a common task (even outside of loops) that C supports a number of shortcuts for that type of change. Consider statements of the following form:

```
var = var op value

// Examples
i = i + 1
y = y * 5
total = total - 1
```

where var is some variable and op is one of the arithmetic operators from Table 2-6. If you are using that pattern in your code, you can use a compound assignment instead:

```
var op= value

// Converted examples
i += 1
```

```
y *= 5
total -= 1
```

Going further, any time you are adding or subtracting 1 from a variable, you can use an even more succinct variation:

```
var++ or var--

// Further converted examples
i++
total--
```

 You may see a "prefix" version of the increment and decrement shortcuts, i.e., ++i or --total. These variations are legal and have a subtle distinction that does not come into play when used in for loops like we're doing.[5]

You don't have to use these compact options, but they are popular and you will certainly encounter them on coding sites like Stack Overflow or in Arduino examples.

for gotchas

Before we tackle the other loop options in C, I want to point out a few details about for loops that can trip you up.

Perhaps the most important element of the for loop syntax is the condition in the middle of the loop's setup. You need to make sure that the condition allows the loop to *start* as well as the more obviously necessary ability to make the loop stop. Consider this loop snippet:

```
for (int x = 1; x == 11; x++) {
    // ....
}
```

The ostensible intent of the loop is to count to 10—by stopping when x is equal to 11. But the condition must evaluate to true for the loop to run, so you can't just watch for the end.

You also need to make sure your condition and adjustment expressions are in sync. One of my favorite mistakes is to create a loop meant to count down or count backward, but I forget to use the decrement operation:

---

5 A quick nerdy detail, if you're curious. *Prefix* operators come before the value or expression they are meant to operate on. The i-- expression contains an example of a *postfix* operator—one that comes after the value or expression. In C, all of the binary operators like + or * or == are *infix* operators, coming "in between" the operands.

```
for (int countdown = 10; countdown > 0; countdown++) {
  // ....
}
```

I obviously should say countdown-- in the last segment of this setup, but incrementing is so common, it's almost muscle memory. Take a look at this loop. Can you see
what is going to happen? Instead of moving toward the stop condition, this loop will
head away and keep going for quite some time. Sadly, the compiler can't really help us
here because this syntax is entirely legal. The error is a logic error, so it falls to you as
the programmer to catch it.

The other big mistake that can be easy to make has to do with the syntax of the for
loop setup. Notice that the expressions are separated by semicolons, not commas:

```
for (int bad = 1, bad < 10, bad++) {
  // ....
}

for (int good = 1; good < 10; good++) {
  // ....
}
```

That detail is easy to miss and you'll probably make that mistake at least once. Here,
the compiler will catch you, though:

```
ch03$ gcc bad_ten.c
ten.c: In function 'main':
ten.c:4:23: error: expected '=', ',', ';', 'asm' before '<=' token
    4 |   for (int bad = 1, bad <= 10, bad++) {
      |                         ^~
ten.c:7:1: error: expected expression before '}' token
    7 | }
      | ^
ten.c:7:1: error: expected expression before '}' token
ten.c:7:1: error: expected expression before '}' token
```

Easy to fix, of course, but something to be mindful of as you are learning. These types
of errors are something you encounter (and then fix!) more often when typing up
code directly rather than cutting and pasting it from an online source. I really do
recommend entering some of the program listings in this book by hand for just this
reason.

The while Statement

Performing a specific number of iterations is certainly a popular task in computer
programming. But looping until some more generic condition is met is easily just as
common. In C, that more generic loop is the while loop. It has a simple condition as
its only real syntactic element. If the condition is true, the body of the loop is executed. Jump back up and check the condition…and repeat.

This type of loop is perfect for input where you cannot predict how many pieces of information you will need to scan. Let's try a simple program to calculate the average of some numbers. Critically, we will allow the user to enter as many (or as few) numbers as they wish. We'll ask them to enter a *sentinel* value to indicate they are done giving us new numbers. A sentinel can be any value that stands out from expected values. We use it in our condition so we know when to stop. For example, let's ask the user for numbers between 1 and 100. We can then use 0 as a sentinel. Here is *ch03/ average.c (https://oreil.ly/KmxH4)*:

```c
#include <stdio.h>

int main() {
  int grade;
  float total = 0.0;
  int count = 0;
  printf("Please enter a grade between 1 and 100. Enter 0 to quit: ");
  scanf("%i", &grade);
  while (grade != 0) {
    total += grade;
    count++;
    printf("Enter another grade (0 to quit): ");
    scanf("%i", &grade);
  }
  if (count > 0) {
    printf("\nThe final average is %.2f\n", total / count);
  } else {
    printf("\nNo grades were entered.\n");
  }
}
```

Here are two sample runs with different inputs:

```
ch03$ gcc average.c
ch03$ ./a.out
Please enter a grade between 1 and 100. Enter 0 to quit: 82
Enter another grade (0 to quit): 91
Enter another grade (0 to quit): 77
Enter another grade (0 to quit): 43
Enter another grade (0 to quit): 14
Enter another grade (0 to quit): 97
Enter another grade (0 to quit): 0

The final average is 67.33

ch03$ ./a.out
Please enter a grade between 1 and 100. Enter 0 to quit: 0

No grades were entered.
```

We get things going by asking the user for the first number. We then use that response in our `while` statement. If they enter a 0 the first time, we're done. Unlike for loops, it is not uncommon for a while loop to never execute. There are reasonable circumstances where you might need to iterate over an optional task, say, turning off all the lights in a smart home. But being optional, sometimes that means you don't do it at all; if the lights are already off, there's nothing to do.

Assuming they give us a valid number, though, we start the loop. We add their input to a separate variable where we keep the running total. (In programming, this is sometimes referred to as an *accumulator*.) We also increment a third variable, count, to keep track of how many numbers the user gives us.

We prompt the user for the next number (or a 0 to quit). We get their input, and again that value will be used in the while loop's condition. If the most recent grade is valid, add it to the total and repeat.

Once we complete the loop, we print the results. We use an if/else statement to wrap that final result in a nice, human-friendly sentence. If they entered a 0 at the beginning, we note that there is no average to print. Otherwise (else) we print the average with two decimal places of precision.

The do/while Variation

The last of the loop statements in C is the do/while (sometimes referred to as just a do loop). As you might guess from the name, it is similar to the while loop, but with one big difference. A do loop automatically guarantees at least one execution of the loop body. It does this by checking the loop condition *after* the body has executed instead of before. This is great where you know you need at least one pass. Our grade averaging program is actually a perfect example. We have to ask the user for a grade at least once. If they give us a 0 right away, we're done and that's fine. If they give us a valid number, we accumulate our total and ask again. Using a do loop and a small adjustment to our count at the end, we can avoid the duplicate scanf() calls in *ch03/average2.c* (*https://oreil.ly/ILhdW*):

```
#include <stdio.h>

int main() {
  int grade;
  float total = 0.0;
  int count = 0;
  do {
    printf("Enter a grade between 1 and 100 (0 to quit): ");
    scanf("%i", &grade);
    total += grade;
    count++;
  } while (grade != 0);
  // We end up counting the sentinel as a grade, so undo that
  count--;
```

```
    if (count > 0) {
      printf("\nThe final average is %.2f\n", total / count);
    } else {
      printf("\nNo grades were entered.\n");
    }
  }
```

And the output is essentially the same:

```
ch03$ gcc average2.c
ch03$ ./a.out
Enter a grade between 1 and 100 (0 to quit): 82
Enter a grade between 1 and 100 (0 to quit): 91
Enter a grade between 1 and 100 (0 to quit): 77
Enter a grade between 1 and 100 (0 to quit): 43
Enter a grade between 1 and 100 (0 to quit): 14
Enter a grade between 1 and 100 (0 to quit): 97
Enter a grade between 1 and 100 (0 to quit): 0

The final average is 67.33
```

Not much of a difference—indeed no difference in the results—but any time you can remove lines of code without harming functionality, you're reducing the chances of bugs cropping up. That's always a good thing!

Nesting

Adding loops and conditional statements to your repertoire greatly expands the problems you can tackle. But it gets even better: you can nest if statements inside loops to watch for error conditions, put a while inside an if to wait on a sensor, or use a for loop inside another for loop to traverse tabular data. Remember that all these control statements are still just statements and they can be used anywhere other, simpler statements are allowed.

Let's use this nesting ability to improve our averaging program further. We know zero is the "done" value, but we said we wanted values between 1 and 100. What happens if the user gives us a negative number? Or a number greater than 100? If you look closely at the code in *average2.c*, you'll see we don't do much about it. We don't exit or throw it out. We can do better if we use an if/else statement inside our loop as in *ch03/average3.c* (*https://oreil.ly/alYI8*):

```
#include <stdio.h>

int main() {
  int grade;
  float total = 0.0;
  int count = 0;
  do {
    printf("Enter a grade between 1 and 100 (0 to quit): ");
    scanf("%i", &grade);
```

```
    if (grade >= 1 && grade <= 100) {
      // Valid! Count it.
      total += grade;
      count++;
    } else if (grade != 0) {
      // Not valid, and not our sentinel, so print an error and continue.
      printf("   *** %d is not a valid grade. Skipping.\n", grade);
    }
  } while (grade != 0);

  if (count > 0) {
    printf("\nThe final average is %.2f\n", total / count);
  } else {
    printf("\nNo grades were entered.\n");
  }
}
```

Cool. We even fixed the little hiccup with our count variable in *average2.c* where we had to decrement count by 1 since we executed the entire body of the do/while loop even if the first entry was 0. Very nice upgrade!

Let's test this program with some simple inputs so we can verify that bad values were not included in the average:

```
ch03$ gcc average3.c
ch03$ ./a.out
Enter a grade between 1 and 100 (0 to quit): 82
Enter a grade between 1 and 100 (0 to quit): -82
   *** -82 is not a valid grade. Skipping.
Enter a grade between 1 and 100 (0 to quit): 43
Enter a grade between 1 and 100 (0 to quit): 14
Enter a grade between 1 and 100 (0 to quit): 9101
   *** 9101 is not a valid grade. Skipping.
Enter a grade between 1 and 100 (0 to quit): 97
Enter a grade between 1 and 100 (0 to quit): 0

The final average is 59.00
```

We can check the math: $82 + 43 + 14 + 97 = 236$. $236 \div 4 = 59$. That matches our result, so our nested if/else is working. Hooray!

As you build more complicated programs with nested control statements, you may bump into situations where you need to get out of a loop before it would normally finish. Happily, the break command you saw in the discussion of the switch statement can be used to immediately exit a loop. Some programmers try to avoid this "cheat," but sometimes I think it actually makes code more readable.

A common use case is encountering an error from user input in the middle of a loop. Rather than try to add extra logic to your loop condition, you can test for the error with an if statement and if you did get the error, just break.

Nested Loops and Tables

Let's try another example. I mentioned using nested for loops for tabular data. We can use this idea to produce the classic multiplication table from grade school in *ch03/multiplication.c* (*https://oreil.ly/mQQbs*):

```
#include <stdio.h>

int main() {
  int tableSize = 10;
  for (int row = 1; row <= tableSize; row++) {
    for (int col = 1; col <= tableSize; col++) {
      printf("%4d", row * col);
    }
    printf("\n"); // final newline to move to the next row
  }
}
```

That's pretty small. This is the type of repetitive task that programs can solve very efficiently. And the resulting table:

```
ch03$ gcc multiplication.c
ch03$ ./a.out
   1   2   3   4   5   6   7   8   9  10
   2   4   6   8  10  12  14  16  18  20
   3   6   9  12  15  18  21  24  27  30
   4   8  12  16  20  24  28  32  36  40
   5  10  15  20  25  30  35  40  45  50
   6  12  18  24  30  36  42  48  54  60
   7  14  21  28  35  42  49  56  63  70
   8  16  24  32  40  48  56  64  72  80
   9  18  27  36  45  54  63  72  81  90
  10  20  30  40  50  60  70  80  90 100
```

Very gratifying! And you aren't limited to just two loops. You could process three-dimensional data with three loops, as in this snippet:

```
for (int x = -5; x <= 5; x++) {
  for (int y = -5; y <= 5; y++) {
    for (int z = -5; z <= 5; z++) {
      // Do something with your 3D (x, y, z) coordinate
      // or use even more nested elements like checking for the origin
      if (x == 0 && y == 0 && z == 0) {
        printf("We found the origin!\n");
      }
    }
  }
}
```

There is (almost) no end to the complexity you can wrap up in your code to solve even the thorniest problems.

Variable Scope

One important thing to remember about nesting statements in C is that the language enforces *variable scope* in its blocks. If you create a variable to use with a for loop, for example, that variable cannot be used *after* the loop has completed. This is true of any variable declared inside a block (e.g., inside a pair of curly braces) or in the setup of a for loop. Once the block ends, the variable is no longer accessible. (Sometimes you'll hear programmers talk about a variable's *visibility*, which is the same idea.)

Most times you don't have to think much about this topic, as you'll naturally tend to use your variables where you declare them and that's great. But in complex code structures, you can lose track of where a variable was declared and that can cause problems.

Let's upgrade our multiplication table program to ask the user what size of table (within reason!) they'd like to produce. We'll allow any table size from 1 to 20. We'll store the user's response in a variable that can be used by both loops. Try the following program (*ch03/multiplication2.c* (*https://oreil.ly/0z424*)) and pay attention to the comments that highlight some potential problem areas where a variable is not visible.

```
#include <stdio.h>

int main() {
  int tableSize;
  printf("Please enter a size for your table (1 - 20): ");
  scanf("%i", &tableSize);
  if (tableSize < 1 || tableSize > 20) {
    printf("We can't make a table that size. Sorry!\n");
    printf("We'll use the default size of 10 instead.\n");
    tableSize = 10;
  }
  for (int row = 1; row <= tableSize; row++) {        ❶
    // row and tableSize are both in scope
    for (int col = 1; col <= tableSize; col++) {      ❶
      // row, col, and tableSize are all in scope
```

```
        printf("%4d", row * col);                            ❷
      }
      // col is now _out_ of scope                           ❸
      printf("\n"); // final newline to move to the next row
    }
    // row is out of scope now, too, but tableSize remains available
}
```

❶ You can see that our `tableSize` variable is visible in both loops.

❷ Clearly, the `row` variable is visible inside the loop drive by the `col` variable.

❸ But once that inner `for` loop finishes printing the values for a given row, the `col` variable goes "out of scope" and cannot be used.

But what happens if you try to access something that has gone out of scope? Well happily, the compiler will usually catch you. For example, if we try printing the final value of `col` where we currently print the newline character to end the row, we'll get an error like this:

```
ch03$ gcc multiplication2.c
multiplication2.c: In function 'main':
multiplication2.c:19:20: error: 'col' undeclared (first use in this function)
   19 |     printf("%d\n", col); // final newline to move to the next row
      |                    ^~~
```

Making these mistakes is never fatal. You just have to read the error message and figure out which bit of code is causing the problem. If you *do* need to use a particular variable after a loop or block concludes, you must define that variable before the block. For example, we could declare both of our loop variables, `row` and `col`, in the same spot where we declare `tableSize` to make all three of them visible everywhere inside our `main()` function. Our initialization step in our `for` loops won't declare those variables with their `int` type, but rather just assign the starting value, like in *ch03/multiplication3.c* (*https://oreil.ly/yTDBc*):

```
#include <stdio.h>

int main() {
  int tableSize, row, col;
  printf("Please enter a size for your table (1 - 20): ");
  scanf("%i", &tableSize);
  if (tableSize < 1 || tableSize > 20) {
    printf("We can't make a table that size. Sorry!\n");
    printf("We'll use the default size of 10 instead.\n");
    tableSize = 10;
  }
  // Notice that since we declared row and col above, we do not
  // include the "int" type declaration inside the for loops below
  for (row = 1; row <= tableSize; row++) {
```

```
    for (col = 1; col <= tableSize; col++) {
      printf("%4d", row * col);
    }
    printf("\n");
  }
  printf("\nFinal variable values:\n");
  printf("  row == %d\n  col == %d\n  tableSize == %d\n", row, col, tableSize);
}
```

If we run our new version with a width of 5, then, here's our output:

```
ch03$ gcc multiplication3.c
ch03$ ./a.out
Please enter a size for your table (1 - 20): 5
   1   2   3   4   5
   2   4   6   8  10
   3   6   9  12  15
   4   8  12  16  20
   5  10  15  20  25

Final variable values:
  row == 6
  col == 6
  tableSize == 5
```

So we can see the final values of row and col that caused the loops to stop. Kind of neat, but also kind of prone to causing problems. Using variables with a broad or global scope is frowned on because of those potential problems. If you have a good reason and need to use a particular variable in different blocks, that's fine, just make sure you declare such variables deliberately and not simply to make the program compile.

Exercises

We've seen the structure of several different flow of control statements in this chapter. Hopefully, you've been trying and tweaking the examples as you've been reading. But nothing helps you get comfortable with a new language or a new statement like using it. Over and over. And over. :) To that end, here are some exercises to try if you like before reading on.

1. Print out a triangle pattern. You can hardcode the size or ask the user, like we did with our multiplication table. For example:

```
exercises$ ./a.out
Please enter a size for your triangle (1 - 20): 5
*
**
***
```

```
****
*****
```

2. Print out a pyramid pattern where the rows of stars are centered, like this:

```
exercises$ ./a.out
Please enter a size for your triangle (1 - 20): 5
    *
   * *
  * * *
 * * * *
* * * * *
```

3. Add row and column labels to our multiplication table, like this:

```
exercises$ ./a.out
Please enter a size for your table (1 - 20): 5
       1   2   3   4   5
   1   1   2   3   4   5
   2   2   4   6   8  10
   3   3   6   9  12  15
   4   4   8  12  16  20
   5   5  10  15  20  25
```

4. Write a number guessing game. For now, just pick a number yourself and store it in a variable like `secret`. (We'll take a look at letting the computer pick a random number for us in Chapter 7.) Tell the user what the bounds of the range are and as they guess, give them clues about whether their guess is lower or higher than the secret. Playing your game might look something like this:

```
exercises$ ./a.out
Guess a number between 1 and 50: 25
Too low! Try again.
Guess a number between 1 and 50: 38
Too low! Try again.
Guess a number between 1 and 50: 44
Too high! Try again.
Guess a number between 1 and 50: 42
*** Congratulations! You got it right! ***
```

5. Try implementing Euclid's algorithm for finding the greatest common divisor shared by two numbers. In *pseudocode* (English statements arranged like code and occasionally using operators like "="; it's meant to be a way of describing the steps of some program without requiring real code), the algorithm goes like this:

```
Start with two positive numbers, a and b
While b is not zero:
  Is a greater than b?
```

```
        Yes: a = a - b
         No: b = b - a
    Print a
```

You can just set the two values in your program or ask the user to input them. To check your program, the greatest common divisor of 3,456 and 1,234 is 2 and the greatest common divisor of 432 and 729 is 27.

If you want to see how I solved these problems, you can look at the various answers in the *ch03/exercises* (*https://oreil.ly/BDw5K*) folder. But I encourage you to try and solve them yourself before looking at my solutions. There are many, many ways to solve each of the exercises, and comparing your own approach to mine can help reinforce the syntax and purpose of the statements we've covered.

Next Steps

The branching and repetition statements we covered in this chapter are the core of a computer program's ability to solve problems. They make it possible to take real-world algorithms and convert them into code. Knowing C's control statements comes with the added benefit of preparing you for other programming languages that often borrow some of C's syntax.

There is more of that syntax to cover, though. In the next chapter, we'll look at how C handles one of the most popular tools for storing big lists of things: the array. With an eye on our goal of writing C code for more limited microcontrollers, we'll also see how C can be used to manipulate the smallest thing in a computer: the bit.

CHAPTER 4

Bits and (Many) Bytes

Before we start building more complex programs with things like functions in Chapter 5, we should cover two more useful storage categories in C: arrays and individual bits. These aren't really distinct types like int or double, but they are useful when dealing with tiny things or with lots of things. Indeed, the notion of an *array*, a sequential list of items, is so useful we had to cheat back in "Getting User Input" on page 24 and use it without much explanation to store user input in the form of a string.

We have also discussed the idea of Boolean values that are either yes or no, true or false, 1 or 0. When dealing with microcontrollers in particular, you will regularly have a small collection of sensors or switches that are providing on/off values. C's normal storage options would mean devoting an entire char (8 bits) or int (16 bits) to keeping track of such tiny values. That feels like a bit (ha!) of a waste, and it is. C has a few tricks you can employ to store this type of information more efficiently. In this chapter, we'll tackle both the big stuff by declaring arrays and then accessing and manipulating their contents, as well as how to work with the smallest bits (ahem). (And I promise not to make more bit puns. Mostly.)

Storing Multiple Things with Arrays

It is almost impossible to find a C program tackling real-world problems that does not use arrays. If you have to work with any collection of values of any type at all, those values will almost certainly wind up in an array. A list of grades, a list of students, the list of US state abbreviations, etc., etc., etc. Even our tiny machines can use arrays to track the colors on a strip of LEDs. It is not an exaggeration to say arrays are ubiquitous in C, so let's take a closer look at how to use them.

Creating and Manipulating Arrays

As I mentioned, we used an array back in Chapter 2 (in "Getting User Input" on page 24) to allow for some user input. Let's revisit that code (*ch04/hello2.c* (*https://oreil.ly/HnAfB*)) and pay more attention to the array of characters:

```c
#include <stdio.h>

int main() {
  char name[20];

  printf("Enter your name: ");
  scanf("%s", name);
  printf("Well hello, %s!\n", name);
}
```

So what exactly does that `char name[20]` declaration do? It creates a variable named "name" with a base type of `char`, but it is an array, so you get space to store multiple `char`s. In this case, we asked for 20 bytes, as illustrated in Figure 4-1.

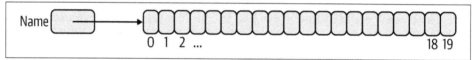

Figure 4-1. An empty array of type `char` called name

And what happens with this array variable when we run the program? When you type in a name and hit Return on your keyboard, the characters you typed get placed in the array. Since we used `scanf()` and its string (`%s`) format field, we will automatically get a trailing null character (`'\0'` or sometimes `'\000'`) that marks the end of the string. In memory, the `name` variable now looks like Figure 4-2.

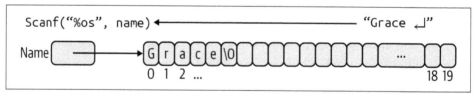

Figure 4-2. A char array with a string

 The null character at the end of the array is a peculiarity of strings; it is not how other types of arrays are managed. Strings are often stored in arrays that are set up before the length of the string is known, and use this `'\0'` sentinel much like we did in "The while Statement" on page 69 to mark the end of useful input. All string-processing functions in C expect to see this terminating character, and you can count on its existence in your own work with strings.

Now when we use the `name` variable again in the subsequent `printf()` call, we can echo back all of the letters that were stored and the null character tells `printf()` when to stop, even if the name doesn't occupy the entire array. Conversely, printing a string that does *not* have the terminating character will cause `printf()` to keep going after the end of the array and likely cause a crash.

Length versus capacity

Didn't we allocate 20 character slots? What are they doing if our name (such as "Grace") doesn't occupy all of the slots? Happily, that final, null character solves this quandary rather neatly. We do indeed have room for longer names like "Alexander" or even "Grace Hopper"; the null character always marks the end, no matter how big the array is.

 If you haven't worked with characters before in C or another language, the notion of a null character can be confusing. It is the character with the numeric value of 0 (zero). That is not the same thing as a space character (ASCII 32) or the digit 0 (ASCII 48) or a newline (`'\n'` ASCII 10). You usually don't have to worry about adding or placing these nulls by hand, but it is important to remember they occur at the end of strings, even though they are never printed.

But what if the name was too long for the allocated array? Let's find out! Run the program again and type in a longer name:

```
ch04$ ./a.out
Enter your name: @AdmiralGraceMurrayHopper
Well hello, @AdmiralGraceMurrayHopper!
*** stack smashing detected ***: terminated
Aborted (core dumped)
```

Interesting. So the capacity we declared is a fairly hard limit—things go wrong if we overflow an array.[1] Good to know! We always need to reserve sufficent space before we use it.[2]

What if we didn't know ahead of time how many slots were in an array? The C `sizeof` operator can help. It can tell you (in bytes) the size of variables or types. For simple types, that is the length of an `int` or `char` or `double`. For arrays, it is the total memory

---

1 Exactly how things go wrong may vary. Your operating system or version, compiler version, or even the conditions on your system at runtime can all affect the output. The point is to be careful not to overflow your arrays.

2 The `gcc` `stack-protector` option can be used to detect some buffer overflows and abort the program before the overflow can be used maliciously. This is a compile-time flag that is off by default.

allocated. That means we can tell how many slots we have in an array as long as we know its base type. Let's try making an array of double values, say, for an accounting ledger. We'll pretend we don't know how many values we can store and use sizeof to find out. Take a look at *ch04/capacity.c* (*https://oreil.ly/O3DfB*):

```
#include <stdio.h>

int main() {
  double ledger[100];
  printf("Size of a double: %li\n", sizeof (double));
  printf("Size of ledger: %li\n", sizeof ledger);
  printf("Calculated ledger capacity: %li\n", sizeof ledger / (sizeof (double)));
}
```

Notice that when asking about the size of a type, you need parentheses. The compiler needs this extra bit of context to treat the keyword as an expression. For variables like ledger that already fit the expression definition, we can leave them off. Let's run our tiny program. Here's the output:

```
ch04$ gcc capacity.c
ch04$ ./a.out
Size of a double: 8
Size of ledger: 800
Calculated ledger capacity: 100
```

Nice. Since we actually do know how big we made our array, we can just compare that chosen size to our calculated results. They match. (Whew!) But there are situations where you are given information from an independent source and won't always know the size of the array. Remember that tools like sizeof exist and can help you understand that information.

Initializing arrays

So far, we've created empty arrays or loaded char arrays with input from the user at runtime. Just like simpler variable types, C allows you to initialize arrays when you define them.

For any array, you can supply a list of values inside a pair of curly braces, separated by commas. Here are a few examples:

```
int days_in_month[12] = { 31, 28, 31, 30, 31, 30, 31, 31, 30, 31, 30, 31 };
char vowels[6] = { 'a', 'e', 'i', 'o', 'u', 'y' };
float readings[7] = { 8.9, 8.6, 8.5, 8.7, 8.9, 8.8, 8.5 };
```

Notice that the declared size of the array matches the number of values supplied to initialize the array. In this situation, C allows a nice shorthand: you can omit the explicit size in between the square brackets. The compiler will allocate the correct amount of memory to fit the initialization list exactly. This means we could rewrite our previous snippet like this:

```
int days_in_month[] = { 31, 28, 31, 30, 31, 30, 31, 31, 30, 31, 30, 31 };
char vowels[] = { 'a', 'e', 'i', 'o', 'u', 'y' };
float readings[] = { 8.9, 8.6, 8.5, 8.7, 8.9, 8.8, 8.5 };
```

Strings, however, are a special case. C supports the notion of *string literals*. This means you can use a sequence of characters between double quotes as a value. You can use a string literal to initialize a `char[]` variable. You can also use it almost anywhere a string variable would be allowed. (We saw this in "The Ternary Operator and Conditional Assignment" on page 63 where we used the terneray operator (`?:`) to print true and false values as words instead of as 1 or 0.)

```
// Special initialization of a char array with a string literal
char secret[] = "password1";

// The printf() format string is usually a string literal
printf("Hello, world!\n");

// And we can print literals, too
printf("The value stored in %s is '%s'\n", "secret", secret);
```

You can also initialize a string by supplying individual characters inside curly braces, but that is generally harder to read. You have to remember to include the terminating null character, and this verbose option doesn't provide any other real advantage over the use of a string literal.

Accessing array elements

Once you have an array created, you can access individual elements inside the array using square brackets. You give an index number inside the square brackets, where the first element has an index value of 0. To print the second vowel or the days in July from our earlier arrays, for example:

```
printf("The second vowel is: %c\n", vowels[1]);
printf("July has %d days.\n", days_in_month[6]);
```

These statements would produce the following output if bundled into a complete program:

```
The second vowel is: e
July has 31 days.
```

But the value we supply inside the square brackets does not need to be a fixed number. It can be any expression that results in an integer. (If you have enough memory, it could be a long or other, larger integer type.) This means you can use a calculation or a variable as your index. For example, if we store the "current month" in a variable and use the typical values for months—January is 1, February is 2, and so on—then we could print the number of days in July using the following code:

```
int month = 7;
printf("July (month %d) has %d days.", month, days_in_month[month - 1]);
```

The ease and flexibility of accessing these members is part of what makes arrays so popular. After a bit of practice, you'll find them indispensible!

 The value inside the square brackets needs to be "in bounds" or you'll get a an error at runtime. For example if you tried printing the days in the 15th month like we tried for July, you'd see something like "Invalid (month 15) has -1574633234 days." C won't stop you—note we did not cause a crash—but neither did we get a usable value. And *assigning* values (which we discuss next) to invalid slots in an array is how you cause a *buffer overflow*. This classic security exploit gets its name from the notion of an array as a storage buffer. You "overflow" it exactly by assigning values to the array outside the actual array. If you get lucky (or are very devious), you can write executable code and trick the computer into running your commands instead of the intended program.

Changing array elements

You can also change the value of a given array position using the square bracket notation. For example, we could alter the number of days in February to accommodate a leap year:

```
if (year % 4 == 0) {
  // Forgive the naive leap year calculation :)
  days_in_month[1] = 29;
}
```

This type of post-declaration assignment is handy (or often even necessary) when you have more dynamic data. With the Arduino projects we'll cover later, for example, you might want to keep the 10 most recent sensor readings. You won't have those readings when you declare your array. So you can set aside 10 slots, and just fill them in later:

```
float readings[10];
// ... interesting stuff goes here to set up the sensor and read it
readings[7] = latest_reading;
```

Just make sure you supply a value of the same type as (or at least compatible with) the array. Our `readings` array, for example, is expecting floating point numbers. If we were to assign a character to one of the slots, it would "fit" in that slot, but it would produce a strange answer. Assigning the letter *x* to `readings[8]` would end up putting the ASCII value of lowercase x (120) in the slot as a `float` value of 120.0.

Iterating through arrays

The ability to use a variable as an index makes working with an entire array a simple loop task. We could print out all the days_in_month counts using a for loop, for example:

```
for (int m = 0; m < 12; m++) {
  // remember the array starts at 0, but humans start at 1
  printf("Days in month %d is %d.\n", m + 1, days_in_month[m]);
}
```

This snippet produces the following output. We can get a sense of just how powerful the combination of arrays and loops could be. With just a tiny bit of code, we get some fairly interesting output:

```
Days in month 1 is 31.
Days in month 2 is 28.
Days in month 3 is 31.
Days in month 4 is 30.
Days in month 5 is 31.
Days in month 6 is 30.
Days in month 7 is 31.
Days in month 8 is 31.
Days in month 9 is 30.
Days in month 10 is 31.
Days in month 11 is 30.
Days in month 12 is 31.
```

You're free to use the elements of your array however you need to. You aren't limited to printing them out. As another example, we could calculate the average reading from our readings array like so:

```
float readings[] = { 8.9, 8.6, 8.5, 8.7, 8.9, 8.8, 8.5 };

// Use our sizeof trick to get the number of elements
int count = sizeof readings / sizeof (float);
float total = 0.0;
float average;
for (int r = 0; r < count; r++) {
  total += readings[r];
}
average = total / count;
printf("The average reading is %0.2f\n", average);
```

This example highlights just how much C you have learned in only a few chapters! If you want some more practice, build this snippet into a complete program. Compile and run it to make sure you have it working. (The average should be 8.70, by the way.) Then add some more variables to capture the highest and lowest readings. You'll need some if statements to help there. You can see one possible solution in *arrays.c* in the examples for this chapter.

Review of Strings

I have noted that strings are really just arrays of type char with some extra features supported by the language itself, such as literals. But since strings represent the easiest way to communicate with users, I want to highlight more of what you can do with strings in C.

Initializing strings

We have already seen how to declare and initialize a string. If you know the value of the string ahead of time, you can use a literal. If you don't know the value, you can still declare the variable and then use scanf() to ask the user what text to store. But what if you wanted to do both? Assign an initial default and then let the user supply an optional new value that overrides the default?

Happily, you can get there, but you do have to plan ahead a little. It might be tempting to use the default value when you first declare your variable, and then let the user provide a different value at runtime if they want. This works, but it requires an extra question to the user ("Do you want to change the background color, yes or no?") and also assumes the user will supply a valid value as an alternative. Such assumptions are often safe as you are likely the only user while you're learning a new language. But in programs you share with others, it's better not to assume what the user will do.

String literals also make it tempting to think you can simply overwrite an existing string just like you can with int or float variables. But a string really is just a char[], and arrays are not assignable beyond the optional initialization when you declare them.

These limitations can all be overcome with the use of things like functions, which we'll explore in Chapter 5. In fact, the need for the functions that make it possible to manipulate strings at runtime are so useful, they have been bundled up into their own library, which I cover in "stdlib.h" on page 150.

For now, I want you to remember that string literals can make the initialization of character arrays simple and readable, but that at their heart, strings in C are not like numbers and individual characters.

Accessing individual characters

But I do want to reiterate that strings are just arrays. You can access individual characters in your string using the same syntax you use to access the members of any other array. For example, we could find out if a given phrase contains a comma by looking at each character in the phrase. Here's *ch04/comma.c* (*https://oreil.ly/UWgY6*):

```c
#include <stdio.h>

int main() {
  char phrase[] = "Hello, world!";
  int i = 0;
  // keep looping until the end of the string
  while (phrase[i] != '\0') {
    if (phrase[i] == ',') {
      printf("Found a comma at position %d.\n", i);
      break;
    }
    // try the next character
    i++;
  }
  if (phrase[i] == '\0') {
    // Rats. Made it to the end of the string without a match.
    printf("No comma found in %s\n", phrase);
  }
}
```

This program actually uses the array nature of the string a few times. Our loop condition depends on accessing a single character of the string just like the if condition that helps answer our original question. And we test an individual character at the very end to see if we found something or not. We'll look at several string-related functions in Chapter 7, but hopefully you see how you could accomplish things like copying or comparing strings using a good loop and the square brackets to march one character at a time through your array.

Multidimensional Arrays

It may not be obvious since strings are already an array, but you can store an array of strings in C. But because there is no "string type" that you can use when declaring such an array, how do you do it? Turns out C supports the idea of a *multidimensional array* so you can create an array of char[] just like other arrays:

```c
char month_names[][];
```

Seems fair. But what is not obvious in that declaration is what the pair of square bracket pairs refer to. When declaring a two-dimensional array like this, the first square bracket pair can be thought of as the row index, and the second is the column. Another way to think about it is the first index tells you *how many* character arrays we'll be storing and the second index tells you *how long* each of those arrays can be.

We know how many months there are and a little research tells us the longest name is September, with nine letters. Add on one more for our terminating null character, and we could precisely define our month_names array like this:

```c
char month_names[12][11];
```

You could also initialize this two-dimensional array since we know the names of the months and don't require user input:

```
char month_names[12][11] = {
  "January", "February", "March", "April", "May", "June", "July",
  "August", "September", "October", "November", "December"
};
```

But here I cheated a little with the initialization by using string literals, so the second dimension of the month_names array isn't readily apparent. The first dimension is the months, and the second (hidden) dimension is the individual characters that make up the month names. If you are working with other data types that don't have this string literal shortcut, you can use nested curly brace lists like this:

```
int multiplication[5][5] = {
  { 0, 0, 0,  0,  0 },
  { 0, 1, 2,  3,  4 },
  { 0, 2, 4,  6,  8 },
  { 0, 3, 6,  9, 12 },
  { 0, 4, 8, 12, 16 }
};
```

It might be tempting to assume the compiler can determine the size of the multi-dimensional structure, but sadly, you must supply the capacity for each dimension beyond the first. For our month names, for example, we could start off without the "12" for how many names, but not without the "11" indicating the maximum length of any individual name:

```
// This shortcut is ok
char month_names[][11] = { "January", "February" /* ... */ };

// This shortcut is NOT
char month_names[][] = { "January", "February" /* ... */ };
```

You'll eventually internalize these rules, but the compiler (and many editors) will always be there to catch you if you make a small mistake.

Accessing Elements in Multidimensional Arrays

With our array of month names, it is straightforward getting access to any particular month. It looks just like accessing the element of any other one-dimensional array:

```
printf("The name of the first month is: %s\n", month_names[0]);

// Output: The name of the first month is: January
```

But how would we access an element in the multiplication two-dimensional array? We use two indices:

```
printf("Looking up 3 x 4: %d\n", multiplication[3][4]);

// Output: Looking up 3 x 4: 12
```

Notice that in this multiplication table, the potentially strange use of zero as the first index value turns out to be a useful element. Index "0" gives us a row—or column—of valid multiplication answers.

And with two indices, you'll need two loops if you want to print out all of the data. We can take the work we did in "Nested Loops and Tables" on page 74 and use it to access our stored values rather than generating the numbers directly. Here's the printing snippet from *ch04/print2d.c* (*https://oreil.ly/3gr8L*):

```
for (int row = 0; row < 5; row++) {
  for (int col = 0; col < 5; col++) {
    printf("%3d", multiplication[row][col]);
  }
  printf("\n");
}
```

And here is our nicely formatted table:

```
ch04$ gcc print2d.c
ch04$ ./a.out
  0  0  0  0  0
  0  1  2  3  4
  0  2  4  6  8
  0  3  6  9 12
  0  4  8 12 16
```

We'll see some other options in Chapter 6 for more tailored multidimensional storage. In the near term, just remember that you can create more dimensions with more pairs of square brackets. While you'll likely use one-dimensional arrays most of the time, tables are common enough and spatial data often fits in three-dimensional "cubes." Few programmers will ever need it, especially those of us concentrating on microcontrollers, but C does support higher orders of arrays.

Storing Bits

Arrays allow us to store truly vast quantities of data with relative ease. At the other end of the spectrum, C has several operators that you can use to manipulate very small amounts of data. Indeed, you can work with the absolute smallest pieces of data: individual bits.

When C was developed in the 1970s, every byte of memory was expensive, and therefore precious. As I noted at the beginning of the chapter, if you had a particular variable that stored Boolean answers, using 16 bits for an int or even just 8 bits for a char would be a little wasteful. If you had an array of such variables, it could become very wasteful. Desktop computers these days can manage that type of waste without blinking an eye (or an LED), but our microcontrollers often need all the storage help they can get.

Binary, Octal, Hexadecimal

Before we tackle the operators in C that access and manipulate bits, let's review some notation for discussing binary values. If we have a single bit, a 0 or a 1 are sufficient and that's easy enough. However, if we want to store a dozen bits inside one int variable, we need a way to describe the value of that int. Technically, the int will have a decimal (base 10) representation, but base 10 does not map cleanly to individual bits. For that, octal and hexadecimal notation is much clearer. (Binary, or base 2, notation would obviously be clearest, but large numbers get very long in binary. Octal and hexadecimal—often just "hex"—are a good compromise.)

When we talk about numbers, we often implicitly use base 10, thanks to the digits (ooh, get it?) on our hands. Computers don't have hands (discounting robots, of course) and don't count in base 10. They use binary. Two digits, 0 and 1, make up the entirety of their world. If you group three binary digits, you can represent the decimal numbers 0 through 7, which is eight total numbers, so this is base 8, or octal. Add a fourth bit and you can represent 0 through 15, which covers the individual "digits" in hexadecimal. Table 4-1 shows these first 16 values in all four bases.

Table 4-1. Numbers in decimal, binary, octal, and hexadecimal

Decimal	Binary	Octal	Hexadecimal	Decimal	Binary	Octal	Hexadecimal
0	0000 0000	000	0x00	8	0000 1000	010	0x08
1	0000 0001	001	0x01	9	0000 1001	011	0x09
2	0000 0010	002	0x02	10	0000 1010	012	0x0A / 0x0a
3	0000 0011	003	0x03	11	0000 1011	013	0x0B / 0x0b
4	0000 0100	004	0x04	12	0000 1100	014	0x0C / 0x0c
5	0000 0101	005	0x05	13	0000 1101	015	0x0D / 0x0d
6	0000 0110	006	0x06	14	0000 1110	016	0x0E / 0x0e
7	0000 0111	007	0x07	15	0000 1111	017	0x0F / 0x0f

You might notice that I always showed eight numbers for the binary column, three for octal, and two for hex. The byte (8 bits) is a very common unit to work with in C. Binary numbers often get shown in groups of four, with as many groups as required to cover the largest number being discussed. So for a full byte of 8 bits, which can store any value between 0 to 255, for example, you would see a binary value with two groupings of four digits. Similarly, octal values with three digits can display any byte's value, and hexadecimal numbers need two digits. Note also that hexadecimal literals are not case sensitive. (Neither is the "x" in the hexadecimal prefix, but an uppercase "X" can be harder to distinguish.)

We'll be using binary notation from time to time when working with microcontrollers in the latter half of this book, but you may have already run into hexadecimal numbers if you have written any styled text in HTML or CSS or similar markup languages. Colors in these documents are often represented with the hex values for a byte of red, a byte of green, a byte of blue, and occasionally a byte of alpha (transparency). So a full red that ignores the alpha channel would be FF0000. Now that you know two hex digits can represent one byte, it may be easier to read such color values.

To help you get accustomed to these different bases, try filling out the missing values in Table 4-2. (You can check your answers with the Table 4-4 table at the end of the chapter.) The numbers are not in any particular order, by the way. I want to keep you on your toes!

Table 4-2. Converting between bases

Decimal	Binary	Octal	Hexadecimal
14		016	
	0010 0000		
		021	11
50			32
		052	
			13
167			
	1111 1001		

Modern browsers can convert bases for you right in the search bar, so you probably won't need to memorize the full 256 values possible in a byte. But it will still be useful if you can estimate the size of a hex value or determine if an octal ASCII code is probably a letter or a number.

Octal and Hexadecimal Literals in C

The C language has special options for expressing numeric literals in octal and hex. Octal literals start with a simple 0 as a prefix, although you can have multiple zeroes if you are keeping all of your values the same width, like we did in our base tables. For hex values, you use the prefix 0x or 0X. You typically match the case of the 'X' character to the case of any of the A-F digits in your hex value, but this is just a convention.

Here's a snippet showing how to use some of these prefixes:

```
int line_feed = 012;
int carriage_return = 015;
int red = 0xff;
int blue = 0x7f;
```

Some compilers support nonstandard prefixes or suffixes for representing binary literals, but as the "nonstandard" qualifier suggests, they are not part of the official C language.

Input and Output of Octal and Hex Values

The printf() function has built-in format specifiers to help you produce octal or hexadecimal output. Octal value can be printed with the %o specifier and hex can be shown with either %x or %X, depending on whether you want lower- or uppercase output. These specifiers can be used with variables or expressions of any of the integer types in any base, which makes printf() a pretty easy way to convert from decimal to octal or hex. We could easily produce a table similar to Table 4-1 (minus the binary column) using a loop and a single printf(). We can take advantage of the width and padding options of the format specifier to get our desired three octal digits and two hex digits. Take a look at *ch04/dec_oct_hex.c* (*https://oreil.ly/59f56*):

```c
#include <stdio.h>

int main() {
  printf(" Dec  Oct  Hex\n");
  for (int i = 0; i < 16; i++) {
    printf(" %3d  %03o  0x%02X\n", i, i, i);
  }
}
```

Notice that we just reuse the exact same variable for each of the three columns. Also notice that when printing the hexadecimal version, I manually added the "0x" prefix —it is not included in the %x or %X formats. Here are a few of the first and last lines:

```
ch04$ gcc dec_oct_hex.c
ch04$ ./a.out
 Dec  Oct  Hex
   0  000  0x00
   1  001  0x01
   2  002  0x02
   3  003  0x03
 ...
  13  015  0x0D
  14  016  0x0E
  15  017  0x0F
```

Neat. Just the output we wanted. On the input side using scanf(), the format specifiers work in an interesting way. They are all still used to get numeric input from the user. The different specifiers now perform base conversion on the number you enter. If you specify decimal input (%d), you cannot use hex values. Conversely, if you specify hex input (%x or %X) and only enter numbers (i.e., you don't use any of the A-F digits), the number will still be converted from base 16.

The specifiers %d and %i are normally interchangeable. In a printf() call, they will result in identical output. In a scanf() call, however, the %d option requires you to enter a simple base 10 number. The %i specifier allows you to use the various C literal perfixes to enter a value in a different base such as 0x to enter a hexadecimal number.

We can illustrate this with a simple converter program, *ch04/rosetta.c* (*https://oreil.ly/ NU9Wc*), that will translate different inputs to all three bases on output. We can set which type of input we expect in the program but use an if/else if/else block to make it easy to adjust. (Although recompiling will still be required.)

```c
#include <stdio.h>

int main() {
  char base;
  int input;

  printf("Convert from? (d)ecimal, (o)ctal, he(x): ");
  scanf("%c", &base);

  if (base == 'o') {
    // Get octal input
    printf("Please enter a number in octal: ");
    scanf("%o", &input);
  } else if (base == 'x') {
    // Get hex input
    printf("Please enter a number in hexadecimal: ");
    scanf("%x", &input);
  } else {
    // assume decimal input
    printf("Please enter a number in decimal: ");
    scanf("%d", &input);
  }
  printf("Dec: %d,  Oct: %o,  Hex: %x\n", input, input, input);
}
```

Here are a few example runs:

```
ch04$ gcc rosetta.c

ch04$ ./a.out
Convert from? (d)ecimal, (o)ctal, he(x): d
Please enter a number in decimal: 55
Dec: 55,  Oct: 67,  Hex: 37

ch04$ ./a.out
Convert from? (d)ecimal, (o)ctal, he(x): x
Please enter a number in hexadecimal: 37
Dec: 55,  Oct: 67,  Hex: 37
```

```
ch04$ ./a.out
Convert from? (d)ecimal, (o)ctal, he(x): d
Please enter a number in decimal: 0x37
Dec: 0,  Oct: 0,  Hex: 0
```

Interesting. The first two runs went according to plan. The third run didn't create an error but didn't really work, either. What happened here is a sort of "feature" of scanf(). It tried very hard to bring in a decimal number. It found the character *0* in our input, which is a valid decimal digit, so it started parsing that character. But it next encountered the *x* character which is *not* valid for a base 10 number. So that was the end of the parsing and our program converted the value 0 into each of the three bases.

Try running this program yourself and switch the mode a few times. Do you get the behavior you expect? Can you cause any errors?

Knowing what we do about the difference between %i and other numeric specifiers in scanf(), can you see how to make this program a little simpler? It should be possible to accept any of the three bases for input without the big if statement. I'll leave this problem to you as an exercise, but you can see one possible solution in the *rosetta2.c* file in the code examples for this chapter.

Bitwise Operators

Starting out on limited hardware like C did means occasionally working with data at the bit level quite apart from printing or reading in binary data. C supports this work with *bitwise operators*. These operators allow you to tweak individual bits inside int variables (or char or long, of course). We'll see some fun uses of these features with the Arduino microcontroller in Chapter 10.

Table 4-3 describes these operators and shows some examples that make use of the following two variables:

```
char a = 0xD; // 1101 in binary
char b = 0x7; // 0111 in binary
```

Table 4-3. Bitwise operators in C

Operator	Name	Description	Example
&	bitwise and	Both bits must be 1 to yield a 1	a & b == 0101
|	bitwise or	Either bit can be 1 to yield a 1	a | b == 1111
!	bitwise not	Yields the opposite of the input bit	~a == 0010
^	bitwise xor	eXclusive OR, bits that don't match yield a 1	a ^ b == 1010
<<	left shift	Move bits to the left by a number of places	a << 3 == 0110 1000
>>	right shift	Move bits to the right by a number of places	b >> 2 == 0001

You can technically apply bitwise operators to any variable type to tweak particular bits. They are rarely used on floating point types, though. You usually pick an integral type that is big enough to hold however many individual bits you need. Because they are "editing" the bits of a given variable, you often see them used with compound assignment operators (op=). If you have five LEDs, for example, you could keep track of their on/off state with a single char type variable, as in this snippet:

```
char leds = 0;  // Start with everyone off, 0000 0000

leds |= 8;     // Turn on the 4th led from the right, 0000 1000
leds ^= 0x1f; // Toggle all lights, 0001 0111
leds &= 0x0f; // Turn off 5th led, leave others as is, 0000 0111
```

Five int or char values likely won't make the difference in whether you can store or run a program on a microcontroller, even ones with only one or two kilobytes of memory, but those small storage needs do add up. If you're tracking a panel of LEDs with hundreds or thousands of lights, it makes a difference how tightly you can store their state. One size rarely fits all, so remember your options and pick one that balances between ease of use and any resource constraints you have.

Mixing Bits and Bytes

We now have enough elements of C under our belts to start writing some really interesting code. We can combine all of our previous discussions on bits, arrays, types, looping, and branching to tackle a popular way of encoding binary data in text. One format for transmitting binary data through networks of devices with potentially limited resources is to convert it to simple lines of text. This is known as "base64" encoding and is still used in things like inline email attachments for images. The 64 comes from the fact that this encoding uses 6-bit chunks, and 2 to the 6th power is 64. We use numbers, lowercase letters, uppercase letters, and other characters more or less arbitrarily chosen, typically the plus (+) and the forward slash (/).[3]

For this encoding, values 0 through 25 are the uppercase letters A through Z. Values 26 through 51 are the lowercase letters a through z. Values 52 through 61 are the digits 0 through 9, and finally, value 62 is the plus sign, and 63 is the forward slash.

But aren't bytes 8 bits long? Yes, they are. That's exactly where all of our recent topics come into play! We can use this new knowledge to change those 8-bit chunks into 6-bit chunks.

---

3 As an example of an alternative pair of extra characters, the *base64url* variation uses a minus ("-") and underscore ("_").

Figure 4-3 shows a small example of converting three bytes into a string of base64 text. These happen to be the first few bytes of a valid JPEG file, but you could work on any source you like. This is a fairly trivial bit of binary data, of course, but it will validate our algorithm.

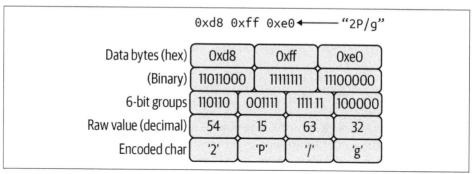

Figure 4-3. Going from 8-bit to 6-bit chunks with encoding

We have nine bytes total to encode in our example, but really we just want to take things three bytes at a time, like the illustration, and repeat. Sounds like a job for a loop! We could use any of our loops, but we'll go with a for loop since we know where to start and end, and we can count up by threes. We'll pull out three bytes from the source array into three variables, just for convenience of discussion.

```
unsigned char source[9] = { 0xd8,0xff,0xe0,0xff,0x10,0x00,0x46,0x4a,0x46 };
char buffer[4] = { 0, 0, 0, 0 };

for (int i = 0; i < 9; i += 3) {
  unsigned char byte1 = source[i];
  unsigned char byte2 = source[i + 1];
  unsigned char byte3 = source[i + 2];
  // ...
}
```

The next big step is getting the four 6-bit chunks into our buffer. We can use our bitwise operators to grab what we need. Look back at Table 4-3. The leftmost six bits of byte1 make up our first 6-bit chunk. In this case, we can just shift those six bits to the right two slots:

```
buffer[0] = byte1 >> 2;
```

Neat! One down, three to go. The second 6-bit chunk, though, is a little messy because it uses the two remaining bits from byte1 and four bits from byte2. There are several ways to do this, but we'll process the bits in order and just break up the assignment to the next slot in buffer into two steps:

```
buffer[1] = (byte1 & 0x03) << 4;   ❶
buffer[1] |= (byte2 & 0xf0) >> 4;  ❷
```

❶ First, take the right two bits from byte1 and scoot them to the left four spaces to make room for the rest of our 6-bit chunk.

❷ Now, take the left four bits from byte2, scoot them to the right four spaces, and put them into buffer[1] without disturbing the upper half of that variable.

Halfway there! We can do something very similar for the third 6-bit chunk:

```
buffer[2] = (byte2 & 0x0f) << 2;
buffer[2] |= (byte3 & 0xc0) >> 6;
```

In this case, we take and scoot the right four bits of byte2 and scoot them over two slots to make room for the left two bits of byte3. But like before, we have to scoot those two bits all the way to the right first. Our last 6-bit chunk is another easy one. We just want the right six bits of byte4, no scooting required:

```
buffer[3] = byte3 & 0x3f;
```

Hooray! We have successfully done the 3x8-bit to 4x6-bit conversion! Now we just need to print out each of the values in our buffer array. Sounds like another loop. And if you recall that we have five ranges for our base 64 "digits," that calls for a conditional of some sort. We could list out all 64 cases in a switch, but that feels tedious. (It would be very self-documenting, at least.) An if/else if chain should do nicely. Inside any particular branch, we'll do a little character math to get the correct value. As you read this next snippet, see if you can figure out how that character math is working its magic:

```
for (int b = 0; b < 4; b++) {
  if (buffer[b] < 26) {
    // value 0 - 25, so uppercase letter
    printf("%c", 'A' + buffer[b]);
  } else if (buffer[b] < 52) {
    // value 26 - 51, so lowercase letter
    printf("%c", 'a' + (buffer[b] - 26));
  } else if (buffer[b] < 62) {
    // value 52 - 61, so a digit
    printf("%c", '0' + (buffer[b] - 52));
  } else if (buffer[b] == 62) {
    // our "+" case, no need for math, just print it
    printf("+");
  } else if (buffer[b] == 63) {
    // our "/" case, no need for math, just print it
    printf("/");
  } else {
    // Yikes! Error. We should never get here.
    printf("\n\n Error! Bad 6-bit value: %c\n", buffer[b]);
  }
}
```

Does the character math make sense? Since char is an integer type, you can "add" to characters. If we add one to the character *A*, we get *B*. Add two to *A* and we get *C*, etc. For the lowercase letters and the digits, we first have to realign our buffered value so it is in a range starting at zero. The last two cases are easy, since we have one value that maps directly to one character. Hopefully, we never hit our else clause, but that is exactly what those clauses are for. If we got something wrong, print out a warning!

Whew! Those are some impressive moving parts. And if you want to build tiny devices that communicate with other tiny devices or the cloud, like a tiny security camera sending a picture to your phone, these are exactly the kind of moving parts you'll bump into.

Let's assemble them in one listing (*ch04/encode64.c* (*https://oreil.ly/Ibp52*)) with the other bits we need for a valid C program:

```c
#include <stdio.h>

int main() {
  // Manually specify a few bytes to encode for now
  unsigned char source[9] = { 0xd8,0xff,0xe0,0xff,0x10,0x00,0x46,0x4a,0x46 };
  char buffer[4] = { 0, 0, 0, 0 };

  // sizeof(char) == 1 byte, so the array's size in bytes is also its length
  int source_length = sizeof(source);
  for (int i = 0; i < source_length; i++) {
    printf("0x%02x ", source[i]);
  }
  printf("==> ");
  for (int i = 0; i < source_length; i += 3) {
    unsigned char byte1 = source[i];
    unsigned char byte2 = source[i + 1];
    unsigned char byte3 = source[i + 2];

    // Now move the appropriate bits into our buffer
    buffer[0] = byte1 >> 2;
    buffer[1] = (byte1 & 0x03) << 4;
    buffer[1] |= (byte2 & 0xf0) >> 4;
    buffer[2] = (byte2 & 0x0f) << 2;
    buffer[2] |= (byte3 & 0xc0) >> 6;
    buffer[3] = byte3 & 0x3f;

    for (int b = 0; b < 4; b++) {
      if (buffer[b] < 26) {
        // value 0 - 25, so uppercase letter
        printf("%c", 'A' + buffer[b]);
      } else if (buffer[b] < 52) {
        // value 26 - 51, so lowercase letter
        printf("%c", 'a' + (buffer[b] - 26));
      } else if (buffer[b] < 62) {
        // value 52 - 61, so a digit
        printf("%c", '0' + (buffer[b] - 52));
```

```
    } else if (buffer[b] == 62) {
        // our "+" case, no need for math, just print it
        printf("+");
    } else if (buffer[b] == 63) {
        // our "/" case, no need for math, just print it
        printf("/");
    } else {
        // Yikes! Error. We should never get here.
        printf("\n\n Error! Bad 6-bit value: %c\n", buffer[b]);
    }
  }
}
printf("\n");
}
```

As always, I encourage you to type in the program yourself, making any adjustments you want or adding any comments to help you remember what you learned. You can also compile the *encode64.c* file and then run it. Here's the output:

```
ch04$ gcc encode64.c
ch04$ ./a.out
0xd8 0xff 0xe0 0xff 0x10 0x00 0x46 0x4a 0x46  ==> 2P/g/xAARkpG
```

Very, very cool. Congratulations, by the way! That is a nontrivial bit of code there. You should be proud. But if you want to really test your skills, try writing your own decoder to reverse this process. If you start with the output above, do you get the original nine bytes? (You can check your answer against mine: *ch04/decode64.c* (*https://oreil.ly/exGqM*).)

Conversion Answers

Whether or not you tackle decoding the base64 encoded string, hopefully you tried converting the values in Table 4-2 yourself. You can compare your answers here. Or use the *rosetta.c* program!

Table 4-4. Base conversion answers

Decimal	Binary	Octal	Hexadecimal
14	0000 1110	016	0E
32	0010 0000	040	20
17	0001 0001	021	11
50	0011 0010	062	32
42	0010 1010	052	2A
35	0001 0011	023	13
167	1010 0111	247	A7
249	1111 1001	371	F9

Next Steps

C's support of simple arrays opens up a wide world of storage and retrieval options for just about any type of data. You do have to pay attention to the number of elements that you expect to use, but within those bounds, C's arrays are quite efficient. And if you are only storing small, yes or no, on or off type values, C has several operators that make it possible to squeeze those values into the individual bits of a larger data type like an `int`. Modern desktops rarely require that much attention to detail, but some of our Arduino options in the latter half of this book care very much!

So what's next? Well, our programs are getting interesting enough that we'll want to start breaking the logic up into manageable slices. Think about this book, for example. It is not made up of one, excessive run-on sentence. It is broken into chapters. Those chapters, in turn, are broken into sections. Those sections are broken into paragraphs. It is usually easier to discuss a single paragraph than it is an entire book. C allows you to perform this type of breakdown for your own logic. And once you have the logic in digestible blocks, you can use those blocks just like we have been doing with the `printf()` and `scanf()` functions. Let's dive in!

CHAPTER 5

Functions

With the various assignment statements and flow of control options we've seen so far, you are now primed to solve just about any problem meant for computers. But solving a problem turns out to be only about half of the, uh, problem. Whether you are coding for work or for fun, you invariably need to go back to code you have already written. You might be fixing a small bug or adding a missing feature. You may be using a previous project as a starting point for a new one. In all of these moments, the maintainability of your code becomes almost as important as the initial effort to get the code working. Breaking up a problem to make it manageable while you are solving it can have a beneficial effect on the code you end up writing—which also has a beneficial effect on its readability and maintainability.

Core to this idea of tackling smaller problems on the way to tackling the whole one is the use of *functions* or *procedures*. Functions help you encapsulate logic—the statements and control structures you are learning to code. In C, you can write and call as many functions as you need.[1] C doesn't really distinguish between the word "function" and the word "procedure," although some languages do. (In those languages, the difference is often whether or not a piece of code returns a value or simply executes a set of statements.) I'll mostly use the term *function*, but if you see discussions of a procedure (or *routine*, same idea) here or in any of your other reading, it still refers to a block of code you can call from some other block of code.

---

1 Within reason, of course. Or rather, within your computer's resource limits. Desktop systems have so much memory these days, it would be difficult to write too many functions. On our microcontrollers, though, we do have to be more careful.

Familiar Functions

We've actually been using functions all along. The `main()` block of code is a function. In our very first "Hello, World" program, we used the `printf()` function to produce some output. We use the `scanf()` function to get input from the user. Both of those functions come from the `stdio.h` library we include in our programs.

Function Flow

What is going on inside these functions? What does it mean to "call" them? Functions and procedures are another form of flow control. They allow you to jump between chunks of code in an orderly way—and return to where you came from when you're done. Figure 5-1 illustrates this flow a little more formally.

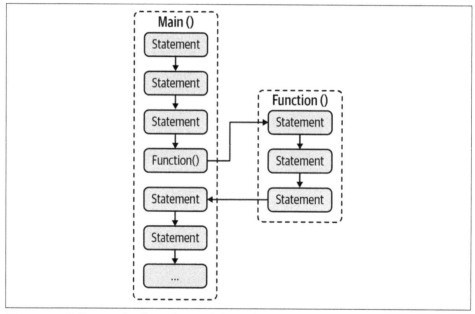

Figure 5-1. Following the flow of control through a function

This flow is what I mean by *calling* a function. You go from your current statement to the first statement of the function. You work your way through the function (which, by the way, can contain calls to other functions) and then come back. On your way back, you can bring along a result, but that's optional. For example, we don't use any return value from our `printf()` and `scanf()` calls. (There is one, but we can safely ignore it.) We do, however, rely on the return value from many functions to know things like whether two strings match, or if a character is a numeric digit, or what the square root of some number is.

We'll look at many of the functions that make up the "standard library" of C in Chapter 7. But we don't have to rely solely on the standard functions, either. C allows us to create our own functions. Figure 5-2 shows the basic structure of a function.

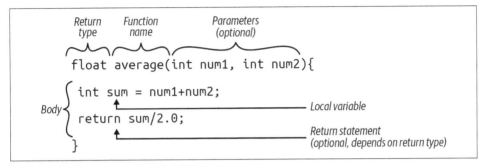

Figure 5-2. The basic parts of a C function

We'll work through all the variations on these key parts of a function in this chapter.

Simple Functions

The simplest form of a C function is one where we only jump to the function, execute its statements, and jump back. We don't pass any information in and we don't expect any information back. This might sound a little boring or even wasteful, but it can be incredibly useful for breaking up large programs into manageable pieces. It also makes it possible to reuse popular chunks of code. For example, your program might come with some helpful instructions. Anywhere the user gets stuck, you print those to the screen to help get them unstuck. You can put those instructions in a function:

```
void print_help() {
    printf("This program prints a friendly greeting.\n");
    printf("When prompted, you can type in a name \n");
    printf("and hit the return key. Max length is 24.\n");
}
```

Note the type of our function; it's a new one. This *void* type tells the compiler this function does not have a return value. C's default is to return an int like our main() function, but functions can return any type of value that C supports—including no value at all, like we do here.

Function names in C follow the same rules as variable names. You have to start with a letter or the underscore, and then you can have any number of following letters, numbers, or underscores. Also, like variables, you cannot use any of the reserved words from Table 2-4.

We can then call this function anytime we need to nudge the user or if they ask for help. Here's the rest of the program, *ch05/help_demo.c* (*https://oreil.ly/LilAh*). We'll print the help information when the program starts, and if the user simply hits the Return key when prompted for a name, we'll print it again.

```c
#include <stdio.h>

void print_help() {
  printf("This program prints a friendly greeting.\n");
  printf("When prompted, you can type in a name \n");
  printf("and hit the return key. Max length is 24.\n");
}

int main() {
  char name[25];

  do {
    // Call our newly minted help function!
    print_help();

    // Now prompt the user, but if they enter an 'h',
    // start over with the help message
    printf("Please enter a name: ");
    scanf("%s", name);
  } while (name[0] == 'h' && name[1] == '\0');

  // Ok, we must have a name to greet!
  printf("Hello, %s!\n", name);
}
```

And here's the output:

```
ch05$ gcc help_demo.c
ch05$ ./a.out
This program prints a friendly greeting.
When prompted, you can type in a name
and hit the return key. Max length is 24.
Please enter a name: h
This program prints a friendly greeting.
When prompted, you can type in a name
and hit the return key. Max length is 24.
Please enter a name: joe
Hello, joe!
```

Notice that in reusing our simple print_help() function, we did not save much by way of lines of code. Sometimes, using a function is more about consistency than reducing space or complexity. If we end up changing how our program works, say, asking the user for their name and address, for example, we can update just this one function and everywhere it gets used will automatically benefit from the new content.

Sending Information to Functions

While there are a surprising number of times where simple functions such as our print_help() come in handy, more often you'll need to pass some information that the function can use to do its work. Think back to our second iteration of saying hello to the user. We prompted them to enter their name and then printed a personalized greeting. We can create a function that has that same tailoring capacity. To do that, we'll specify a function *parameter*.

Parameters go inside the pair of parentheses and look a lot like variable declarations. In a very real sense, they are variable declarations. But there are a few key differences between parameters and variables. First, you must supply a type for each parameter. You can't "piggyback" on another parameter's type, even though the second type is the same. Secondly, you cannot initialize a parameter. Parameters get their initial value from the *arguments* you supply when you call the function. Here are a few valid and invalid examples:

```
// Correct and valid parameter declarations:
void average(double v1, double v2, double v3) { ...
void plot(int x, int y) { ...
void printUser(char *name, long id) { ...

// Incorrect declarations:
void bad_average(double v1, v2, v3) { // every parameter needs a type
void bad_plot(int x; int y) { // separate parameters with commas
void bad_print(char *name, long id = 0) { // do not initialize a parameter
```

The names "parameter" and "argument" are just programmer-speak for variables and values. But it's useful to have distinct names when talking about the structure of your program with other developers. When you say "parameter," other programmers know you are talking about defining a function and its inputs. By contrast, when you talk about arguments, it is clear you mean the values passed to an already defined function that you are calling. Knowing this terminology can also help you ask better questions when you search online for help.

Passing Simple Types

Let's try passing some things to a function and using them. A canonical function with parameters is one that calculates a numeric average. We can define a function that accepts two floating point numbers and prints out the average like this:

```
void print_average(float a, float b) {
  float average = (a + b) / 2;
  printf("The average of %.2f and %.2f is %.2f\n", a, b, average);
}
```

We can now call `print_average()` from some other part of our program like this:

```
float num1, num2;
printf("Please enter two numbers separated by a space: ");
scanf("%f %f", &num1, &num2);
print_average(num1, num2);
```

Notice that our parameters, a and b, do not share a name with the variables we use as arguments, num1 and num2. It is not the names of things that tie arguments to parameters, it is their position. The first argument, whether it is a literal value, a variable, or even an expression, must match the type of the first parameter and will be used to give that first parameter its starting value. The second argument goes with the second parameter, and so on. All of the following calls to `print_average()` are valid:

```
float x = 17.17;
float y = 6.2;
print_average(3.1415, 2.71828);
print_average(x, y);
print_average(x * x, y * y);
print_average(x, 3.1415);
```

Passing arguments to functions is fundamental to C programming. We won't go through the output here, but take a look at *ch05/averages.c* (*https://oreil.ly/v9VLq*). Run it and see if you get the output you expect. Try adding some of your own variables or use `scanf()` to get more input, and then print some more averages. This is definitely a case where practice will pay off!

Passing Strings to Functions

But what about our personalized greeting function? We can pass strings (again, really just an array of char) more or less like we pass other types. As with other parameters, we do not give array parameters an initial value, so the square brackets are always empty:

```
void greet(char name[]) {
  printf("Hello, %s\n", name);
}
```

When we go to call `greet()`, we'll use the whole array as the argument, similar to how we pass string variables to the `scanf()` function. We reused the variable name because it makes sense for our program and our `greet()` function. It is not required that arguments and parameters match like this. In fact, such alignment is rare. We'll look at this distinction between the parameters in a function and the arguments passed to it in "Variable Scope" on page 118.

You will often see array parameters declared with a "*" prefix rather than the "[]" bracket suffix (e.g., void greet(char *name)). This is valid notation centering on the use of pointers. We'll tackle pointers in Chapter 6 where I'll cover how array variables work in more detail, both in terms of their memory allocation and using them with functions.

Here's a complete program, *ch05/greeting.c* (*https://oreil.ly/FTudJ*) that defines and uses greet():

```c
#include <stdio.h>

void print_help() {
  printf("This program prints a friendly greeting.\n");
  printf("When prompted, you can type in a name \n");
  printf("and hit the return key. Max length is 24.\n");
}

void greet(char name[]) {
  printf("Hello, %s\n", name);
}

int main() {
  char name[25];

  // First, tell them how to use the program
  print_help();

  // Now, prompt them for a name (just the once)
  printf("Please enter your name: ");
  scanf("%s", name);

  // Finally, call our new greeting function with our name argument
  greet(name);
}
```

And here is the output of a few runs:

```
ch05$ gcc greeting.c
ch05$ ./a.out
This program prints a friendly greeting.
When prompted, you can type in a name
and hit the return key. Max length is 24.
Please enter your name: Brian
Hello, Brian
ch05$ ./a.out
This program prints a friendly greeting.
When prompted, you can type in a name
and hit the return key. Max length is 24.
Please enter your name: Vivienne
Hello, Vivienne
```

Hopefully, nothing too surprising there. As noted above, we'll revisit passing arrays as arguments in Chapter 6. There's nothing wrong with how we specify our `char[]` parameter in this example, but it isn't the only way to do it.

Multiple Types

It might be obvious, but I want to point out that the parameter list in a function definition can mix and match types. You are not restricted to one type. For example, we can write a `repeat()` function that takes a string to print and a `count` to tell us how many times to print the string:

```
void repeat(char thing[], int count) {
  for (int i = 0; i < count; i++) {
    printf("%d: %s\n", i, thing);
  }
}
```

Neat! If we call `repeat()` with the word "Dennis" and the number 5, we will get the following output:

```
// repeat("Dennis", 5);
0: Dennis
1: Dennis
2: Dennis
3: Dennis
4: Dennis
```

 Well, the answer to this little quiz is a tip, at least. :) Can you think of a way to print the index numbers in the output above so that they start at 1 and go to 5 instead of the less human-friendly 0 to 4 that we have now?

Exiting a Function

A common problem every programmer faces is making sure that the inputs to functions are appropriate. In the case of our nifty `repeat()` function, for example, we want a `count` that is a positive number so that we actually get some output. What do we do if we get a bad number and don't want to finish the rest of the function? Fortunately, C provides a way to exit a function at any time: the `return` statement.

We can upgrade `repeat()` to check for a good `count` before trying to run the printing loop:

```
void repeat(char thing[], int count) {
  if (count < 1) {
    printf("Invalid count: %d. Skipping.\n", count);
    return;
  }
```

```
  for (int i = 0; i < count; i++) {
    printf("%d: %s\n", i, thing);
  }
}
```

Much better. The first version of `repeat()` wouldn't crash or anything if a negative count was supplied, but the user would not see any output and would not know why. Testing for legal or expected values is usually a good idea—especially if you are writing code that other people might also end up using.

Returning Information

Functions can also return information. You specify one of the data types, such as `int` or `float`, in the definition, and then use the `return` statement to send back an actual value. When you call such a function, you can store that returned value in a variable or use it anywhere a value or an expression is allowed.

For example, we could take `print_average()` and turn it into a function that calculates the average and simply returns it, rather than printing anything out. That way you are free to print the average yourself with a custom message. Or you can use the average in some other calculation.

Here's a simple version of such a function:

```
float calc_average(float a, float b) {
  float average = (a + b) / 2;
  return average;
}
```

Instead of `void` for a type, we now have `float`. So our `return` statement should include a float value, variable, or expression. In this example, we calculate the average and store it in a temporary variable called `average`. We then use that variable with the `return`. It's important to note that what gets returned is a *value*. The `average` variable disappears when we're done with the function, but its final value is sent back.

Since we do return a value, it is common for functions like `calc_average()` to skip the temporary variables. You can perform this simple calculation right with the `return` like so:

```
float calc_average(float a, float b) {
  return (a + b) / 2;
}
```

You don't lose any readability here, but that is probably because this is such a straightforward calculation. For larger or more complex functions, feel free to use whichever approach is more comfortable or seems more maintainable.

Using Returned Values

To capture that average, we put the call to the `calc_average()` function somewhere we would normally see a literal or expression. We can assign it to a variable. We could use it in a `printf()` statement. We could include it inside a larger calculation. Its type is `float`, so anywhere you could use a floating point value or variable, you can call `calc_average()`.

Here are a few examples from *ch05/averages2.c* (*https://oreil.ly/ALwA3*):

```
float avg = calc_average(12.34, 56.78);
float triple = 3 * calc_average(3.14, 1.414);
printf("The first average is %.2f\n", avg);
printf("Our tripled average is %.2f\n", triple);
printf("A direct average: %.2f\n", calc_average(8, 12));
```

In each of these statements, you can see how `calc_average()` gets used in place of a `float` value. Figure 5-3 illustrates the flow of that first assignment statement.

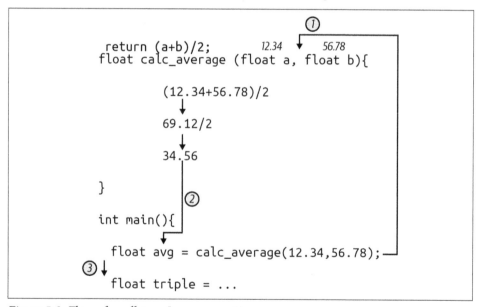

Figure 5-3. Flow of a call to `calc_average()`

❶ Call to `calc_average()` transfers control to the function; its parameters are initialized from the arguments.

❷ Once the function completes its work, return control to the main function along with the result to be stored in `avg`.

❸ Resume processing statements in the original function.

If you build your own program with the `calc_average()` function and the previous snippet, you should see something like this output:

```
ch05$ gcc averages2.c
ch05$ ./a.out
The first average is 34.56
Our tripled average is 6.83
A direct average: 10.00
```

You can create your own file, or compile and run *averages2.c* if you would like to try these examples. As an exercise, how could you expand the `calc_average()` function to produce the average of three inputs?

Ignoring Returned Values

You are not required to make use of a return value in C if it isn't useful. I didn't mention this when introducing the `printf()` function, but it actually returns an `int`: the count of how many bytes were written out. Don't believe it? Try it! I dropped this snippet in *ch05/printf_bytes.c* (*https://oreil.ly/rDKBc*) if you don't want to write it up yourself:

```
printf("This is a typical print statement.\n");
int total_bytes = printf("This is also a print statement.\n");
printf("The previous printf displayed %d bytes.\n", total_bytes);
```

This snippet would produce the following output:

```
ch05$ gcc printf_bytes.c
ch05$ ./a.out
This is a typical print statement.
This is also a print statement.
The previous printf displayed 32 bytes.
```

C is happy with all three of those calls to `printf()`. The first and the third call also return a count, but we ignore it (with no ill effect). We grab the count from the second call just to show that `printf()` does in fact return a value. Usually, you call a function that returns a value precisely because you want that returned value. Some functions, however, come with side effects that are the real target, rather than the returned value. `printf()` is just such a function. It is occasionally useful to keep track of how many bytes your program has written (a microcontroller that reports sensor readings to a cloud service, for example, might have a daily or monthly limit it cannot surpass), but you probably used `printf()` because you wanted some text to show up on the screen.

Nested Calls and Recursion

If you look at any of the complete program files for this chapter like *ch05/greeting.c* (*https://oreil.ly/fBCrG*) or *ch05/averages2.c* (*https://oreil.ly/BPwIl*), you will likely notice that we follow a simple pattern: define a function, define the main() function, and call our first function from inside main(). But that is not the only valid arrangement. As I'll show you in Chapter 11, with just a little extra code, you could swap the position of main() and calc_average(), for example.

We also have the freedom to call our functions from inside yet other functions. We could create a new program that reproduces the same exact output as the original print_average() function from *averages.c*, but do it using the calc_average() function from *averages2.c* to get the actual average value.

Here's the complete *ch05/averages3.c* (*https://oreil.ly/c3Ssi*) so you can see where we place the different functions and where those functions are called:

```
#include <stdio.h>

float calc_average(float a, float b) {
  return (a + b) / 2;
}

void print_average(float a, float b) {
  float average = calc_average(a, b);
  printf("The average of %.2f and %.2f is %.2f\n", a, b, average);
}

int main() {
  float num1, num2;
  printf("Please enter two numbers separated by a space: ");
  scanf("%f %f", &num1, &num2);
  print_average(num1, num2);

  float x = 17.17;
  float y = 6.2;
  print_average(3.1415, 2.71828);
  print_average(x, y);
  print_average(x * x, y * y);
  print_average(x, 3.1415);
}
```

If you run it, the output will be similar to the first example back in "Passing Simple Types" on page 107:

```
ch05$ gcc averages3.c
ch05$ ./a.out
Please enter two numbers separated by a space: 12.34 56.78
The average of 12.34 and 56.78 is 34.56
The average of 3.14 and 2.72 is 2.93
```

```
The average of 17.17 and 6.20 is 11.68
The average of 294.81 and 38.44 is 166.62
The average of 17.17 and 3.14 is 10.16
```

Clever. We've actually been relying on this feature all along. In our very first "Hello, World" program, we call the `printf()` function—which is indeed a real function, just one defined by the built-in standard I/O library—from within our `main()` function.

All C programs out there solving real-world problems will use this basic pattern. Functions are written to tackle some small portion of a bigger problem. Other functions call those functions to assemble the small answers into a bigger whole. Some problems are so large that you will have several layers of functions that call functions that call functions. But we're getting ahead of ourselves. We'll keep practicing with simpler functions. As you get comfortable defining and calling them, you'll naturally start to build more complex hierarchies as you solve more complex problems.

Recursive Functions

It may not be obvious unless you have worked with other languages, but a C function is allowed to call itself, too. This is called *recursion* and such a self-calling function is known as a *recursive* function. If you've spent any time around programmers, perhaps you have heard the surprisingly accurate joke about the definition of recursion: "I looked up recursion in the dictionary. It said: 'See recursion.'" Who says nerds don't have a sense of humor? ;-)

But the joke definition does hint at exactly how you write a recursive function in C. There is just one big caveat: you need to have a way to stop the recursion. If the subject in the joke were a computer, it would be in an endless cycle of looking up the word only to be told to look up the word only to be told to look up the word, etc., etc., ad infinitum. If you write such a function in C, eventually the program will consume all the memory in your computer and crash.

To avoid that crash, recursive functions have at least two branches. One branch, a *base case*, terminates. It produces a concrete value and completes. The other branch does some sort of calculation and recurses. That "some sort of calculation" must eventually lead to the base case. If that sounds a little confusing, don't panic![2] We can better illustrate this process with actual code.

Perhaps one of the most famous recursive algorithms is one that calculates the Fibonacci numbers. You may recall these from high school math. Named for a 13th century Italian mathematician, they are part of a sequence that builds up from a simple starting point of two numbers, either a zero and a one, or two ones. You add those

---

2 If you want to experience the pinnacle of nerdy humor, check out *The Hitchhiker's Guide to the Galaxy* by Douglas Adams. The words "Don't Panic" feature prominently in large, friendly letters.

two numbers to produce the third. You add the second and the third to produce the fourth, and so on. So the nth Fibonacci number is the sum of the previous number, and the previous previous number. A more formal way to say that goes like this:

```
F(n) = F(n - 1) + F(n - 2)
```

Here, the function *F()* is defined in terms of the function *F()*. Aha! Recursion! So what does this look like in C? Let's take a look.

We'll start by defining a function that takes one int as a parameter and returns an int. If the value passed to us is a zero or a one, we return a zero or a one, respectively, as part of the definition of the sequence. (So F(0) == 0 and F(1) == 1, more formally.) That sounds pretty easy:

```c
int fibonacci(int n) {
  // Base case 0
  // We'll cheat and return zero for negative numbers as well
  if (n <= 0) {
    return 0;
  }
  // Base case 1
  if (n == 1) {
    return 1;
  }
  // recursive call will go here
}
```

We have the critical part: the base case (or cases, like our 0 and 1) that has a definite answer. If we get some integer greater than one, we will fall to the recursive call. What does that look like? Just like any other function call. What makes it special is that we call the function we are in the middle of defining, fibonacci() in our case. The "some sort of calculation" we mentioned when introducing recursion is the n - 1 and n - 2 elements from our formal definition:

```c
// recursive call
return fibonacci(n - 1) + fibonacci(n - 2);
```

Let's put that all together in a complete program (*ch05/fib.c* (*https://oreil.ly/8xBXV*)) that prints a few sample Fibonacci numbers:

```c
#include <stdio.h>

int fibonacci(int n) {
  // Base case 0
  // We'll lazily return zero for negative numbers as well
  if (n <= 0) {
    return 0;
  }
  // Base case 1
  if (n == 1) {
    return 1;
```

```
  }

  // recurring call
  return (fibonacci(n-1) + fibonacci(n-2));
}

int main() {
  printf("The 6th Fibonnaci number is: %d\n", fibonacci(6));
  printf("The 42nd Fibonnaci number is: %d\n", fibonacci(42));
  printf("The first 10 Fibonacci numbers are:\n");
  for (int f = 0; f < 10; f++) {
    printf("  %d", fibonacci(f));
  }
  printf("\n");
}
```

If we run it, we'll get the following output:

```
ch05$ gcc fib.c
ch05$ ./a.out
The 6th Fibonnaci number is: 8
The 42nd Fibonnaci number is: 267914296
The first 10 Fibonacci numbers are:
  0  1  1  2  3  5  8  13  21  34
```

Very cool. But how does it work? It would seem impossible to assign a value coming from a function that needs that very same function to calculate the value! Figure 5-4 shows what's happening inside fibonacci() using the tiny value of 4.

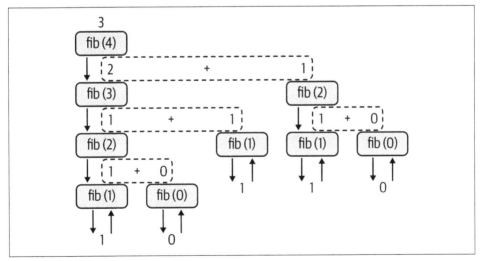

Figure 5-4. A recursive call stack

If this process still seems a little convoluted, give it time. The more you work with functions in general, the easier it will become to read (and create!) more interesting functions like our recursive Fibonacci example.

But it *is* convoluted for the computer. Recursion can go too deep and cause the computer to run out of memory. Even if your recursive code doesn't go that deep, it can still take quite a while to process. Try changing the program to show the 50th Fibonacci number instead of the 42nd. Notice it pause at that step? If not, congrats on your powerful system! Try bumping it up to 60 or 70. You will eventually go high enough that the sheer number of function calls will clog your CPU. Just remember that recursion is best in moderation.

 It is also worth pointing out that most recursive algorithms have counterparts that use more mundane tricks like loops. But sometimes using loops turns out to be much more complex than the recursive option. In the right circumstances, recursion makes solving some problems simpler by literally breaking them into smaller problems. The Fast Fourier Transform (FFT), so common in processing audio and video streams, for example, is a fairly complex algorithm that has a recursive solution that is easier to understand and implement.

Variable Scope

I didn't highlight this detail explicitly in our average-calculating functions, but you can declare any variables of any type you need inside a function. These are often referred to as *local* variables because they are located inside a function and are removed when the function finishes. Let's revisit that first `print_average()` function we wrote in "Passing Simple Types" on page 107:

```
void print_average(float a, float b) {
  float average = (a + b) / 2;
  printf("The average of %.2f and %.2f is %.2f\n", a, b, average);
}
```

Here, the variables `a` and `b` are the function's parameters, and `average` is a local variable. There's nothing terribly special about local variables, but because they are kept inside the function where they are defined, you can reuse names between different functions. Consider two functions that calculate the average for two and three parameters:

```
void print_average_2(float a, float b) {
  float average = (a + b) / 2;
  printf("The two numbers average out to %.2f\n", average);
}

void print_average_3(float a, float b, float c) {
```

```
    float average = (a + b + c) / 3;
    printf("The three numbers average out to %.2f\n", average);
}
```

Both functions declare a local variable named average, but they are two wholly separate variables. Even though they share a name, the compiler never confuses them. Indeed, even if the calling function also has an average variable, they won't be confused. Each local variable is contained entirely within its function:

```
float calc_average_2(float a, float b) {
    float average = (a + b) / 2;
    return average;
}

int main() {
    float avg1 = calc_average_2(18.5, 21.1);
    float avg2 = calc_average_2(16.3, 19.4);
    float average = calc_average_2(avg1, avg2);
    printf("The average of the two averages is: %.2f\n", average);
}
```

Wonderful. That means we can concentrate on using names appropriate to whatever work we're doing in a given function. We don't have to keep track of what variables were used in other functions or even in main(). That makes our job as programmers much easier.

Global Variables

As a programmer, though, you will undoubtedly encounter *global* variables as well as local ones. A global variable is sort of the opposite of a local variable. Where local variables are contained inside a function or a loop block, global variables are visible everywhere. Where local variables disappear when the loop or function is done, global variables persist.

This visibility and persistence can make global variables very attractive for any value that is shared or reused in several functions. But it is frustratingly easy to corrupt a global variable precisely because any function can see it—and modify it. Here's an example (*ch05/globals.c* (*https://oreil.ly/5tgaO*)) with a global variable that we use inside a function and inside main():

```
#include <stdio.h>

char buffer[30];

void all_caps() {
    char diff = 'a' - 'A';
    for (int b = 0; b < 30 && buffer[b] != 0; b++) {
        if (buffer[b] >= 'a' && buffer[b] <= 'z') {
            // We have a lowercase letter, so change this slot
            // in the char array to its uppercase cousin
```

```
      buffer[b] -= diff;
    }
  }
}

int main() {
  printf("Please enter a name or phrase: ");
  scanf("%[^\n]s", buffer);
  printf("Before all_caps(): %s\n", buffer);
  all_caps();
  printf("After all_caps(): %s\n", buffer);
}
```

And here's the output from running the program:

```
ch05$ gcc globals.c
ch05$ ./a.out
Please enter a name or phrase: This is a test.
Before all_caps(): This is a test.
After all_caps(): THIS IS A TEST.
```

Notice that we never alter the value of the variable in main(), but we see (and can print) the changes that were made inside the all_caps() function.

 The format string I use in *globals.c* probably looks strange. On its own, scanf("%s", buffer) would stop scanning for a string at the first bit of white space. In the sample output, that would mean only the word "This" would be captured into buffer. The [^\n] qualifier borrows some syntax from the world of regular expressions (*https://oreil.ly/3A61l*) and means "any character except a newline." This allows us to type in a phrase with spaces and capture every word up to the newline as a single string.

Sometimes working with a global variable is legitimately useful. Especially on smaller systems like the Arduino, this arrangement can occasionally save you a few bytes. But you really do have to be careful. If too many functions use and alter a global variable, debugging what is happening when things go wrong gets really messy. If you don't have a compelling reason to use a global variable, I recommend passing shared values as parameters to any function that needs them.

Masking global variables

One other important gotcha with respect to global variables is that you can still declare a local variable inside a function with the same name as the global variable. Such a local variable is said to *mask* the global variable. Any printing or calculating or manipulating you do inside the function only affects the *local* variable. And if you also need to access the global one, you are out of luck. Look at *ch05/globals2.c* (*https:// oreil.ly/KO8Fe*):

```
#include <stdio.h>

char buffer[30];

void all_caps() {
  char buffer[30] = "This is a local buffer!";
  char diff = 'a' - 'A';
  for (int b = 0; b < 30 && buffer[b] != 0; b++) {
    if (buffer[b] >= 'a' && buffer[b] <= 'z') {
      // We have a lowercase letter, so change this slot
      // in the char array to its uppercase cousin
      buffer[b] -= diff;
    }
  }
  printf("Inside all_caps(): %s\n", buffer);
}

int main() {
  printf("Please enter a name or phrase: ");
  scanf("%[^\n]s", buffer);
  printf("Before all_caps(): %s\n", buffer);
  all_caps();
  printf("After all_caps(): %s\n", buffer);
}
```

And compare the output from the previous *globals.c* to this output:

```
ch05$ gcc globals2.c
ch05$ ./a.out
Please enter a name or phrase: A second global test.
Before all_caps(): A second global test.
Inside all_caps(): THIS IS A LOCAL BUFFER!
After all_caps(): A second global test.
```

You can see here that back in the main() method, the global buffer variable was not updated, even though that may have been what we wanted. Again, I don't recommend using global variables unless it is necessary. Sometimes their convenience will win you over, and that's fine. Just be vigilant and deliberate.

The main() Function

We've mentioned the main() function a number of times in this chapter as we expand our knowledge of C functions. main() is indeed a real, regular C function with the main (ha!) distinction of being the function where an executable C program starts. Since it is "just a function," can we return a value from it? Can we pass it parameters? If so, where would the arguments used to fill those parameters come from? You can indeed return values and declare parameters. This last section covers main() in more detail if you're interested. Luckily, the simple main() we've been using so far will continue to suffice for our lean examples.

Return values and main()

But we haven't really dug into the details of our main() declarations. You may have already been wondering about the fact that we give a type (int) to the main() function although we have never written a return statement in that function. But it turns out we could!

Most operating systems use some mechanism for determining whether a program you run has completed successfully or failed for some reason. Unix and its derivatives, as well as MS DOS, use numeric values for this purpose. A return value of zero is generally considered success and anything else a failure. "Anything else" leaves a pretty wide range of failure options, which some programs do use. If you write shell scripts or DOS batch files, you may have used these return values to suss out exactly why a particular command failed, and mitigate the problem if possible.

I have not included a return in the main() function in any of our examples so far. So what has been going on? The compiler has simply built a program that implicitly provides 0 as the int return value. Let's take a look by checking the exit status of our very first program, *hello.c*.

First, let's compile and run the program. Now we can follow up and ask the operating system about that return value. On Unix/Linux and macOS systems, you check the $? special variable:

```
ch01$ gcc -o hello hello.c
ch01$ ./hello
Hello, world
ch01$ echo $?
0
```

On Windows systems, you can check the %ERRORLEVEL% variable:

```
C:\Users\marc\Documents\smallerc> gcc -o hello.exe hello.c

C:\Users\marc\Documents\smallerc> hello
Hello world

C:\Users\marc\Documents\smallerc>echo %ERRORLEVEL%
0
```

But that "0" might feel a little unconvincing since that is a common value for undefined or uninitialized variables. Let's write a new program, *ch05/exitcode.c* (*https://oreil.ly/vHOfd*), that returns an explicit, non-zero value to prove something is being returned.

We'll prompt the user to see if they want to succeed or fail. It's a silly prompt, but it allows you to try the two options without recompiling:

```
#include <stdio.h>

int main() {
  char answer;
  printf("Would you like to succeed (s) or fail (f)? ");
  scanf("%c", &answer);
  if (answer == 's') {
    return 0;
  } else if (answer == 'f') {
    return 1;
  } else {
    printf("You supplied an unsupported answer: %c\n", answer);
    return 2;
  }
}
```

Let's compile and run this one with a few different answers to see what we get when checking the exit code via the operating system. (For brevity, I'll just show the Linux output, but both macOS and Windows would be similar.)

```
ch05$ gcc exitcode.c
ch05$ ./a.out
Would you like to succeed (s) or fail (f)? s
ch05$ echo $?
0
ch05$ ./a.out
Would you like to succeed (s) or fail (f)? f
ch05$ echo $?
1
ch05$ ./a.out
Would you like to succeed (s) or fail (f)? invalid
You supplied an unsupported answer: i
ch05$ echo $?
2
```

This simple program hints at how more complex programs might use these exit codes to provide more details on what happened. Notice, though, that in the end the program still exited. These values are optional but can be useful if you plan to write utilities that will end up in scripts.

Command-Line Arguments and main()

What about passing arguments to main()? Happily, you can use the command line and a second option for defining main that helps with that exact task. This alternate version looks like this:

```
int main(int argc, char *argv[]) { // ...
```

The argc parameter is the "argument count," and the argv string array is the list of "argument values." The asterisk in the type of argv might be a little surprising. The argv variable is indeed an array of character arrays, similar to the two-dimensional char arrays in "Multidimensional Arrays" on page 89, but this is a more flexible version. It is an array of char *pointers* (denoted by that askterisk). We'll cover pointers next in Chapter 6, where we can dive into details. For now, think of argv as an array of strings.

You stock the argv array from the command line when you start your program. Everything comes in as a string, but you can convert them to other things (well, numbers or characters) if that's what you need. Here's a short program, *ch05/argv.c* (*https://oreil.ly/1SiYk*), to illustrate accessing the arguments with a common check for a "help flag." If the first command-line argument is -h, we'll print a help message and ignore the rest of the arguments. Otherwise we'll list them all out, one per line:

```
#include <stdio.h>

void print_help(char *program_name) {
  printf("You can enter several command-line arguments like this:\n");
  printf("%s this is four words\n", program_name);
}

int main(int argc, char *argv[]) {
  if (argc == 1) {
    printf("Only the name of the program '%s' was given.\n", argv[0]);
  } else if (argc == 2) {
    // Might be a request for help
    int len = sizeof(argv[1]);
    if (len >= 2 && argv[1][0] == '-' && argv[1][1] == 'h') {
      print_help(argv[0]);
    } else {
      printf("Found one, non-help argument: %s\n", argv[1]);
    }
  } else {
    printf("Found %c command-line arguments:\n", argc);
    for (int i = 0; i < argc; i++) {
      printf("  %s\n", argv[i]);
    }
  }
}
```

When you run *argv.c* with a few random words, you should see them listed out:

```
ch05$ gcc argv.c
ch05$ ./a.out this is a test!
Found  command-line arguments:
  ./a.out
  this
  is
  a
  test!
```

But if you use just the special -h argument, you should get our help message:

```
ch05$ ./a.out -h
You can enter several command-line arguments like this:
./a.out this is four words
ch05$ gcc -o argv argv.c
ch05$ ./argv -h
You can enter several command-line arguments like this:
./argv this is four words
```

Try running it a few times yourself. If you want to try a fairly advanced exercise, create a function that converts a string of digits to an integer. Then use that function to add up all of the numbers you pass on the command line. Here's an example of the expected output:

```
./sum 22 154 6 73
The sum of these 4 numbers is 255
```

You can check my solution in the *sum.c* file if you want to see how I tackled it.

 You might suppose converting strings to numbers is a common task and that C would already have a function for it, and you'd mostly be right. There is a function called `atoi()` (ascii to integer) that is part of the standard library, *stdlib.h*. We'll look into libraries in Chapter 7, but this small addition saves a lot of manual labor. If you are up for another quick exercise, try including the `stdlib.h` header and use the `atoi()` function to complete an alternate variation. Or feel free to just peek at my solution in *sum2.c*.

Next Steps

We've got all of the biggest building blocks out of the way now. You can start building some really interesting programs to solve real-world problems with the various control structures from previous chapters and the functions we covered here. But C can do more, and as we start to look forward to working on microcontrollers, some of that "more" will be critical.

In the next two chapters, we'll tackle pointers and using libraries to round out our C skills. Then we can dive into the world of Arduino and have a world of fun!

CHAPTER 6

Pointers and References

Reasonably direct access to memory is one of C's biggest features for folks who work on low-level problems like device drivers or embedded systems. C gives you the tools to micromanage your bytes. That can be a real boon when you need to worry about every bit of free memory, but it can also be a real pain to worry about every bit of memory you use. When you want that control, though, it's great to have the option. This chapter covers the basics of finding out where things are located in memory (their *address*) as well as storing and using those locations with *pointers*, variables that store the address of other variables.

Addresses in C

We've touched on the notion of pointers when we discussed using `scanf()` to read in base types like integers and floats versus reading in a string as a character array. You may recall for numbers, I mentioned the required & prefix. That prefix can be thought of as an "address of" the operator or function. It returns a numeric value that tells you where the variable following the & is located in memory. We can actually print that location out. Take a look at *ch06/address.c* (*https://oreil.ly/z9TrR*):

```
#include <stdio.h>

int main() {
  int answer = 42;
  double pi = 3.1415926;
  printf("answer's value: %d\n", answer);
  printf("answer's address: %p\n", &answer);
  printf("pi's value: %0.4f\n", pi);
  printf("pi's address: %p\n", &pi);
}
```

In this simple program, we create two variables and initialize them. We use a few `printf()` statements to show both their values and their locations in memory. If we compile and run this example, here's what we'll see:

```
ch06$ gcc address.c
ch06$ ./a.out
answer's value: 42
answer's address: 0x7fff2970ee0c
pi's value: 3.1416
pi's address: 0x7fff2970ee10
```

 I should say here is *roughly* what we'll see; your setup will likely differ from mine, so the addresses likely won't match exactly. Indeed, simply running this program successively will almost certainly result in different addresses as well. Where a program is loaded into memory depends on myriad factors. If any of those factors are different, the addresses will probably be different as well.

In all of the examples that follow, it is more useful to pay attention to which addresses are close to which other addresses. The exact values are not important.

Getting the value stored in `answer` or `pi` is straightforward and something we've been doing since Chapter 2. But playing with the address of a variable is new. We even needed a new `printf()` format specifier, `%p`, to print them! The mnemonic for that format specifier is "pointer," which is closely related to "address." Typically, *pointer* refers to a variable that stores an address, even though you will see people talk about a specific value as a pointer. You will also run across the term *reference*, which is synonymous with pointer but is more often used when talking about function parameters. For example, tutorials online will say things like "when you pass a reference to this function...." They mean you are passing the address of some variable to the function rather than the value of the variable.

But back to our example. Those printed pointer values sure look like big numbers! This won't always be the case, but on systems with gigabytes or even terabytes of RAM that use logical addresses to help separate and manage multiple programs, it's not uncommon. What do those values represent? They are the slots within our process's memory where our variables' values are kept. Figure 6-1 illustrates the basic setup in memory of our simple example.

Even without figuring out the exact decimal value of the addresses, you can see they are close together. In fact, the address for `pi` is four bytes bigger than the address for `answer`. An `int` on my machine is four bytes, so hopefully you can see the connection. A `double` is eight bytes on my system. If we added a third variable to our example, can you guess what address it would have?

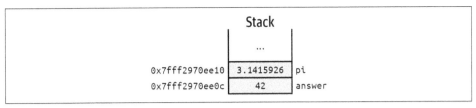

Figure 6-1. Variable values and addresses

Let's go ahead and try it together. The program *ch06/address2.c* (*https://oreil.ly/6gdjU*) adds another int variable and then prints its value and address:

```
#include <stdio.h>

int main() {
    int answer = 42;
    double pi = 3.1415926;
    int extra = 1234;
    printf("answer's value: %d\n", answer);
    printf("answer's address: %p\n", &answer);
    printf("pi's value: %0.4f\n", pi);
    printf("pi's address: %p\n", &pi);
    printf("extra's value: %d\n", extra);
    printf("extra's address: %p\n", &extra);
}
```

And here's the output of our three-variable version:

```
ch06$ gcc address2.c
ch06$ ./a.out
answer's value: 42
answer's address: 0x7fff9c827498
pi's value: 3.1416
pi's address: 0x7fff9c8274a0
extra's value: 1234
extra's address: 0x7fff9c82749c
```

Hmm, actually the variables are not stored in the order we declared them. How strange! If you look closely, you can see that answer is still stored first (address 0x...498), followed by extra four bytes later (0x...49c), followed by pi four bytes after that (0x...4a0). The compiler will often arrange things in a way it deems efficient—and that efficient ordering won't always line up with our source code. So even though the order is a little surprising, we can still see that the variables all stack on top of each other with exactly as much space as their type dictates.

The NULL Value and Pointer Errors

The *stdio.h* header includes a handy value, NULL, that we can use whenever we need to talk about an "empty" or uninitialized pointer. You can assign NULL to a pointer variable or use it in a comparison to see if a particular pointer is valid. If you like always assigning an initial value to your variables when you declare them, NULL is the value to use with pointers. For example, we could declare two variables, one double and one pointer to a double. We'll initialize them with "nothing," but then fill them in later:

```
double pi = 0.0;
double *pi_ptr = NULL;
// ...
pi = 3.14156;
pi_ptr = &pi;
```

You should check for NULL pointers anytime you can't trust where a pointer came from. Inside a function where a pointer was passed to you, for example:

```
double messyAreaCalculator(double radius, double *pi_ptr) {
  if (pi_ptr == NULL) {
    printf("Could not calculate area with a reference to pi!\n");
    return 0.0;
  }
  return radius * radius * (*pi_ptr);
}
```

Not the easiest way to calculate the area of a circle, of course, but the if statement at the beginning is a common pattern. It's a simple guarantee that you have something to work with. If you forget to check your pointer and try dereferencing it anyway, your program will (usually) halt, and you'll probably see an error like this:

```
Segmentation fault (core dumped)
```

Even if you can't do anything about the empty pointer, if you check before using it, you can give the user a nicer error message and avoid crashing.

Arrays

What about arrays and strings? Will those go on the stack just like simpler types? Will they have addresses in the same general part of memory? Let's create a couple array variables and see where they land and how much space they take up. *ch06/address3.c* (*https://oreil.ly/UA5ZK*) has our arrays. I've added a size printout so that we can easily verify how much space is allocated:

```
#include <stdio.h>

int main() {
  char title[30] = "Address Example 3";
  int page_counts[5] = { 14, 78, 49, 18, 50 };
  printf("title's value: %s\n", title);
  printf("title's address: %p\n", &title);
  printf("title's size: %lu\n", sizeof(title));
  printf("page_counts' value: {");
  for (int p = 0; p < 5; p++) {
    printf(" %d", page_counts[p]);
```

```
    }
    printf(" }\n");
    printf("page_counts's address: %p\n", &page_counts);
    printf("page_counts's size: %lu\n", sizeof(page_counts));
}
```

And here is our output:

```
title's value: Address Example 3
title's address: 0x7ffe971a5dc0
title's size: 30
page_counts' value: { 14 78 49 18 50 }
page_counts's address: 0x7ffe971a5da0
page_counts's size: 20
```

The compiler rearranged our variables again, but we can see that the page_counts array is 20 bytes (5 x 4 bytes per int) and that title gets an address 32 bytes after page_counts. (You can ignore the common parts of the address and do a little math: 0xc0 – 0xa0 == 0x20 == 32.) So what's in the extra 12 bytes? There is some overhead for an array, and the compiler has kindly made room for it. Happily, we (as programmers or as users) do not have to worry about that overhead. And as programmers we can see the compiler definitely sets aside enough room for the array itself.

Local Variables and the Stack

So where exactly is that "room" being set aside? In the largest terms, the room is allocated from our computer's memory, its RAM. In the case of variables defined in a function (and remember from "The main() Function" on page 121 that main() is a function), the space is allocated on the *stack*. That's the term for the spot in memory where all local variables are created and kept as you make various function calls. Organizing and maintaining these memory allocations is one of the primary jobs of your operating system.

Consider this next small program, *ch06/do_stuff.c* (*https://oreil.ly/C5xCP*). We have the main() function as usual, and another function, do_stuff(), that, well, does stuff. Not fancy stuff, but it still creates and prints the details of an int variable. Even boring functions use the stack and help illustrate how function calls fit together in memory!

```
#include <stdio.h>

void do_stuff() {
  int local = 12;
  printf("Our local variable has a value of %d\n", local);
  printf("local's address: %p\n", &local);
}

int main() {
  int count = 1;
```

```
    printf("Starting count at %d\n", count);
    printf("count's address: %p\n", &count);
    do_stuff();
}
```

And here's the output:

```
ch06$ gcc do_stuff.c
ch06$ ./a.out
Starting count at 1
count's address: 0x7fff30f1b644
Our local variable has a value of 12
local's address: 0x7fff30f1b624
```

You can see the addresses of count in main() and local in do_stuff() are near each other. They are both on the stack. Figure 6-2 shows the stack with a little more context.

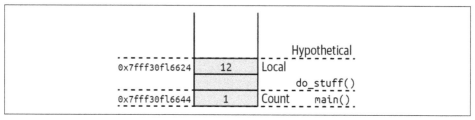

Figure 6-2. Local variables on the stack

This is where the name "stack" comes from: the function calls stack up. If do_stuff() were to call some other function, that function's variables would pile on top of local. And when any function completes, its variables are popped off the stack. That stacking can go on quite awhile, but not forever. If you don't provide a proper base case for a recursive function like those in "Recursive Functions" on page 115, for example, this runaway stack allocation is what eventually causes your program to crash.

You might have caught that the addresses in Figure 6-2 are actually decreasing. The start of the stack can either be at the beginning of the memory allocated to our program and addresses will count up, or at the end of the allotted space and addresses will count down. Which version you see depends on the architecture and operating system. The idea of the stack and its growth, though, remains the same.

The stack also houses any parameters that get passed to a function as well as any loop or other variables that get declared later in the function. Consider this snippet:

```
float average(float a, float b) {
    float sum = a + b;
    if (sum < 0) {
        for (int i = 0; i < 5; i++) {
            printf("Warning!\n");
        }
```

```
        printf("Negative average. Be careful!\n");
    }
    return sum / 2;
}
```

In this snippet, the stack will include space for the following elements:

- the float return value from average() itself
- the float parameter a
- the float parameter b
- the float local variable sum
- the int variable i for the loop (only if sum < 0)

The stack is pretty versatile! Pretty much anything having to do with a particular function will get its memory from the stack.

Global Variables and the Heap

But what about global variables that are not connected to any particular function? They get allocated in a separate part of memory called the *heap*. If "heap" sounds a little messy, it is. Any bit of memory your program needs that isn't part of the stack will be in the heap. Figure 6-3 illustrates how to think about the stack and the heap.

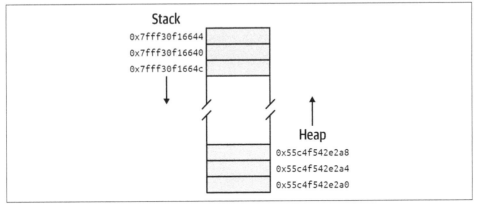

Figure 6-3. Stack versus heap memory

The stack and the heap share one logical lump of memory given to your program when you run it. As you make function calls, the stack will grow (down from the "top" in this case). As functions complete their call, the stack shrinks. Global variables make the heap grow (up from the "bottom"). Large arrays or other structures may also be allocated in the heap. ("Managing Memory with Arrays" on page 138 in this chapter looks at how you can manually use memory in this space.) You can free up some parts of the heap to make it shrink, but global variables remain as long as your program is executing.

We'll look in more detail at how these two parts of memory interact in "Stacks and heaps" on page 209. As both the stack and the heap grow, the free space in the middle gets smaller and smaller. If they meet, you're in trouble. If the stack cannot grow any further, you won't be able to call any more functions. If you call a function anyway, you will likely crash your program. Similarly, if there is no space left for the heap to grow, but you try to request some space, the computer has no choice but to halt your program.

Managing to stay out of this trouble is your job as the programmer. C won't stop you from making a mistake, but in turn, it gives you room to be quite clever when circumstances dictate. Chapter 10 looks at several of those circumstances on microcontrollers and discusses some tricks for navigating them.

Pointer Arithmetic

Regardless of where your variables store their contents, C allows you to work directly with the addresses in a powerful (and potentially dangerous) way. We aren't limited to printing out the address of a variable for simple inspection. We can store it in another variable. And we can use that other variable to get to the same bit of data and manipulate it.

Take a look at *ch06/pointer.c* (*https://oreil.ly/ONjNE*) to see an example of using a variable that points to another variable. I've called out a few key concepts in working with pointers:

```
#include <stdio.h>

int main() {
  double total = 500.0;                    ❶
  int count = 34;
  double average = total / count;
  printf("The average of %d units totaling %.1f is %.2f\n",
    count, total, average);

  // Now let's reproduce some of that work with pointers
  double *total_ptr = &total;              ❷
  int *count_ptr = &count;
  printf("total_ptr is the same as the address of total:\n");
  printf("  total_ptr %p == %p &total\n", total_ptr, &total);

  // We can manipulate the value at the end of a pointer
  // with the '*' prefix (dereferencing)
  printf("The current total is: %.1f\n", *total_ptr);
  // Let's pretend we forgot two units and correct our count:
  *count_ptr += 2;                         ❸
```

```
    average = *total_ptr / *count_ptr;
    printf("The corrected average of %d units totaling %.1f is %.2f\n",
        count, total, average);                    ❹
}
```

❶ We start with a normal set of variables and perform a simple calculation.

❷ Next, we create new variables with corresponding pointer types. E.g., we create
    `total_ptr` of type `double *` as a pointer to our `total` variable of type `double`.

❸ You can dereference pointers to use or alter the things they point to.

❹ Lastly, we prove that the original, non-pointer variables were in fact changed by
    the work we did with their pointer counterparts.

Here's the output:

```
ch06$ gcc pointer.c
ch06$ ./a.out
The average of 34 units totaling 500.0 is 14.71
total_ptr is the same as the address of total:
    total_ptr 0x7ffdfdc079c8 == 0x7ffdfdc079c8 &total
The current total is: 500.0
The corrected average of 36 units totaling 500.0 is 13.89
```

That output isn't very exciting, but again, it proves we were able to edit the value of
variables like `count` via the `count_ptr` pointer. Manipulating data through pointers is
pretty advanced stuff. Don't worry if this topic still feels a little overwhelming. Keep
trying the examples and you'll get more comfortable with the syntax, which in turn
will help you think about using pointers with your own future projects.

Array Pointers

We have actually worked with a pointer already, although it was very cleverly dis-
guised as an array. Recall our expanded use of the `scanf()` function in "scanf() and
Parsing Inputs" on page 38. When we wanted to scan in a number, we had to use &
with the name of the numeric variable. But scanning strings did not require that syntax—we simply gave the name of the array. That is because arrays in C are already
pointers, just pointers with an expected structure to make reading and writing array
elements easy.

It turns out that you can work with the contents of an array *without* the convenience
of the square brackets. You can use exactly the same dereferencing we just saw in the
previous example. With dereferencing, you can add and subtract simple integers to
the array variable to get at individual elements in that array. But this type of thing is
best discussed over code. Check out *ch06/direct_edit.c* (*https://oreil.ly/GPhxA*):

```
#include <stdio.h>

int main() {
  char name[] = "a.c. Programmer";          ❶
  printf("Before manipulation: %s\n", name);
  *name = 'A';                               ❷
  *(name + 2) = 'C';                         ❸
  printf("After manipulation: %s\n", name);  ❹
}
```

❶ We declare and initialize our string (`char` array) as usual.

❷ We can dereference the array variable to read or alter the first character. This is equivalent to `name[0]` = `A`.

❸ We can also dereference an expression involving our array variable. We can add or subtract `int` values, which translates to moving forward or backward in the array by one element. In our code, this line is equivalent to `name[2]` = `C`.

❹ And you can see the array variable itself is "unharmed," although we did successfully edit the string.

Go ahead and compile and run the program. Here's the output:

```
ch06$ gcc direct_edit.c
ch06$ ./a.out
Before manipulation: a.c. Programmer
After manipulation: A.C. Programmer
```

This type of math and dereferencing works on arrays of other types, as well. You might see pointer arithmetic in loops that process arrays, for example, where incrementing the array pointer amounts to moving to the next element in the array. This use of pointers can be remarkably efficient. But while the simple manipulations in *direct_edit.c* might have been faster historically, modern C compilers are very (very!) good at optimizing your code.

 I recommend concentrating on getting the answer you want before worrying about performance. Chapter 10 looks at memory and other resources on the Arduino platform where such worrying is a bit more justified. Even there, optimizing won't be your first concern.

Functions and Pointers

Where pointers really start to make a difference in your day-to-day life as a programmer is when you attach them to the parameters or return values of functions. This feature allows you to create a piece of shareable memory without making it global. Consider the following functions from *ch06/increment.c* (*https://oreil.ly/JJLV4*):

```
void increment_me(int me, int amount) {
  // increment "me" by the "amount"
  me += amount;
  printf("  Inside increment_me: %d\n", me);
}

void increment_me_too(int *me, int amount) {
  // increment the variable pointed to by "me" by the "amount"
  *me += amount;
  printf("  Inside increment_me_too: %d\n", *me);
}
```

The first function, increment_me(), should feel familiar. We have passed values to functions before. Inside increment_me(), we can add amount to me and get the correct answer. However, we did pass only the *value* of count from our main() method. That should mean that the original count variable will remain untouched.

But increment_me_too() uses a pointer. Instead of a simple value, we can now pass a *reference* to count. In this approach, we should find that count has been updated once we return to main(). Let's test that expectation. Here's a minimal main() method that tries both functions:

```
int main() {
  int count = 1;
  printf("Initial count: %d\n", count);
  increment_me(count, 5);
  printf("Count after increment_me: %d\n", count);
  increment_me_too(&count, 5);
  printf("Count after increment_me_too: %d\n", count);
}
```

And here's what we get for output:

```
ch06$ gcc increment.c
ch06$ ./a.out
Initial count: 1
  Inside increment_me: 6
Count after increment_me: 1
  Inside increment_me_too: 6
Count after increment_me_too: 6
```

Excellent. We got exactly the behavior we wanted. The increment_me() function does not affect the value of count passed in from main(), but increment_me_too() does affect it. You will often see the terms "pass by value" and "pass by reference" to distinguish the way a function handles the arguments passed to it. And note that in the case of `increment_me_too()`, we have one reference parameter and one value parameter. There is no restriction on mixing the types. As the programmer, you just have to make sure you use your function correctly.

Functions can also return a pointer to something they have created in the heap. This is a popular trick in external libraries, as we'll see in Chapters 9 and 11.

Managing Memory with Arrays

If you know ahead of time you want a large chunk of memory, say, to store image or audio data, you can allocate your own arrays (and structures; see "Defining Structures" on page 141). The result of the allocation is a pointer that you can then pass to any functions that might need to work with your data. You don't duplicate any storage this way, and you can check to make sure you got all the memory you need *before* you have to use it. That is a definite boon when working with content from unknown sources. If sufficient memory is not available, you can provide a polite error message and ask the user to try again rather than simply crashing without an explanation.

Allocating with malloc()

While we'll typically reserve heap work for larger arrays, you can allocate anything you want there. To do so, you use the `malloc()` function and provide it a quantity in bytes that you need. The `malloc()` function is defined in another header, `stdlib.h`, so we have to include that header, similar to how we include `stdio.h`. We'll see more of the functions that `stdlib.h` provides in "stdio.h" on page 150, but for now, just add this line at the top, below our usual `include`:

```
#include <stdio.h>
#include <stdlib.h>

// ...
```

With this header included, we can create a simple program that illustrates the memory allocation of global and local variables as well as our own, custom bit of memory in the heap. Take a look at *ch06/memory.c* (*https://oreil.ly/zAK5y*):

```
#include <stdio.h>
#include <stdlib.h>

int result_code = 404;
char result_msg[20] = "File Not Found";

int main() {
  char temp[20] = "Loading ...";
  int success = 200;
```

```
char *buffer = (char *)malloc(20 * sizeof (char));

// We won't do anything with these various variables,
// but we can print out their addresses
printf("Address of result_code:  %p\n", &result_code);
printf("Address of result_msg:   %p\n", &result_msg);
printf("Address of temp:         %p\n", &temp);
printf("Address of success:      %p\n", &success);
printf("Address of buffer (heap): %p\n", buffer);
}
```

The global declarations of `result_code` and `result_msg` as well as the local variables `temp` and `success` should be familiar. But look at how we declared `buffer`. You can see the use of `malloc()` in a real program. We asked for 20 characters of space. You can specify a simple number of bytes if you want, but it is usually safer (indeed, often necessary) to use `sizeof`, as shown in this example. Different systems will have different rules regarding type sizes and memory allocation, and `sizeof` provides an easy guard against unwitting mistakes.

Let's take a look at the addresses of our variables in the output:

```
ch06$ gcc memory.c
ch06$ ./a.out
Address of result_code:   0x55c4f49c8010
Address of result_msg:    0x55c4f49c8020
Address of temp:          0x7fffc84f1840
Address of success:       0x7fffc84f1834
Address of buffer (heap): 0x55c4f542e2a0
```

Again, don't worry about the exact value of those addresses. What we're looking for here is their general location. Hopefully, you can see that the global variables and the `buffer` pointer we created in the heap manually with `malloc()` are all in roughly the same spot. Likewise, the two variables local to `main()` are similarly grouped, but in a separate spot.

So `malloc()` makes room for your data in the heap. We'll make use of this allocated space in "Pointers to Structures" on page 142, but we need to look at a closely related function, `free()`, first. When you allocate memory using `malloc()`, you are responsible for returning that space when you are done.

Deallocating with free()

As you might recall in the discussion of Figure 6-3, if you use up too much of the stack or the heap—or enough of both—you will run out of memory and your program will crash. One of the benefits of working with the heap is that you have control over when and how memory is allocated from and returned to the heap. Of course, as I just noted, the flipside of this benefit is that you have to remember to do the "giveing back" part yourself. Many newer languages work to relieve the programmer of that burden, as it is all too easy to forget to clean up after yourself. Perhaps you have even heard of the quasi-official term for this issue: a memory leak.

To return memory and avoid such leaks in C, you use the `free()` function (also from *stdlib.h*). It's pretty straightforward to use—you just pass the pointer returned from your corresponding `malloc()` call. So to free up `buffer` when you're done using it, for example:

```
free(buffer);
```

Easy! But again, it's remembering to use `free()` that is the difficulty. That might not seem like such a problem, but it gets increasingly tricky when you start using functions to create and remove bits of data. How many times did you call the create functions? Did you call a reciprocal remove function for each one? What if you try to remove something that was never allocated? All of these questions make keeping track of your memory usage as troublesome as it is vital.

C Structures

As you tackle more interesting problems, your data storage needs will get more complex. If you are working with LCD displays, for example, you will work with pixels that need a color and a location. That location itself will be made up of x and y coordinates. While you can create three separate arrays (one for all the colors, one for all the x coordinates, and finally one for the y coordinates), that collection will be difficult to pass to and from functions and opens up several avenues for bugs—like adding a color but forgetting one of the coordinates. Fortunately, C includes the `struct` facility to create better containers for your new data needs.

To quote K&R: "A *structure* is a collection of one or more variables, possibly of different types, grouped together under a single name for convenient handling."[1] They go on to note that other languages support this idea as a *record*. Searching online today you would also encounter the term *composite type*. Whatever you call it, this variable grouping feature is very powerful. Let's see how it works.

---

1 That convenient handling turns out to be very convenient. Kernighan and Ritchie devote an entire chapter of *The C Programming Language* to this topic. Obviously they go into more detail than I can here, so here's one more plug for picking up this classic.

Defining Structures

To create your own structures, you use the struct keyword and name followed by your list of variables inside curly braces. Then you can access those variables by name much like you access the elements of an array by index. Here's a quick example we could use with a program for bank accounts:

```
struct transaction {
  double amount;
  int day, month, year;
};
```

We now have a new "type" we can use with our variables. Instead of int or char[], we have struct transaction:

```
int main() {
  int count;
  char message[] = "Your money is safe with us!";
  struct transaction bill, deposit;
  // ...
}
```

The count and message declarations should look familiar. The next line declares two more variables, bill and deposit, who share the new struct transaction type. You can use this new type anywhere you have been using native types like int. You can create local or global variables with struct types. You can pass structures to functions or return them from functions. Working with structures and functions tends to rely more on pointers, but we'll look at those details in "Functions and Structures" on page 143.

Your structure definitions can be quite complex. There is no real restriction on how many variables they can contain. A structure can even contain nested struct definitions! You don't want to go overboard, of course, but you do have freedom to create just about any kind of record you can imagine.

Assigning and Accessing Structure Members

Once your structure type is defined, you can declare and initialize variables of that type using syntax similar to how we handle arrays. For example, if you know a structure's values ahead of time, you can use curly braces to initialize your variable:

```
struct transaction deposit = { 200.00, 6, 20, 2021 };
```

The order of the values inside the braces needs to match the order of the variables you listed in the struct definition. But you can also create a structure variable and fill it in after the fact. To indicate which field you want to assign, you use the "dot" operator. You give the structure variable's name (bill or deposit in our current example), a period, and then the member of the structure you are interested in, like day or amount. With this approach, you can make assignments in any order you like:

```
bill.day = 15;
bill.month = 7;
bill.year = 2021;
bill.amount = 56.75;
```

Regardless of how you filled the structure, you use the same dot notation to access a structure's contents anytime you need them. For example, to print any details from a transaction, we specify the transaction variable (bill or deposit in our case), the dot, and the field we want, like this:

```
printf("Your deposit of $%0.2f was accepted.\n", deposit.amount);
printf("Your bill is due on %d/%02d\n", bill.month, bill.day);
```

We can print these inner elements to the screen. We can assign new values to them. We can use them in calculations. You can do everything with the pieces inside your structure that you do with other variables. The point of the structure is simply to make it easier to keep related pieces of data together. But these structures also keep data *distinct*. Consider assigning the amount variable in both our bill and our deposit:

```
deposit.amount = 200.00;
bill.amount = 56.75;
```

There is never any confusion over which amount you mean, even though we used the amount name in both assignments. If we add some tax to our bill after it was set up, for example, that will not affect how much money we include in our deposit:

```
bill.amount = bill.amount + bill.amount * 0.05;

printf("Our final bill: $%0.2f\n", bill.amount); // $59.59
printf("Our deposit: $%0.2f\n", )                // $200.00
```

Hopefully, that separation makes sense. With structures, you can talk about bills and deposits as entities in their own right, while understanding that the details of any individual bill or deposit remain unique to that transaction.

Pointers to Structures

If you build a good composite type that encapsulates just the right data, you will likely start using these types in more and more places. You can use them for global and local variables or as parameter types or even function return types. In the wild, however, you will more often see programmers working with pointers to structures rather than structures themselves.

To create (or destroy) pointers to structures, you can use exactly the same operators and functions that are available for simple types. If you already have a struct variable, for example, you can get its address with the & operator. If you created an instance of your structure with malloc(), you use free() to return that memory to the heap. Here are a few examples of using these features and functions with our struct transaction type:

```
struct transaction tmp = { 68.91, 8, 1, 2020 };
struct transaction *payment;
struct transaction *withdrawal;

payment = &tmp;
withdrawal = malloc(sizeof(struct transaction));
```

Here, tmp is a normal struct transaction variable and we initialize it using curly braces. Both payment and withdrawal are declared as pointers. We can assign the address of a struct transaction variable like we do with payment, or we can allocate memory on the heap (to fill in later) like we do with withdrawal.

When we go to fill in withdrawal, however, we have to remember that we have a pointer, so withdrawal requires dereferencing before we can apply the dot. Not only that, the dot operator has a higher order of precedence than the dereference operator, so you have to use parentheses to get the operators applied correctly. That can be a little tedious, so we often use an alternate notation for accessing the members of a struct pointer. The "arrow" operator, ->, allows us to use a struct pointer without dereferencing it. You place the arrow between the structure variable's name and the name of the intended member just like with the dot operator:

```
// With dereferencing:
(*withdrawal).amount = -20.0;

// With the arrow operator:
withdrawal->day = 3;
withdrawal->month = 8;
withdrawal->year = 2021;
```

This difference can be a little frustrating, but eventually you'll get used to it. Pointers to structures provide an efficient means of sharing relevant information between different parts of your program. Their biggest advantage is that pointers do not have the overhead of moving or copying all of the internal pieces of their structures. This advantage becomes apparent when you start using structures with functions.

Functions and Structures

Consider writing a function to print out the contents of a transaction in a nice format. We could pass the structure as is to a function. We just use the struct transaction type in our parameter list and then pass a normal variable when we call it:

```
void printTransaction1(struct transaction tx) {
  printf("%2d/%02d/%4d: %10.2f\n", tx.month, tx.day, tx.year, tx.amount);
}
// ...
printTransaction1(bill);
printTransaction1(deposit);
```

Pretty simple, but recall our discussion of how function calls work with the stack. In this example, all of the fields of bill or deposit will have to be put on the stack when we call printTransaction1(). That takes extra time and space. Indeed, in the very earliest versions of C, this wasn't even allowed! That's obviously not true any longer, but passing pointers to and from functions is still faster. Here's a pointer version of our printTransaction1() function:

```
void printTransaction2(struct transaction *ptr) {
  printf("%2d/%02d/%4d: %10.2f\n",
      ptr->month, ptr->day, ptr->year, ptr->amount);
}
// ...
printTransaction2(&tmp);
printTransaction2(payment)
printTransaction2(withdrawal);
```

The only thing required to go on the stack was the address of one struct transaction object. Much cleaner.

Passing pointers this way has an interesting, intended feature: we can change the contents of a structure in the function. Recall from "Passing Simple Types" on page 107 that without pointers, we end up passing values via the stack that initialize the parameters of the function. Nothing we do to those parameters while inside the function affects the original arguments from wherever the function was called.

If we pass a pointer, however, we can use that pointer to change the insides of the structure. And those changes persist because we are working on the actual structure, not a copy of its values. For example, we could create a function to add tax to any transaction:

```
void addTax(struct transaction *ptr, double rate) {
  double tax = ptr->amount * rate;
  ptr->amount += tax;
}

// ... back in main
  printf("Our bill amount before tax: $%.2f\n", bill.amount);
  addTax(&bill, 0.05);
  printf("Our bill amount after tax: $%.2f\n", bill.amount);
  // ...
```

Notice that we do not change `bill.amount` in the `main()` function. We simply pass its address to `addTax()` along with a tax rate. Here's the output of those `printf()` statements:

```
Our bill amount before tax: $56.75
Our bill amount after tax: $59.59
```

Exactly what we were hoping for. Because it proves so powerful, passing structures by reference is very common. Not everything needs to be in a structure, and not every structure has to be passed by reference, but in large programs, the organization and efficiency you get are definitely appealing.

 This ability to alter the contents of a structure using a pointer is usually desirable. But if for some reason you *don't* want to change a member while you're using a pointer to its structure, be sure not to assign anything to that member. You can, of course, always put a copy of that member's value into a temporary variable first, and then work with the temporary variable.

Pointer Syntax Recap

I introduced enough new and somewhat esoteric bits of C's syntax in this chapter that I wanted to recap things here for quick reference:

- We defined new data types with the `struct` keyword.
- We used the "dot" operator (`.`) for accessing the contents of a structure.
- We used the "arrow" operator (`->`) for accessing the contents of a structure though a pointer.
- We allocated our own space for data using `malloc()`.
- We worked with that space using the `&` ("address of") and `*` ("dereference") operators.
- When we're done with the data, we can release its space using `free()`.

Let's see these new concepts and definitions in context. Consider the following program, *ch06/structure.c* (*https://oreil.ly/xeqqL*). Rather than use callouts in this slightly longer listing, I have added several inline comments to highlight key points. That way you can look up these details quickly here in the book, or in your code editor if you're working on one of your own programs:

```
// Include the usual stdio, but also stdlib for access
// to the malloc() and free() functions, and NULL
#include <stdio.h>
#include <stdlib.h>
```

```
// We can use the struct keyword to define new, composite types
struct transaction {
  double amount;
  int month, day, year;
};

// That new type can be used with function parameters
void printTransaction1(struct transaction tx) {
  printf("%2d/%02d/%4d: %10.2f\n", tx.month, tx.day, tx.year, tx.amount);
}

// We can also use a pointer to that type with parameters
void printTransaction2(struct transaction *ptr) {
  // Check to make sure our pointer isn't empty
  if (ptr == NULL) {
    printf("Invalid transaction.\n");
  } else {
    // Yay! We have a transaction, print out its details with ->
    printf("%2d/%02d/%4d: %10.2f\n", ptr->month, ptr->day, ptr->year,
        ptr->amount);
  }
}

// Passing a structure pointer to a function means we can alter
// the contents of the structure if necessary
void addTax(struct transaction *ptr, double rate) {
  double tax = ptr->amount * rate;
  ptr->amount += tax;
}

int main() {
  // We can declare local (or global) variables with our new type
  struct transaction bill;

  // We can assign initial values inside curly braces
  struct transaction deposit = { 200.00, 6, 20, 2021 };

  // Or we can assign values at any time after with the dot operator
  bill.amount = 56.75;
  bill.month = 7;
  bill.day = 15;
  bill.year = 2021;

  // We can pass structure variables to functions just like other variables
  printTransaction1(deposit);
  printTransaction1(bill);

  // We can also create pointers to structures and use them with malloc()
  struct transaction tmp = { 68.91, 8, 1, 2020 };
  struct transaction *payment = NULL;
  struct transaction *withdrawal;
  payment = &tmp;
```

```
    withdrawal = malloc(sizeof(struct transaction));

    // With a pointer, we either have to carefully dereference it
    (*withdrawal).amount = -20.0;
    // Or use the arrow operator
    withdrawal->day = 3;
    withdrawal->month = 8;
    withdrawal->year = 2021;

    // And we are free to pass structure pointers to functions
    printTransaction2(payment);
    printTransaction2(withdrawal);

    // Add tax to our bill using a function and a pointer
    printf("Our bill amount before tax: $%.2f\n", bill.amount);
    addTax(&bill, 0.05);
    printf("Our bill amount after tax: $%.2f\n", bill.amount);

    // Before we go, release the memory we allocated to withdrawal:
    free(withdrawal);
}
```

As with most new concepts and bits of syntax, you'll get more comfortable with pointers and malloc() as you use them more in your own programs. Creating a program from scratch that solves a problem you are interested in always helps cement your understanding of a new topic. I officially give you permission to go play around with pointers!

Next Steps

We covered some pretty advanced stuff in this chapter. We looked at where data is stored in memory as your program is running and the operators (&, *, ., and ->) and functions (malloc() and free()) that help you work with the addresses of that data. Many books on intermediate and advanced programming will spend multiple chapters on these concepts, so don't be discouraged if you need to read through some of this material a few more times. As always, running the code with some of your own modifications is a great way to practice your understanding.

We have an impressive array of tools in our C kit now! We can start tackling complex problems and have a good shot at solving them. But in many cases, our problems are not actually novel. In fact, a lot of problems (or at least a lot of the subproblems we find when we break up our real task into manageable pieces) have already been encountered and solved by other programmers. The next chapter looks at how to take advantage of those external solutions.

CHAPTER 7

Libraries

One of C's best qualities is the minimal adornment present in its compiled code. A favorite snipe at some more modern languages like Java is the size of the "Hello, World" program. Our very first program back in "Creating a C 'Hello, World'" on page 15 takes up a little over 16Kb on my Linux machine without any optimizations. Achieving the same output from a standalone executable on the same system using Java, though, requires tens of megabytes and much, much more effort to build. That's not an entirely fair comparison since the Java hello application needs the entire Java runtime baked into the executable, but that's also the point: C makes it easy to create lean code for a given system.

That ease is great when we're tackling small things like "Hello, World" or even most of the examples from past chapters. But as we get ready to jump into the world of microcontrollers and Arduino, we're left worrying about re-creating our own solutions to some pretty mundane problems. For example, we've written some of our own functions to compare strings. We wrote a fancier program to encode base64 content. That stuff is fun, but do we always have to do this type of work from scratch?

Happily, the answer to that question is: no. C supports the notion of using a *library* for quick, friendly expansion of its capabilities—without losing its lean profile for the final executable. A library is a bundle of code that can be imported into your projects to add new capabilities, like working with strings or talking to a wireless network. But the key to using libraries is that you only need to add the one that contains the features you need. That Java hello application would have latent support for creating an entire graphical interface and opening network connections, even though they would not be used just to print some text in a terminal window.

With Arduino, for example, you'll find libraries for most of the popular sensors like temperature components or light-level resistors and outputs like LEDs and LCD displays. You won't have to write your own device driver to use a piece of electronic paper or change the color of an RGB LED. You can load up a library and get to work on *what* you want to display on that e-paper, and not worry about *how*.

The C Standard Library

We have already used a couple libraries on our path to this point in the book. Even our very first program needed the *stdio.h* header for access to the printf() function. And our most recent work on pointers in Chapter 6 required the malloc() function found in the *stdlib.h* header. We didn't have to do much to get access to those bits. Indeed, we just wrote an #include statement at the top of our program and off we went!

The reason these functions are so easy to incorporate is that they belong to the C standard library. Every C compiler or development environment will have this library available. It may be packaged differently on different platforms (such as including or excluding the math functions), but you can always count on the overall content being ready for inclusion. I can't cover everything in the library, but I do want to highlight some useful functions and the headers that provide them. In "Putting It Together" on page 161, I'll also cover where to look for other libraries that tackle a wider range of features.

stdio.h

Obviously we've been using the *stdio.h* header from the very start. We have already used the two most useful functions (for our purposes): printf() and scanf(). The other functions in this header revolve around access to files. The microcontrollers we'll be working with in the coming chapters do sometimes have filesystems, but the types of programs we'll be writing won't need that particular feature. Still, if you do want to work with files on a desktop or high-powered microcontroller, this header is a good place to start!

stdlib.h

We have also seen a few functions from *stdlib.h*, namely malloc() and free(). But this header has a few more useful tricks worth mentioning.

atoi()

In "Command-Line Arguments and main()" on page 123, I gave you an exercise to convert a string to a number. The "extra credit" note mentioned using *stdlib.h* to get access to C's standard conversion function: atoi(). There are two other converters for other base types: atol() converts to a long value, and atof() converts to a floating point type, but contrary to the final letter in the function's name, atof() returns a double value. (You can always cast that to the lower-precision float type if needed.)

The solution to that extra exercise, *ch07/sum2.c* (*https://oreil.ly/x8J8O*), highlights just how simple converting can be if you include the necessary header file:

```
#include <stdio.h>
#include <stdlib.h>

int main(int argc, char *argv[]) {
  int total = 0;
  for (int i = 1; i < argc; i++) {
    total += atoi(argv[i]);
  }
  printf("The sum of these %d numbers is %d\n", argc - 1, total);
}
```

Pretty easy! Which is, of course, the hope in using a library function like this. You *could* write this conversion code yourself, but you can save a lot of time (and a fair amount of debugging) if you can find an appropriate library function to use instead.

 Do be a little careful with these functions. They stop parsing the string when they hit a nondigit character. If you attempt to convert the word "one" to a number, for example, that parsing stops immediately and `atoi()` (or the others) will return a 0 without any errors. If 0 can appear as a legitimate value in your string, you'll need to add your own validity checks before calling them.

rand() and srand()

Random values play a fun role in many situations. Want to vary the colors of your LED lamp? Want to shuffle a virtual deck of cards? Need to simulate potential communication delays? Random numbers to the rescue!

The `rand()` function returns a pseudorandom number between 0 and a constant (well, technically a *macro*; more on these in "Special Values" on page 190), RAND_MAX, also defined in *stdlib.h*. I say "pseudorandom" because the "random" number you get back is the product of an algorithm.[1]

A related function, `srand()`, can be used to *seed* the random number generating algorithm. The "seed" value is the starting point for the algorithm before it goes hopping around producing a nice variety of values. You can use `srand()` to supply new values every time your program runs—using the current timestamp, for example—or you can use the seed to produce a known list of numbers. That might seem like a strange thing to want, but it can be useful in testing.

---

1 That algorithm is deterministic and while that's fine for most developers, it is not truly random.

Let's try out these two functions to get a feel for their use. Take a look at *ch07/random.c* (*https://oreil.ly/sst4C*):

```
#include <stdio.h>
#include <stdlib.h>
#include <time.h>

int main() {
  printf("RAND_MAX: %d\n", RAND_MAX);
  unsigned int r1 = rand();
  printf("First random number: %d\n", r1);
  srand(5);
  printf("Second random number: %d\n", rand());
  srand(time(NULL));
  printf("Third random number: %d\n", rand());
  unsigned int pin = rand() % 9000 + 1000;
  printf("Random four digit number: %d\n", pin);
}
```

And let's compile and run it to see the output:

```
ch07$ gcc random.c
ch07$ ./a.out
RAND_MAX: 2147483647
First random number: 1804289383
Second random number: 590011675
Third random number: 1205842387
Random four digit number: 7783

ch07$ ./a.out
RAND_MAX: 2147483647
First random number: 1804289383
Second random number: 590011675
Third random number: 612877372
Random four digit number: 5454
```

On my system, then, the maximum value returned by rand() is 2147483647. The first number we generate should be between 0 and 2147483647, and so it is. The second number we generate will be in the same range, but it comes after we provide a new seed value to srand(), so hopefully it's different than r1, and that bears out.

But look at those first two "random" numbers in the output of our second run. They're exactly the same! Hardly random. As I mentioned, rand() is a pseudo-random generator. The default seed for the generating algorithm is 1 if you never call srand(). But if you call it with a constant like 5, that's no better. It will be a different sequence of numbers, but every time you run the program it will be the same "different" sequence.

So, in order to get different pseudorandom numbers, you need to provide a seed that changes every time you run your program. The most common trick is to do what I did by including yet another header, *time.h* (see "time.h" on page 159) and pull in the current timestamp (seconds since January 1, 1970). As long as we don't manage to start the program twice in one second, we'll get new sequences each run. You can see that seed turned out fine in the two runs above as the third number is indeed different between them.

With that better seed[2] in place, subsequent calls to rand() should look random from execution to execution. We can see that benefit with the PIN we generate for our final random number. The PIN is bounded using a popular trick for getting a random number in a range. You use the remainder operator to make sure you get an appropriately limited range, and then add a base value. For the PIN to have exactly four digits, we use a base of 1000 and a range of 9000 (0 to 8999 inclusive).

exit()

The final function from *stdlib.h* that I want to highlight is the exit() function. In "Return values and main()" on page 122 we looked at using the return statement to end your program and optionally return a value from the main() function to provide some status information to the operating system.

There is also a separate exit() function that takes an int argument that is used for the same exit code value as the return statement in the main() method. The difference between using exit() and returning from main() is that exit() can be called from any function and immediately quits the application. For example, we could write a "confirmation" function that asks the user if they are sure they want to quit. If they answer with a *y*, then we can use exit() at that point rather than returning some sentinel value to main() and then using return. Take a look at *ch07/areyousure.c* (*https://oreil.ly/W5lIr*):

```c
#include <stdio.h>
#include <stdlib.h>

void confirm() {
  char answer;
  printf("Are you sure you want to exit? (y/n) ");
  scanf("%c", &answer);
  if (answer == 'y' || answer == 'Y') {
    printf("Bye\n\n");
    exit(0);
    printf("This will never be printed.\n");
  }
}
```

---

2 I don't have space to cover good generators, but searching online for "C random generator" will net you some interesting options. There are better algorithms such as Blum Blum Shub or a Mersenne Twister, but you can also find hardware-dependent generators that are better still.

```
int main() {
  printf("In main... let's try exiting.\n");
  confirm();
  printf("Glad you decided not to leave.\n");
}
```

And here is the output from two runs:

```
ch07$ gcc areyousure.c
ch07$ ./a.out
In main... let's try exiting.
Are you sure you want to exit? (y/n) y
Bye

ch07$ ./a.out
In main... let's try exiting.
Are you sure you want to exit? (y/n) n
Glad you decided not to leave.
```

Notice that when we use exit(), we don't go back to the main() function or even finish the code in our confirm() function itself. We really do exit the program and supply an exit code to the operating system.

Inside main(), by the way, it mostly doesn't matter whether you use return or exit(), although the former is more "polite." (For example, any cleanup from completing the main() function will still run if you use return. That same cleanup would be skipped if you use exit().) It is also worth noting that simply making it to the end of the main() body as we have been doing all along is a fine and popular way to finish your program when there were no errors.

string.h

Strings are so common and so useful that they even have their own header file. The *string.h* header can be added to any program where you need to compare or manipulate strings beyond simply storing and printing them. This header describes more functions than we have time to cover here, but there are some import utilities we want to highlight in Table 7-1.

Table 7-1. Useful string functions

Function	Description
strlen(char *s)	Calculate the length of a string (not including the final null character)
strcmp(char *s1, char *s2)	Compare two strings. Return -1 if s1 < s2, 0 if s1 == s2, and 1 if s1 > s2
strncmp(char *s1, char *s2, int n)	Compare at most n bytes of s1 and s2 (results similar to strcmp)
strcpy(char *dest, char *src)	Copy src to dest
strncpy(char *dest, char *src, int n)	Copy at most n bytes of src to dest

Function	Description
strcat(char *dest, char *src)	Append src to dest
strncat(char *dest, char *src, int n)	Append at most n bytes of src to dest

We can demonstrate all of these functions in a simple program, *ch07/fullname.c* (*https://oreil.ly/dzycy*), by asking the user for their full name in pieces and (safely!) putting it together at the end. If we find we're interacting with Dennis M. Ritchie, we'll thank him for writing C.

```c
#include <stdio.h>
#include <string.h>

int main() {
  char first[20];
  char middle[20];
  char last[20];
  char full[60];
  char spacer[2] = " ";

  printf("Please enter your first name: ");
  scanf("%s", first);
  printf("Please enter your middle name or initial: ");
  scanf("%s", middle);
  printf("Please enter your last name: ");
  scanf("%s", last);

  // First, assemble the full name
  strncpy(full, first, 20);
  strncat(full, spacer, 40);
  strncat(full, middle, 39);
  strncat(full, spacer, 20);
  strncat(full, last, 19);

  printf("Well hello, %s!\n", full);

  int dennislen = 17;  // length of "Dennis M. Ritchie"
  if (strlen(full) == dennislen &&
      strncmp("Dennis M. Ritchie", full, dennislen) == 0)
  {
    printf("Thanks for writing C!\n");
  }
}
```

And an example run:

```
ch07$ gcc fullname.c
ch07$ ./a.out
Please enter your first name: Alice
Please enter your middle name or initial: B.
Please enter your last name: Toklas
Well hello, Alice B. Toklas!
```

Give this program a try yourself. If you do enter Dennis's name (including the period after his middle initial: "M."), do you get the thank-you message as expected?

 It's a common mistake to set the maximum number of characters to concatenate in `strncat()` to the length of the source string. Instead, you should set it to the maximum number of characters remaining in your destination. Your compiler may warn you about this mistake with a "specified bound X equals source length" message. (X, of course, would be the bound you specified when calling `strncat()`.) It's just a warning, and you might well have exactly the length of your source remaining. But if you see the warning, double-check that you didn't use the source length by accident.

As another example, we can revisit the notion of default values and overwriting arrays from "Initializing strings" on page 88. You can delay the initialization of a character array until you know what the user has done. We can declare—but not initialize—a string, use it with `scanf()`, and then go back to the default if the user didn't give us a good alternate value.

Let's try this with a question about the background color of some future, amazing application. We might assume a dark theme with a black background. We can prompt the user for a different value, or have them simply hit the Return key without entering a value if they want to keep the default. Here's *ch07/background.c* (*https://oreil.ly/a89Jd*):

```
#include <stdio.h>
#include <string.h>

int main() {
  char background[20];                                          ❶
  printf("Enter a background color or return for the default: ");
  scanf("%[^\n]s", background);                                 ❷
  if (strlen(background) == 0) {                                ❸
    strcpy(background, "black");
  }
  printf("The background color is now %s.\n", background); ❹
}
```

❶ Declare a string with enough capacity, but don't set it to anything.

❷ Get input from the user and store it in our array.

❸ If the array is empty after prompting the user, store our default.

❹ Show the final value, either from the user or from our default.

And here are some sample runs, including one where we keep the black background:

```
ch07$ gcc background.c
ch07$ ./a.out
Enter a background color or return for the default: blue
The background color is now blue.
ch07$ ./a.out
Enter a background color or return for the default: white
The background color is now white.
ch07$ ./a.out
Enter a background color or return for the default:
The background color is now black.
```

If you are inviting the user to supply a value, just remember to allocate sufficient room in your array to contain whatever response the user might give you. If you can't trust your users, scanf() has another trick that you can deploy. Just like the format specifiers in printf(), you can add a width to any input field in scanf(). For our previous example, say, we could change to an explicit limit of 19 (saving room for that final '\0' character):

```
scanf("%19[^\n]s", background);
```

Easy peasy. It does look quite dense, but it's a nice option for limited devices where you might not be able to allocate a lot of extra space in case of verbose users.

math.h

The *math.h* header declares several useful functions for performing a variety of arithmetic and trigonometric calculations. Table 7-2 includes several of the more popular functions. All of these functions return a double value.

Table 7-2. Handy functions from math.h

Function	Description
Trigonometric Functions	
cos(double rad)	Cosine
sin(double rad)	Sine
atan(double rad)	Arctangent
atan2(double y, double x)	Two-argument arctangent (angle between positive X axis and point (x,y))
Roots and Exponents	
exp(double x)	e^x
log(double x)	Natural logarithm (base *e*) of x
log10(double x)	Common logarithm (base 10) of x
pow(double x, double y)	x^y
sqrt(double x)	Square root of x

Function	Description
Rounding	
ceil(double x)	Ceiling function, next bigger integer from x
floor(double x)	Floor function, next smaller integer from x
Signs	
fabs(double x)[a]	Return the absolute value of x

[a] Oddly, the absolute value function for integer types, abs(), is declared in *stdlib.h*.

For any situation where you want an int or long answer, you just have to cast. For example, we could write a simple program (*ch07/rounding.c (https://oreil.ly/rEMTv)*) to average several integers and then round them to the nearest int value like this:

```
#include <stdio.h>
#include <math.h>

int main() {
  int grades[6] = { 86, 97, 77, 76, 85, 90 };
  int total = 0;
  int average;

  for (int g = 0; g < 6; g++) {
    total += grades[g];
  }
  printf("Raw average: %0.2f\n", total / 6.0);
  average = (int)floor(total / 6.0 + 0.5);
  printf("Rounded average: %d\n", average);
}
```

Since we (may) need to help the compiler with this library, let's take a look at the compile command:

```
gcc rounding.c -lm
```

Again, *math.h* declares functions in the C standard library, but those functions are not necessarily implemented in the same place as other functions. The binary containing most of the functions we're discussing is *libc* (or *glibc* for GNU's version). However, on many systems, the math functions live in a separate binary, *libm*, which requires that trailing -lm flag to make sure the compiler knows to link in the math library.

Your system may differ. There's no harm in trying to compile without the -lm option to see if your system automatically includes *libm* (or has all of the functions already included in *libc*). If you try compiling without the flag and you don't get any errors, you're in good shape! If you do need the library flag, you'll see something like this:

```
ch07$ gcc rounding.c
/usr/bin/ld: /tmp/ccP1MUC7.o: in function `main':
rounding.c:(.text+0xaf): undefined reference to `floor'
collect2: error: ld returned 1 exit status
```

Try it yourself (with or without the library flag as needed). You should get 85 as an answer. If rounding is something you do often, you can write your own function to simplify things and avoid littering your code with the slightly clunky business of adding the 0.5 value before calling `floor()` and casting the result.

time.h

This header gives you access to a number of utilities to help with determining and displaying time. It uses two types of storage for handling dates and times: a simple timestamp (with a type alias, `time_t`, representing the number of seconds since January 1, 1970, UTC) and a much more detailed structure, `struct tm`, with the following definition:

```
struct tm {
   int tm_sec;   // seconds (0 - 60; allow for leap second)
   int tm_min;   // minutes (0 - 59)
   int tm_hour;  // hours (0 - 23)
   int tm_mday;  // day of month (1 - 31)
   int tm_mon;   // month (0 - 11; WARNING! NOT 1 - 12)
   int tm_year;  // year (since 1900)
   int tm_wday;  // day of week (0 - 6)
   int tm_yday;  // day of year (0 - 365)
   int tm_isdst; // Daylight Saving Time flag
                 // This flag can be in one of three states:
                 // -1 == unavailable, 0 == standard time, 1 == DST.
}
```

I won't be using this nifty structure with all the separated fields, but it can be useful if you are doing any work with dates and times, like you might find in a calendaring application. I will be using timestamps from, uh, time to time, as we've already seen in "rand() and srand()" on page 151 for supplying a changing seed to the `srand()` function. Table 7-3 shows some functions that work with these simple values:

Table 7-3. Working with timestamps

Function	Description
`char *ctime(time_t *t)`	Return a string of the local time
`struct tm *localtime(time_t *t)`	Expand a timestamp into the detailed structure
`time_t mktime(struct tm *t)`	Reduce a structure to a timestamp
`time_t time(time_t *t)`	Return the current time as a timestamp

The definition of that last function, `time()`, might look a little weird. It both takes and returns a `time_t` pointer. You can call `time()` with either a `NULL` value or with a valid pointer to a variable of type `time_t`. If you use `NULL`, the current time is simply returned. If you supply a pointer, the current time is returned, but the variable pointed to is also updated with the current time. We only need the `NULL` option for our work with random numbers, but you'll stumble on a few utility functions that use this pattern. It can be useful if you are working with heap memory.

ctype.h

Many situations where you process input from users require you to validate that the input conforms to some expected type or value. For example, a ZIP code should be five digits and a US state abbreviation should be two uppercase letters. The *ctype.h* header declares several handy functions for checking individual characters. It also has two helper functions that convert between upper- and lowercase. Table 7-4 highlights several of these functions.

Table 7-4. Working with characters using ctype.h

Function	Description
Testing	
`isalnum(int c)`	Is c a numeric character or a letter
`isalpha(int c)`	Is c a letter
`isdigit(int c)`	Is c a decimal digit
`isxdigit(int c)`	Is c a hexadecimal digit (case-insensitive)
`islower(int c)`	Is c a lowercase letter
`isupper(int c)`	Is c an uppercase letter
`isspace(int c)`	Is c a space, tab, newline, carriage return, vertical tab, or form feed
Conversion	
`tolower(int c)`	Return the lowercase version of c
`toupper(int c)`	Return the uppercase version of c

Don't forget your Boolean operators! You can easily expand these tests to ask questions like "is not whitespace" with the ! operator:

```
if (!isspace(answer)) {
  // Not a blank character, so go ahead
  ...
}
```

As with the math functions and getting a `double` result where you need an `int`, the conversion functions in *ctype.h* return an `int`, but you can easily cast it to a `char` as needed.

Putting It Together

Let's pull in a few of these new headers and use some of the topics from previous chapters to make a more rounded example. We'll create a structure to store information on a simple bank account. We can use the new *string.h* utilities to add a name field to each account. And we'll use the *math.h* functions to calculate a sample compound interest payment on the balance of the account. Here are the includes this example will require:

```
#include <stdio.h>
#include <stdlib.h>
#include <string.h>
#include <math.h>
```

With our headers ready, let's dive in and get the program itself going.

Filling In Strings

Let's start our example by creating our account type including a string "name" field. The new `struct` is simple enough:

```
struct account {
  char name[50];
  double balance;
};
```

We can now use our string functions to load up `name` with actual content after our structure is created. We can also use `malloc()` to create that structure in a function and return the address of our account. Here's the new function, with some of the safety checks omitted just for readability:

```
struct account *create(char *name, double initial) {
  struct account *acct = malloc(sizeof(struct account));
  strncpy(acct->name, name, 49);
  acct->balance = initial;
  return acct;
}
```

Notice I chose to use `strncpy()` here. The idea is that I cannot guarantee the incoming `name` parameter will fit. Since I wrote the entire program, of course, I certainly can guarantee that detail, but that's not the point. I want to make sure if I ever allow user input, say, by prompting the user for details, my `create()` function has some safeguards in place.

Let's go ahead and create a function to print our account details. Hopefully, this code looks familiar from our work in Chapter 6. We can also start our `main()` function to try out everything we've written so far:

```
void print(struct account *a) {
  printf("Account: %s\n", a->name);
  printf("Balance: $%.2f\n", a->balance);
}

int main() {
  struct account *checking;
  checking = create("Bank of Earth (checking)", 200.0);
  print(checking);
  free(checking);
}
```

Let's compile and run *ch07/account1.c* (*https://oreil.ly/i8vvr*). Here's our output:

```
ch07$ gcc account1.c
ch07$ ./a.out
Account: Bank of Earth (checking)
Balance: $200.00
```

Hooray! So far, so good. Next up is figuring out an interest payment.

Finding Our Interest

Using the `pow()` function from the *math.h* library, we can calculate a monthly compounded interest in one expression. I know I was taught this formula in high school, but I still have to look it up online any time I actually need to use it. Then we'll update `main()` to add a year's worth of interest (at 5%) to our account and print out the details again. Here are the new parts from *ch07/account2.c* (*https://oreil.ly/EAOwS*):

```
void add_interest(struct account *acct, double rate, int months) {
  // Put our current balance in a local var for easier use
  double principal = acct->balance;
  // Convert our annual rate to a monthly percentage value
  rate /= 1200;
  // Use the interest formula to calculate our new balance
  acct->balance = principal * pow(1 + rate, months);
}

int main() {
  struct account *checking;
  checking = create("Bank of Earth (checking)", 200.0);
  print(checking);

  add_interest(checking, 5.0, 12);
  print(checking);

  free(checking);
}
```

That's looking pretty good! Let's compile and run *account2.c*. If your system needs the `-lm` math library flag, be sure to add it when you compile:

```
ch07$ gcc account2.c -lm
ch07$ ./a.out
Account: Bank of Earth (checking)
Balance: $200.00
Account: Bank of Earth (checking)
Balance: $210.23
```

Everything worked! Although you are reading the final output from my code *after* I fixed the various little mistakes I made while writing it. I reversed the order of the source and destination strings in `strncpy()`, for example. It's rare to get everything right the first time. The compiler will usually let you know what you got wrong. You just head back to your editor and fix it. Getting comfortable with mistakes—and with fixing them!—is one of the reasons I encourage you to type in some of these examples. Nothing like actually writing code to get better at writing code.

Finding New Libraries

There are many more libraries out there for your consumption than I can possibly cover here. Indeed, there are more functions just in the C standard library; you can dig much deeper with the GNU C Library (*https://oreil.ly/58fLM*) documentation online.

Beyond the standard library, though, there are other libraries that can help with your projects. For those situations where you want a specialized library, your best bet these days is to search online. If you want to interact directly with a USB-connected device, for example, you could search for "C USB library" and wind up with the nifty *libusb* from *https://libusb.info*.

You can also find some lists of popular libraries, but those lists vary in quality and upkeep. Sadly, there is no central repository for "all things C" like one has with some languages. My advice is to look over the search results for links to reputable sites like GitHub (*https://github.com*) or gnu.org (*https://gnu.org*). And don't be afraid to just read through the source code of the library. If anything you see raises a flag, pay attention. Most times you'll be getting exactly what you expected, but a little caution is always advisable when using things you find online.

Coming to a Folder Near You

I also want to point out that most development environments have several of the more common libraries ready for use by you and other applications installed on your system right out of the gate. Where the header files for these libraries get stored varies from system to system, but Linux systems have the */usr/include* and */usr/local/include* folders as popular locations.

On macOS, you can find many headers in */usr/local/include* but most will be in an ungainly path below your Xcode application, such as */Applications/Xcode.app/Contents/Developer/Platforms/MacOSX.platform/Developer/SDKs/MacOSX.sdk/usr/include*.

On Windows, it depends largely on how you installed GCC, but you will often find similar *usr\include* or *usr\local\include* folders under the install folder for your compiler. For example, on my Windows 10 machine, I can use a normal *cmd.exe* window and navigate to *C:\msys64\usr\include*. On a different machine with Cygwin, that folder is *C:\cygwin65\lib\gcc\x86_64-pc-cygwin\10\include*.

Next Steps

Helping you get better at writing code is certainly one of the goals for this book. We've covered a number of the more common and popular libraries (and the header files that we must include to make use of their functions) in this chapter. There are certainly more libraries out there! Hopefully, you see how libraries and headers interact with your own code.

We'll be tackling microcontrollers next, and we'll start looking at writing *tighter* code along the way. Good code isn't necessarily a prerequisite for doing optimization work, but it sure helps. Feel free to review some of the examples from past chapters before forging ahead. Try making some changes. Try breaking things. Try fixing the things you broke. Every successful compile should count as a notch in your programmer belt.

CHAPTER 8

Real-World C With Arduino

We've seen our C skills grow from compiling a short list of simple statements to passing pointers to functions with nested flow of control. But so far we've been printing results in our terminal windows. That's great for proving that our logic works and that our program is doing what we expect, but eventually we'll want code that runs somewhere other than a terminal in order to take advantage of all the great hardware out there. In the rest of this book, we're going to write code aimed at microcontrollers. And what better microcontroller to start with than an Arduino.

The Arduino family of microcontrollers has been around for over 15 years. Starting with 8-bit Atmel AVR (*https://oreil.ly/EH7un*) controllers designed specifically to facilitate learning and tinkering, these gadgets have exploded in popularity. These days, you can find a wealth of development boards preloaded with all manner of sensors and connections. WiFi, GPS, Bluetooth, even radio options can be added easily. The ecosystem of inputs, outputs, and containers is truly mind-boggling. For us, that makes this platform a perfect target. You can grab an inexpensive controller and LEDs to start, and expand into robotics or weather stations or radio control or just about any other electronics niche that tickles your fancy.[1]

"Getting the Hardware: Adafruit" on page 276 includes information on all the microcontrollers and peripherals I'll be using throughout the rest of the book. But any Arduino-compatible microcontroller will work with the majority of our examples.

---

[1] For more (much more!) information on the details of Arduino, check out *Arduino: A Technical Reference* by J. M. Hughes (O'Reilly).

Arduino IDE (Win, Mac, Linux)

Way back in "Compiling Your Code" on page 17, we learned how to compile C source code into an executable for our operating system on our machine. And while it might be possible to run a C compiler on an Arduino controller, we can use the notion of a *cross-compiler* to let our fancy laptops and desktops do the hard work of compiling, yet still produce a binary built for Arduino.

You can find tools like gcc-avr to run from the command line as we did with gcc, but fortunately there is a nifty IDE that does what it says on the label. The Arduino IDE is an integrated development environment where you can edit your source code, compile it, load to a microcontroller, and watch a serial console for help debugging. See an error in that console? Fix the source, recompile, and reload. And it runs on all three major platforms.

No matter your platform, head to the Arduino Software (*https://oreil.ly/jMXH0*) page (see Figure 8-1) and download the appropriate version. If you want background on the features of the IDE, you can look over the IDE Environment Guide (*https://oreil.ly/FKreY*) online.

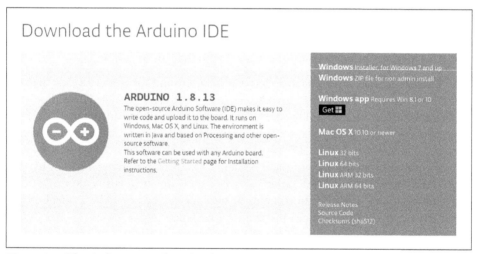

Figure 8-1. The Arduino IDE download site

Let's take a look at the installation details for Windows, macOS, and Linux. Mostly the Arudino IDE is a mature tool with a typical installer, but there are a few platform-specific steps and gotchas I want to point out.

Installing on Windows

From the download page, be sure to grab one of the downloads that come direct from arduino.cc, either the ZIP file or the Windows 7 and up installer.

 If you use the Microsoft Store for apps, you may have noticed the Arduino IDE there as well. Regrettably, there are many reports of difficulties using this version of the IDE. It is older, and the store listing does not seem to be well maintained. We recommend avoiding this version, even though a link to the store is available on the downloads page.

The online guide (*https://oreil.ly/Fa8kZ*) has detailed instructions for installing the Arduino IDE through the *.exe* file you downloaded. It's a fairly standard Windows installer; our only suggestion is to install all of the components available when prompted. (If you don't want shortcuts on your desktop or in your start menu, you can certainly uncheck those.) You may also be prompted to install some ports and drivers, which we recommend using as well. If all goes well, you can launch the IDE and see an empty document, as shown in Figure 8-2.

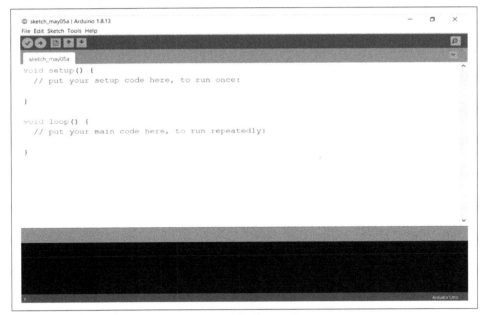

Figure 8-2. The Arduino IDE running on Windows 10

Once your IDE is running, go ahead and try the first project in "Your First Arduino Project" on page 169.

Installing on macOS

The macOS version of Arduino IDE is delivered as a simple *.zip* file. Many browsers will automatically unzip the download, but you can always double-click the file yourself to unzip. The only thing in the *.zip* file is the macOS application. Go ahead and drag the application to your *Applications* folder. (This may require you to enter your administrative password.) That's it! If it worked, you should see the standard startup in Figure 8-3.

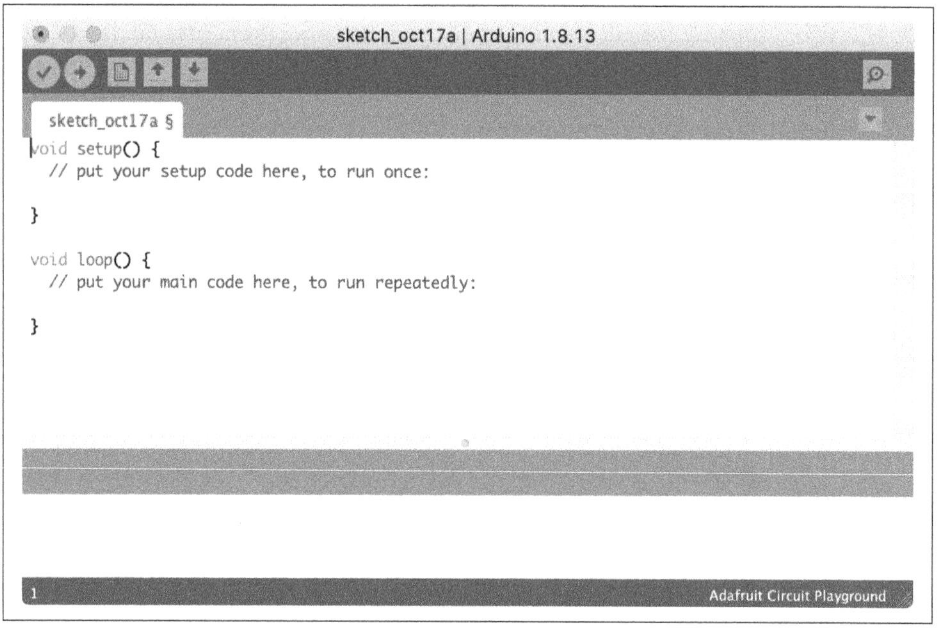

Figure 8-3. The Arduino IDE running on macOS

Once your IDE is running, go ahead and try the first project in "Your First Arduino Project" on page 169.

Installing on Linux

For Linux, you also receive the application as a simple archive, *.tar.xz* in this case. Most distributions have an archive manager app that will happily unpack your download with a double-click. If you don't have such an accommodating app already, you can try your version of tar as it can automatically decompress most types of archives:

```
$ tar xf arduino-1.8.13-linux64.tar.xz
```

(Of course your filename may be different depending on your platform and the currently released version of the app itself.)

Place the unpacked folder (named *arduino-1.8.13*, again, depending on the version you downloaded) wherever you want to keep the application. That might be in a shared location or just in your own user directory somewhere. Once you have it in your preferred spot, change into that *arduino-1.8.13* folder and run **./install.sh**. That script will do its best to add shortcuts to your start menu and desktop. Go ahead and start the app to make sure the installation worked. You should end up with something like Figure 8-4, similar to that for the other operating systems.

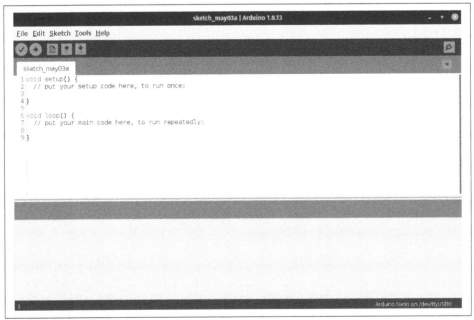

Figure 8-4. The Arduino IDE running on Linux (with Gnome)

Hooray! Let's get that first program running on our microcontroller.

Your First Arduino Project

Of course, with microcontrollers like Arduino, the IDE is only half of the equation. You need an actual Arduino controller! Or at least one of its many siblings. You can get these boards from a wide variety of sellers and manufacturers. I'll toss out an unpaid plug for Adafruit (*https://adafruit.com*) as they have a fantastic array of both boards and peripherals—plus everything else that goes into building actual electronics projects. Their Trinkets and Feathers and ultra dimunitive QT Py pack some great features in some small packages.

Selecting Your Board

Whatever microcontroller you choose, you'll need to specify that choice in the Arduino IDE. Under the Tools menu, look for the Board: item. Then comes a long, long list of supported boards ready for you to use, as shown in Figure 8-5. You can see that I have the "Adafruit ESP32 Feather" board selected. That's just the most recent project I was tackling—an ESP32 WiFi-enabled LED project. It really is amazing what fits on a microcontroller these days! If you don't see a matching board in this list, go back to the top for the "Boards Manager..." option. That option opens a dialog where you can browse for other supported boards.

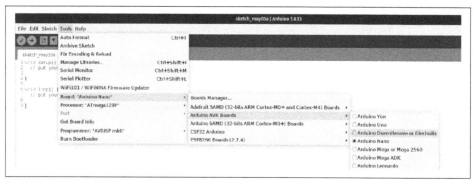

Figure 8-5. Supported development boards

For most of the examples in this book, I'll be using a Metro Mini from Adafruit (*https://oreil.ly/6oe6O*), as shown in Figure 8-6. It has a 16MHz ATmega328P with 2K of RAM and 32K of flash. With lots of I/O pins, we'll be free to tackle a good range of interesting projects getting input from sensors and switches while providing output through LEDs, LCDs, and servos.

Figure 8-6. The Metro Mini microcontroller from Adafruit

The Metro Mini is pin-compatible with the Arduino UNO, so let's select that as our board option. Figure 8-7 shows the Boards list again with our UNO selected. A *pin*, by the way, is what you call the things that stick out of the microcontroller and fit into your breadboard (engineer-speak for the nifty, perforated base that simplifies connecting components). Even when you connect your Arduino using something else like alligator clips or just soldering a wire directly, "pin" is still the term for a named or numbered connection to the microcontroller. A "pin-out diagram" is a sort of cheat sheet for matching up those names and numbers to actual connecting points on the device.

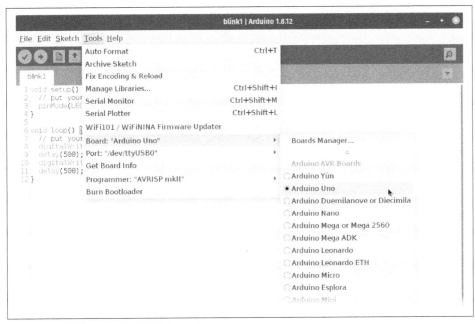

Figure 8-7. Selecting the UNO board

 Chances are pretty high that you'll have a different microcontroller. There are so many wonderful options out there for makers and anyone else tinkering with electronics. Hopefully, you see your board in the list and can simply select it like we did with the UNO. Sadly, we can't cover every option or even predict the most popular ones. The Arduino Help Center (*https://oreil.ly/bgyMM*) has some great documentation and FAQs. Their community is top-notch as well.

Hello, LED!

In Arduinoland, making an LED blink is the electronics equivalent of our "Hello, World" program from "Creating a C 'Hello, World'" on page 15. We'll do our best to lay out any circuitry and connections we build, but you'll have to adjust as needed for your own controller and components.

Many development boards include an LED with an appropriate resistor right on the board itself. We'll start by blinking the LED on our Metro Mini to make sure our C code can be uploaded and then run on our microcontroller. Back in the Arduino IDE, select the File → New option. You should now have a new *sketch* tab. "Sketch" is the term for the compiled bundle meant for executing on a microcontroller. (More on sketches in "C++ Objects and Variables" on page 182.) You'll see two empty functions, setup() and loop(). These two functions serve as the microcontroller version of the main() function from our desktop C programs.

The setup() function is the entry point for our code and is run once, typically when power is first supplied to the board or after the user presses a reset button (if such a button is part of the board). Here we set up any global information we need or run any initializations that are required of our hardware such as resetting a servo position or specifying how we plan to use the I/O pins.

The loop() function then takes over to repeat your program indefinitely. Microcontrollers are typically used to do one task (or perhaps a modest few) over and over as long as they have power. They can continuously read a sensor. They can drive an LED animation. They can read a sensor and use that value to alter an LED animation. They can nudge a clock hand forward. But they all repeat some flow or other until you cut the power, so loop() is an aptly named function.

While there is a lot more going on behind the scenes, it's reasonable to imagine the standard main() function for Arduino projects defined like this:

```
int main() {
  setup();
  while (1) {
    loop();
  }
}
```

Note that our while loop "condition" is just the value 1. Recall that "not zero" is considered to be true in these Boolean contexts. So this while loop runs forever. Just what we need for Arduino.

For our blinking hello program, we'll use setup() to tell our board we want to use the built-in LED for output (meaning we'll "write" on and off values to the pin associated with the LED). Then we'll use loop() to do that writing along with some small delays to make the blinking readily visible to humans. Here's our first iteration using constants described in the Arduino docs (*https://oreil.ly/Qt6DM*):

```
void setup() {
  // put your setup code here, to run once:
  // Tell our board we want to write to the built-in LED
  pinMode(LED_BUILTIN, OUTPUT);
}

void loop() {
  // put your main code here, to run repeatedly:
  // A high value is 'on' for an LED
  digitalWrite(LED_BUILTIN, HIGH);
  // Now wait for 500 milliseconds
  delay(500);
  // And write a low value to turn our LED off
  digitalWrite(LED_BUILTIN, LOW);
  // and wait another 500ms
  delay(500);
}
```

The all-caps names like LED_BUILTIN and HIGH were defined in headers that are included automatically by the Arduino IDE. They are technically preprocessor macros, and we'll look at those in more detail in "Preprocessor Directives" on page 238. They are quite handy and very easy to use in your own code: #define PIN 5 defines the word PIN to be the value 5. It's a lot like a variable or a constant. The difference is that the preprocessor will go through your code before the compiler (hence the "pre-" prefix) and replace every spot it finds PIN with the literal number 5. A typical variable or constant would reserve a slot in memory and could be initialized at runtime, perhaps after you have gathered some necessary information from the user.

Go ahead and type this simple program in. You can also open the *ch08/blink1/blink1.ino* (*https://oreil.ly/p6eGd*) project directly in the IDE.

Before trying it on your board, you can use the IDE's Verify button (shown in Figure 8-8) to make sure the code compiles. Verifying your code also checks to make sure your finished program will fit on the controller you selected. If you have used too many variables or simply have too much logic, you'll see warnings and errors in the bottom status area. Try leaving off a semicolon on some statement like we did in "Statements in C" on page 21. Click Verify again and you can see the type of message you might encounter as you write your own code going forward.

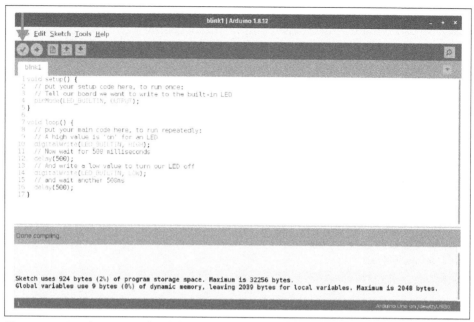

Figure 8-8. Verifying your sketch before uploading

After verifying your code is OK, you can ship it over to your microcontroller using the Upload shortcut button next to Verify or select the appropriate item from the Sketch menu. Uploading will compile the code (even if you have recently verified it) and then write it to your board. The Arduino IDE works great with the Metro Mini on this step—it's all delightfully automatic. Some development boards need to be manually configured for upload. Again, the Arduino Help Center (*https://oreil.ly/csLX6*) is your friend here.

Once the upload completes, you should see your LED start blinking at half-second intervals. While less impressive on the printed page, Figure 8-9 shows the on/off states of our nifty LED.

Figure 8-9. Our "Hello, World" LED blinking

An External LED Upgrade

We are focusing on the software side of Arduino projects, but it is impossible to work with an Arduino and not use *some* external components. Let's upgrade our simple blinker to use an external LED.

Figure 8-10 shows the simple circuit we're using. We have our controller, one LED, and a resistor. For this setup, we can rely on the power being supplied over USB.

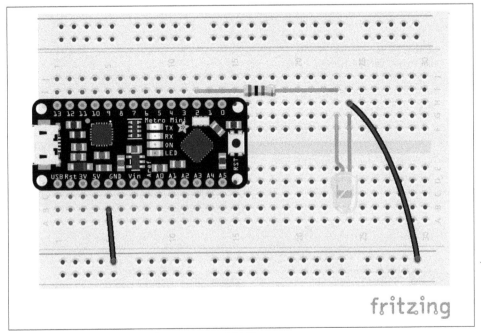

Figure 8-10. Simple circuit for an external LED

We can pick a pin to use and learn more about the voltage supplied over the pins by reading the specs for our microcontroller. In the case of our Metro Mini, we looked at the Pinouts page (*https://oreil.ly/H2wNN*) on the Adafruit site. The details tell us which pins on our board map to the UNO's pins. Along the "top" of our board (the tiny print on the chip is right side up) are several digital I/O pins, and in particular, pins 2 through 12 are exactly what we need. We'll start with 2, since it's such a nice number. Different boards will likely have different configurations, but for ours, pins 0 through 13 map directly to digital pins 0 through 13. So we can either use our own #define and attach a nice name (yay!) or just use the value 2 in our pinMode() and digitalWrite() calls.

The Metro Mini provides 5V on its digital pins. Using the specs provided by the LED manufacturer, we know our blue LED has a forward voltage drop of 2.5V. If we want to supply 30mA of current for a bright light, Ohm's law (*https://oreil.ly/6ihdc*) tells us a 100Ω resistor will work fine. With everything wired up, we can make a new sketch (or just tweak the first one). Here's *ch08/blink2/blink2.ino* (*https://oreil.ly/xpo2a*) as it stands:

```
#define D2 2

void setup() {
  // put your setup code here, to run once:
  // Tell our board we want to write to digital pin 2
  pinMode(D2, OUTPUT);
}

void loop() {
  digitalWrite(D2, HIGH);
  delay(2000);
  digitalWrite(D2, LOW);
  delay(1000);
}
```

Notice I went with the preprocessor `#define` feature to designate which digital pin we are using with our LED (D2). You can see this simple configuration up and running in Figure 8-11. Hooray!

Figure 8-11. Our external LED blinking

There is something extra satisfying in these small, physical projects. The "Hello, World" programs are all designed to prove your development environment works and that you can produce some output. That's all we've done here, but gosh it's fun seeing the LED light turn on. Every time I throw the switch on a new project, it feels a bit like Dr. Frankenstein screaming, "It's alive!" in his lab. :-)

Arduino Libraries

We're not done making blinking lights just yet. While you can do an amazing amount of work with these microcontrollers right out of the box, quite often you'll be building projects with some interesting accessories like multicolor LEDs, LCD screens, e-ink, sensors, servos, keypads, or even game controllers. Many of those components have handy chunks of code already written for them. These chunks are collected into a library that you can add to the Arduino IDE. Some of the libraries are "official" and come from the component maker; others are produced by fellow hobbyists. Whatever the provenance, libraries can speed up devlopment on your projects.

Let's take a look at finding and managing libraraies through the IDE. Doing so properly will help ensure your sketch does not contain any unused libraries.

Managing Libraries

The Tools menu of the Arduino IDE has an entry to "Manage Libraries..." that pulls up a dialog for searching and installing libraries. We're going to add an Adafruit library and try lighting up one of their fantastic NeoPixels—individually addressable, three-color LEDs that come in a wide variety of form factors for just about any possible use. They can even be chained together to build fancier rigs. For this example, though, we'll be sticking with one of the simplest form factors: the Flora (*https://oreil.ly/JEuFF*).

In the Library Manager dialog, enter the term "neopixel" in the search box at the top. You should get several results; we want the simple "Adafruit NeoPixel" entry. Click the Install button (or Update if you happen to have an older version of this library already installed as we do in Figure 8-12), and that's it! The IDE downloads the library and does the appropriate work to make it available behind the scenes.

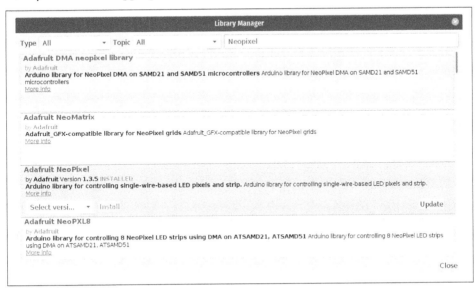

Figure 8-12. Finding a NeoPixel library

The physical circuit for using NeoPixels is similar to what we use for simple LEDs, but they have three wires rather than two. You have standard V+ and Ground connectors for the basic power needs, and the third wire provides the "data" to the pixel or strip. The data does flow in a particular direction, so if you decide to try this circuit, pay attention to where you connect the data input. Like our simple LED, we also want a small resistor (470Ω in our case) before the data signal gets to the NeoPixel. You can see the full setup in Figure 8-13.

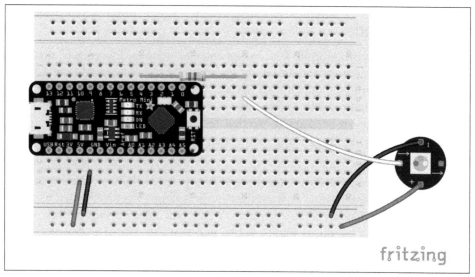

Figure 8-13. A simple NeoPixel setup

 You can follow along with this project without NeoPixels, by the way. You can use any other addressable LEDs. If you have some of your own WS281x or APA102 or other lights, they'll likely work with the excellent FastLED (*http://fastled.io*) library. You'll have to do a little more independent reading, but all of the concepts are the same. FastLED has nice documentation on GitHub. For example, the work we'll do in the next section with NeoPixels is covered in FastLED's Basic Usage (*https://oreil.ly/eupDp*) page.

Using Arduino Libraries

So how do we pull an Arduino library into our sketch? We use the familiar #include preprocessor command just like we did with the various header files from the C standard library in previous chapters. For the NeoPixels, our include looks like this:

```
#include <Adafruit_NeoPixel.h>
```

The IDE even helps confirm you have the library installed by bolding and coloring the name of the header file. Take a look at the comparison in Figure 8-14 where we used a lower-case "p" when spelling NeoPixel. The nice, bold color disappears. So if your library is correctly installed and the name stands out in your include line, you are ready to go!

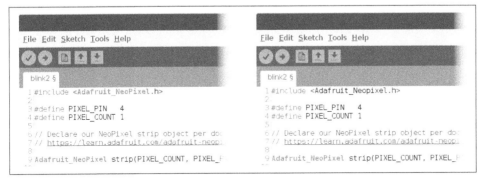

Figure 8-14. Noticing library name mistakes

 You can use multiple libraries within any given sketch. It's entirely reasonable to have a library for things like your LEDs as well as one for servos or for an LCD screen. The only real limitation is memory—a ubiquitous concern when working with microcontrollers.

When you verify a sketch, check the messages in the lower section of the IDE. You'll get a report on the memory used as well as how much remains (assuming you have the correct board selected.) Happily, most folks and companies writing libraries for Arduino are very aware of how limited memory is. For example, adding this NeoPixel library took our blinking sketch from a little under 1K (964 bytes) to about 2.5K (2636 bytes). While you could say it tripled the amount of flash required to store, getting all of the niceties of the library for less than 2K seems a fair trade-off!

Arduino Sketches and C++

To put this NeoPixel library to use, we need to take a tiny detour into C++, a successor to C with an object orientation (compared to C's procedural orientation). Sketches are actually C++ projects. Happily, since C++ grew out of C, C code is legal C++ code as well. As programmers, we don't have to learn much C++ if we don't want to.

But notice that "much" qualifier in that last sentence. Many libraries—including our NeoPixel library—are written as C++ classes (a *class* is the organizing unit of object-oriented languages.) These libraries often take advantage of some nifty features of C++. In particular, you'll find *constructors* and *methods* used all over the place.

Constructors are functions that initialize an *object*. An object, in turn, is an encapsulation of both data and functions meant to access and manipulate that data. Those functions defined for an object are referred to as the object's methods.

To see where constructors and methods show up in an Arduino library, let's go ahead and finish our next iteration of the blinking light. Recall the setup shown in Figure 8-13. We can write a new sketch, *blink3*, that cycles the NeoPixel through its primary colors: red, green, and blue. Here's the full code, including (no pun intended!) the appropriate #include line, *ch08/blink3/blink3.ino* (*https://oreil.ly/Ughez*):

```
#include <Adafruit_NeoPixel.h>

#define PIXEL_PIN    4
#define PIXEL_COUNT 1

// Declare our NeoPixel strip object per documentation from Adafruit
// https://learn.adafruit.com/adafruit-neopixel-uberguide/arduino-library-use

Adafruit_NeoPixel strip(PIXEL_COUNT, PIXEL_PIN);            ❶

void setup() {
  strip.begin();            // Get things ready            ❷
  strip.setBrightness(128); // Set a comfortable brightness ❸
  strip.show();             // Start with all pixels off    ❹
}

void loop() {
  // Show red for 1 second on the first pixel (start counting at 0)
  strip.setPixelColor(0, 255, 0, 0);  ❺
  strip.show();                       ❻
  delay(1000);
  // Show green for 1 second
  strip.setPixelColor(0, 0, 255, 0);
  strip.show();
  delay(1000);
  // Show blue for 1 second
  strip.setPixelColor(0, 0, 0, 255);
  strip.show();
  delay(1000);
}
```

❶ Our constructed variable, strip. Its class (roughly analagous to its type) is Ada fruit_NeoPixel. The name "strip" here is common, but a little wrong for our single Flora. But technically we are allocating a strip that is simply one pixel long.

❷ An example of a method: begin() is a function that applies to strip. The begin() method gets our strip of lights ready by filling in default values and performing other miscellaneous startup tasks.

❸ The setBrightness() method controls a premultiplied max brightness on strip.

❹ Another example of a method. show() causes the current colors in memory to be displayed on the actual LEDs of strip.

❺ The setPixelColor() method takes four arguments: which pixel on strip to set (starting at 0), and the red, green, and blue values to apply. Color values range from 0 (off) to 255 (full brightness, though the final value is adjusted by that set Brightness() call we made in setup()).

❻ To see our new pixel color on strip, we repeat our call to show().

Try uploading this with your NeoPixel connected. Hopefully, you'll see it run through red, green, and blue colors, as shown in Figure 8-15.

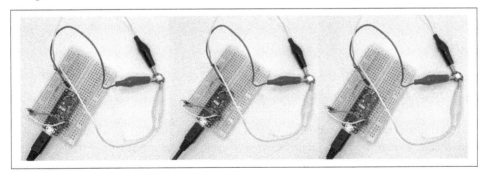

Figure 8-15. Our blinking NeoPixel

Neat! Feel free to play around with the color or blink patterns. It can be surprisingly fun getting just the right hue. It really is magic. And now, you too know the right incantations!

C++ Objects and Variables

When you create an object variable, the declaration and initialization look a little funny. In C, we can create a variable and give it some starting value like this:

```
int counter = 1;
```

If we had a C++ class named `Integer`, trying the same type of setup might look like this:

```
Integer counter(1);
```

The parentheses give you a clue that a function is being called. That's the constructor. If you decide to go on and study C++ down the road, you'll learn all the clever things that can be done in constructors. For now, though, we just want you to be aware of the syntax so that you're comfortable creating variables that refer to objects.

The `strip.begin()` and `strip.setPixelColor()` lines that we called out are examples of calling an object's functions (again, object-oriented languages use the term "methods"). The idea is the `strip` is what we want to work on, and `begin()` or `set PixelColor()` represents the work to be done.

One way to think about this syntax is that it is a sort of transformation. In pure C, we could imagine writing normal functions for `begin()` and `setPixelColor()`. But we'd have to tell those functions which strip of NeoPixels we want to set up or change. So we would need an extra argument to pass a reference to the correct strip like so:

```
void setup() {
  begin(&strip);
  // ...
}

void loop() {
  // ...
  setPixelColor(&strip, 0, 255, 0, 0);
}
```

But again, for our work in this book, you mostly just need to get comfortable with statements that create a new object from a library, and then remember that using the methods of objects follows the `object.method()` pattern.

What Are *.ino* Files?

If you look in your computer's filesystem for the files being saved from the Arduino IDE, you'll discover there are folders matching the sketch names (e.g., *blink1*, *blink2*, etc.). Inside each folder is a *.ino* file with the same base name as the sketch as well. But what are *.ino* files? They are actually rebranded C++ files. (Do you see the suffix from A-r-d-u-***ino***?) To compile a valid application, you still need a `main()` function as a launch point. The IDE is doing some magic behind the scenes to incorporate our *.ino*

---

content into a broader package that has a few standard includes and an appropriate `main()` function. That function will "do the right thing" to get our Arduino code up and running. It will call `setup()` at the start, then move on and call `loop()` inside, well, a loop.

For our projects, we don't really need to worry about these files. The IDE manages them for us. We will be looking at writing more complex projects and creating our own libraries in Chapter 11, but the majority of our projects will fit in the standard `setup()` and `loop()` functions of a single file. I do want you to be aware of where things are stored so that you are familiar with the structure of these Arduino projects. That familiarity can be useful when you get advanced enough that single-file projects no longer cover your needs.

More Practice with Objects

Before we move on to other aspects of coding for microcontrollers, let's make one more blinking application with an eye toward reinforcing the object syntax. We'll try using some actual strips of LEDs with more than one LED. In particular, we'll be using a small stick (*https://oreil.ly/yeieS*) of 8 NeoPixels and a ring (*https://oreil.ly/1CTcw*) of 24 NeoPixels. To make things even more fun, we'll be using them at the same time!

To keep the code simple, we'll make a blink program that shows one pixel at a time on each strip. This will also keep the power requirement down so that we can continue to use what we get from our USB connection. (If you are familiar with larger LED setups and already know how to add external power, feel free to create your own arrangement.) Figure 8-16 shows our new setup. We removed the blue LED and the previous "strip" of the lonely NeoPixel Flora.

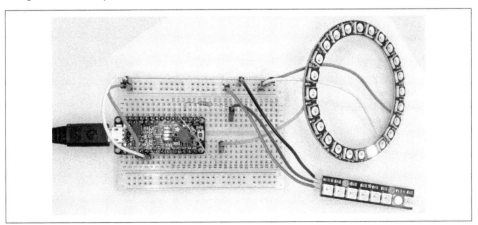

Figure 8-16. A more interesting NeoPixel setup

We are reusing the same output pins for the data line, though. In this arrangement, the stick is using pin 2 and the ring is using pin 4.

Without further ado, here is the code for our two-strip blink extravaganza, *blink4*. We'll dive into the callouts after the snippet to make sure the steps we take here make sense. Before reading those callouts, though, try going through *ch08/blink4/blink4.ino* (*https://oreil.ly/19dUL*) and see if you can guess how the objects work.

```
#include <Adafruit_NeoPixel.h>

#define STICK_PIN    2
#define STICK_COUNT 8
#define RING_PIN     4
#define RING_COUNT 24

// Declare our NeoPixel strip object per documentation from Adafruit
// https://learn.adafruit.com/adafruit-neopixel-uberguide/arduino-library-use

Adafruit_NeoPixel stick(STICK_COUNT, STICK_PIN);          ❶
Adafruit_NeoPixel ring(RING_COUNT, RING_PIN, NEO_GRBW);   ❷

void setup() {
  stick.begin();            // Initialize our stick      ❸
  stick.setBrightness(128);
  stick.show();
  ring.begin();             // Initialize our ring       ❹
  ring.setBrightness(128);
  ring.show();
}

void loop() {
  // our stick and ring have different LED counts, so we have
  // to be a little clever with our loop. There are several
  // ways to do this. We'll use modulus (remainder) math, but
  // can you think of other solutions that would achieve
  // the same pattern?
  for (int p = 0; p < RING_COUNT; p++) {
    stick.clear();
    stick.setPixelColor(p % STICK_COUNT, 0, 0, 255);      ❺
    ring.clear();
    ring.setPixelColor(p, 0, 255, 0, 0);                  ❻
    stick.show();                                         ❼
    ring.show();
  }
}
```

❶ Here we create an Adafruit_NeoPixel object named stick similar to how we created strip in "Arduino Sketches and C++" on page 179.

❷ And now we create a second, distinct object named ring. (The ring uses a fancier
LED configuration with a white component so we add a third argument to the
constructor. You can find this value in the NeoPixel documentation.)

❸ We initialize our stick just as we did before with the strip.

❹ We also initialize our ring; notice we use the begin() method on both objects.

❺ Now we set the color of one of the pixels on our stick.

❻ We use a similar method with a fifth argument to set the color on our ring. (The
arguments here are which pixel, red, green, blue, and white. The ring will blink
green.)

❼ Last but not least, show both changes.

Hopefully, seeing two objects in use side by side helps illustrate how the object-
oriented syntax works. Again, our for loop is pure C. We dip into the C++ syntax on
an as-needed basis.

C++ Considerations

There is definitely more to the role of object-oriented programming in Arduino
development. OO programming is a fairly natural fit for an environment where so
many of things we get to work with are physical objects. C++ also offers several features that are well suited to bundling up code to share with others. If you interact
with your microcontrollers primarily through the Arduino IDE, it's worth spending
some time investigating C++.

Diving into C++ will teach you about classes and members and methods. You'll create
constructors and destructors. As your understanding of objects improves, you'll likely
start breaking down your projects along object lines rather than along functional
ones. You will certainly find things you like about C++ and probably a few that you
don't. Some libraries will be easier to use if you understand C++, but none of them
will be out of your reach even if you never crack an official C++ book.

The C language on its own remains a powerful core in Arduino programming, and I'll keep the focus of the remaining chapters on using functions and other basic C features to code up our projects. Where we use any third-party libraries for specific peripherals, I'll try to use the minimum of object notation. I'll also try to highlight any spots where C++ syntax stands out.

To reiterate the most common object-oriented patterns you'll see in the remaining chapters, here is a recap from our NeoPixel example in "Arduino Sketches and C++" on page 179:

```
// Using a library written in C++ still requires the same C "#include"
// directive to bring in the associated header file.
#include <Adafruit_NeoPixel.h>

#define PIXEL_PIN    4
#define PIXEL_COUNT 1

// Common example of a C++ constructor call that creates an object.
// Our NeoPixel "strip" is the created object in this case.
Adafruit_NeoPixel strip(PIXEL_COUNT, PIXEL_PIN);

void setup() {
  // Common example of using the method "begin()" from our object "strip".
  strip.begin();

// ...
```

Hopefully, you'll grow more comfortable with these small dips into C++. I also hope that comfort grows into curiosity about what more you can do with C++! But don't worry if you never really get curious or even comfortable. One of the things I most enjoy about coding for microcontrollers is that a little code goes a long way. You can still get a lot of satisfaction out of your programming efforts without mastering C++. A brief scan of my own projects shows that I stuck with C more than 90% of the time, even though every one of those projects also uses a library written in C++.

Object Homework

If you'd like a little more practice with the object notation we've already seen and will bump into occasionally in the coming chapters, try creating some of these ideas:

- Blink every other pixel on the stick so that the even pixels turn on, then the odd pixels, back and forth.
- Blink each pixel on the ring once for every pixel on the stick, like a counter. (I.e., keep one pixel showing on the stick as you march around the ring. Then move to the next pixel on the stick, and march around the ring again. Repeat!)

- Working with just the stick, try "filling" it from left to right. Then clear all the pixels and let it fill again.

- Take a look at the documentation for NeoPixels (*https://oreil.ly/GxxxI*) (or Fas-tLED (*https://oreil.ly/9Ln6A*), or whatever library you are using) and see if there are any methods to turn the entire strip one color with a single call. Use that method to turn the entire stick red, then green, then blue, similar to our *blink3* program that used the single Flora.

Next Steps

We now have the basics of an Arduino project up and running. We've worked with the Arduino IDE and we've seen where C++ might crop up in our code. Putting it all together, we turned on an LED! While that is exciting, there is a lot more fun to be had.

In the next chapter, we'll explore some of the many inputs and outputs available for use with a microcontroller. We certainly can't cover every sensor or button or speaker or display, but we can (and will!) look at several good examples of these peripherals. We'll concentrate on getting these disparate gadgets to work together so you have a solid foundation to rely on as you tackle your own projects down the road.

CHAPTER 9

Smaller Systems

Now that we have the Arduino IDE ready to go, we can embark on the physically satisfying world of writing C code to control things! LED things. Sensor things. Button things. So many things! We'll also dip our toes into the Internet of Things (IoT) in "IoT and Arduino" on page 268.

In this chapter, I'll touch on several Arduino peculiarities (most of them helpful, some of them frustrating) while building some small but complete projects that you can try yourself. "Getting the Hardware: Adafruit" on page 276 contains links for all the various components and microcontrollers I use in case you want to replicate any of the projects exactly.

The Arduino Environment

I'm sure you noticed that we did not write "complete" C programs in Chapter 8. We had no `main()` function, and for the earlier examples, we didn't even import the usual header files. Yet we clearly had access to new functions and things like the `HIGH` and `LOW` values we used to blink our first LED.

Where did those extras come from? It can feel at times like the IDE is providing a bit of magic. It's not, of course, but it is doing a lot of work behind the scenes in the hopes of making you more productive. I want to point out some of that hidden work so that you have a better understanding of the distinction between C itself and the supporting elements provided by the Arduino IDE. Inevitably, you'll head to the web to search for examples of new topics as you build more of your own projects. Knowing the difference between the language and the tools can make those searches more fruitful.

The Arduino IDE quietly includes several headers for you to make up what can loosely be called the "Arduino language." It's not a distinct language like Python, but it certainly feels like something more than just the C-with-headers-and-libraries we've seen so far. The Arduino language is more a collection of useful pieces (values and functions) that make programming microcontrollers easier. I'll be showing you several of the more immediately beneficial parts, but you can get the complete list online. The Language Reference (*https://oreil.ly/wlwhf*) at the Arduino site contains a simple index of included features as well as links to details and examples.

Special Values

We relied on some of these "language" extensions just to make our first LED blink. Let's revisit that code but with more discussion of the named values (the Arduino Language Reference calls these *constants*) that are specific to the Arduino environment.[1]

```
void setup() {
  // put your setup code here, to run once:
  // Tell our board we want to write to the built-in LED
  pinMode(LED_BUILTIN, OUTPUT);          ❶ ❷
}

void loop() {
  // put your main code here, to run repeatedly:
  // A high value is 'on' for an LED
  digitalWrite(LED_BUILTIN, HIGH);       ❸
  // Now wait for 500 milliseconds
  delay(500);
  // And write a low value to turn our LED off
  digitalWrite(LED_BUILTIN, LOW);        ❹
  // and wait another 500ms
  delay(500);
}
```

❶ The LED_BUILTIN constant represents the number of the pin connected to the LED found on most development boards. It won't always be the same number for every controller, but the IDE grabs the correct value based on the board you select.

❷ OUTPUT is the value we use to indicate we will send information to something like an LED or a motor. We'll see analogous INPUT and INPUT_PULLUP constants when we tackle sensors and buttons.

---

1 Generic C calls these named values *symbolic constants*. I'll use the unqualified "constant" to match the Arduino documentation.

❸ HIGH is a reference to the increased voltage used to "switch on" the device attached to the pin. What "on" means depends on said device. It's pretty self-explanatory for an LED. :)

❹ And LOW is the decreased voltage counterpart to HIGH, turning the LED off.

These named values are not variables. They are technically *preprocessor macros*. The preprocessor is a step your code goes through before it is compiled.[2] You create these entities with the define directive. (The prefix might look familiar from #include, and it should. Both "commands" are handled by the preprocessor.) We'll go into more depth on this directive in "Preprocessor Directives" on page 238, but its syntax is simple:

```
#define LED_BUILTIN 13
#define HIGH 1
#define LOW  0
```

The C preprocessor simply catches every instance of the macro's name in your code and replaces that name with the defined value. If we had a new controller with fewer pins, for example, we could change our #define to, say, 8. Then we wouldn't have to change any of the other parts of our program where we turn the onboard LED on or off.

Constants: const versus #define

In computer programming, a *constant* is a variable or other reference to a value that does not change at runtime. (That is different from a *literal* like the numbers and strings discussed in "Literals" on page 33.) Using this generic definition, it's reasonable to refer to the #define entries we've seen as constants.

In C, we can also use the const keyword to create a regular variable (of any type) and assign it some value. Once that value is assigned, the compiler will make sure we never try to assign a new value. Such a declaration would go like this:

```
const double lo_res_pi = 3.14;
```

For a lot of the work we'll do with Arduino, which approach you choose won't really matter. In many cases, the compiler will analyze how your const variable is used and substitute the actual value as an optimization, just as if you had used #define. But sometimes it is useful to have a known, explicit type. In those situations, const is often the easiest approach.

---

2 This is true for GCC, but some compilers use wholly separate executables for preprocessing and compiling.

And to be clear, #define *is* part of C (via the preprocessor). You can use it in your own code whether you are writing for a microcontroller or for a desktop. It's the specific constants like OUTPUT that are part of the Arduino setup. Table 9-1 shows some of the constants we'll be using in our projects.

Table 9-1. Useful constants defined for Arduino

Name	Description
LED_BUILTIN	If the selected board has a built-in LED, this represents the pin number for that LED
INPUT	For pins that can perform both input and output, expect input
INPUT_PULLUP	Similar to INPUT, but use an internal pull-up resistor to report HIGH on something like an unpressed push button, and LOW while it is pressed
OUTPUT	For pins that can perform both input and output, expect output
HIGH	Friendly name for 1, meant for use with digital reading and writing
LOW	Friendly name for 0, meant for use with digital reading and writing

You can get more details on these constants on the official Arduino Reference (*https://oreil.ly/pS11s*) page.

Special Types

Beyond those constants, the headers that are loaded for your Arduino sketches also include a number of other data types that I want to highlight, as you might find them useful. These aren't really new types and aren't even restricted to use in Arduino, but again, your sketches have access to these and you will likely see them used in examples you find online.

Table 9-2 lists several of these types with their sizes and a brief description.

Table 9-2. Useful constants defined for Arduino

Type	Description
bool	Boolean type; bool variables can be assigned either true or false
byte	Unsigned 8-bit integer type
size_t	Integer type corresponding to maximum size (in bytes) of an object on the selected board. The value you get from sizeof, for example, is of type size_t.
String	An object-oriented way of handling strings (note the capital "S" in the type) with several convenience functions available
int8_t, int16_t, int32_t	Signed integer types with explicit sizes (8, 16, and 32 bits, respectively)
uint8_t, uint16_t, uint32_t	Unsigned integer types with explicit sizes (8, 16, and 32 bits, respectively)

With the exception of String, these types are actually *aliases* of other types. This is done with C's typedef and is fairly straightforward. For example, the byte type is an alias for unsigned char and can be defined like this:

```
typedef unsigned char byte;
```

We'll do more work with typedef in "Preprocessor Macros" on page 239, but several of the types are pretty handy. I use byte in particular in many of my own projects as it makes more sense (and takes fewer keystrokes) than unsigned char, but that's just a personal preference. Either type defines an 8-bit slot capable of storing values from 0–255.

"Built-In" Functions

The Arduino environment includes several headers that make some popular functions available to you. You can make use of the functions shown in Table 9-3 without any explicit #include in your sketch.

Table 9-3. Functions available in Arduino

Function	Description
Input/Output	
void pinMode(pin, mode)	Set the specified pin to input or output mode
int digitalRead(pin)	Return value will be HIGH or LOW
void digitalWrite(pin, value)	Value should be HIGH or LOW
int analogRead(pin)	Returns 0–1023 (some boards offer 0–4095)
void analogWrite(pin, value)	Value is 0–255, must use PWM-capable pin
Time	
void delay(ms)	Pause execution for specified number of milliseconds
void delayMicroseconds(micros)	Pause execution for specified number of microseconds
unsigned long micros()	Returns number of microseconds since program started
unsigned long millis()	Returns number of milliseconds since program started
Math (Unlisted return types depend on the type of the arguments)	
abs(x)	Returns absolute value of x (int or float)
constrain(x, min, max)	Returns x, but bounded by min and max
map(x, fromLow, fromHigh, toLow, toHigh)	Returns x converted from "from" range to "to" range
max(x, y)	Returns the larger of x or y
min(x, y)	Returns the smaller of x or y
double pow(base, exp)	Returns base raised to the exp power
double sq(x)	Returns the square of x

Function	Description
`double sqrt(x)`	Returns the square root of x
`double cos(rad)`	Returns the cosine of the angle given in radians
`double sin(rad)`	Returns the sine of the angle given in radians
`double tan(rad)`	Returns the tangent of the angle given in radians
Random Numbers	
`void randomSeed(seed)`	Initializes the generator; seed is an unsigned long
`long random(max)`	Returns a random long between 0 and max - 1
`long random(min, max)`	Returns a random long between min and max - 1

The many character tests from *ctype.h* such as `isdigit()` or `isupper()` are also available automatically.[3] See Table 7-4 for the full list.

Trying Out the Arduino "Stuff"

Let's put all of these new ideas into a project and see just how they work (and work together). To do this, we'll create a more interesting LED sketch. We'll make the LED "breathe" using the `analogWrite()` function and a little math.

The LED in question is not actually an analog device. It still has just the on and off states. But many output devices like LEDs can simulate "degrees" of on with a technique known as *Pulse Width Modulation* or PWM. The idea is that you can turn the LED on and off rapidly in such a way that it appears dimmer. (Or working with something like a motor, it might seem to turn slower.)

It's important to note that not all pins on all controllers can do PWM output. You need to check the datasheet or pinout diagram for your controller.[4] On the Metro Mini I've been using in the projects so far, for example, only pins 3, 5, 6, 9, 10, and 11 support PWM.

We'll use a different RGB LED this time. It has four pins: one ground, and one each for the red, green, and blue channels. Each color will need its own connection to the controller, so we'll define some constants for those pins. We'll also define a few values for the breathing rate and our maximum number of radians, $(2 * \pi)$. Figure 9-1 shows the wiring I used in this example. Remember that using `analogWrite()` requires

---

3 The Arduino Language provides some alternate names for these functions with slightly different casing that you might find more readable, like `isDigit()` and `isUpperCase()`.

4 On typical pinout diagrams, digital pins that can do PWM often have a ~ prefix or other distinguishing mark.

paying attention to which pins you connect. (I won't bother with a picture for this project; the fun is in running it yourself to see the change in brightness!)

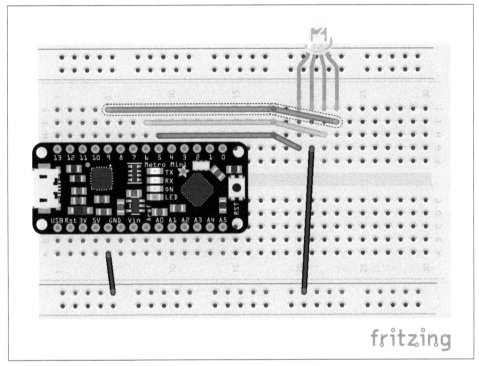

Figure 9-1. Wiring diagram for our breathing LED example

And now we can get to coding! As always, I encourage you to start a new sketch and type this in yourself, but you can also just pop open *breathe.ino* and follow along.

For our `setup()`, we'll get our color pin modes set to `OUTPUT` and pick a random color for the LED. We'll show that color on the LED for a few seconds before starting the animation.

Our `loop()` function will drive the animation. We can use the `millis()` function to get an ever-increasing number. We'll use our breathing rate and our max radians value to turn those milliseconds into radians. With the radians in hand, we'll use the `sin()` function to get a nice fractional brightness that grows and fades. Finally, we'll apply that brightness to the LED and pause a few milliseconds before animating the next step. Here's the complete listing of *ch09/breathe/breathe.ino* (*https://oreil.ly/FHdP8*):

```
// Output pins, have to make sure they support PWM
#define RED    5
#define GREEN  6
#define BLUE   9
```

```
// Some helper values
#define RATE 5000
#define PI_2 6.283185

// Color channel values for our LED
byte red;
byte green;
byte blue;

void setup() {
  // Set our output pins
  pinMode(RED, OUTPUT);
  pinMode(GREEN, OUTPUT);
  pinMode(BLUE, OUTPUT);

  // Start the LED "off"
  digitalWrite(RED, 0);
  digitalWrite(GREEN, 0);
  digitalWrite(BLUE, 0);

  // Get our PRNG ready, then pick our random colors
  randomSeed(analogRead(0));

  // And pick our random color, but make sure it's relatively bright
  red = random(128,255);
  green = random(128,255);
  blue = random(128,255);

  // Finally show the LED for a few seconds before starting the animation
  analogWrite(RED, red);
  analogWrite(GREEN, green);
  analogWrite(BLUE, blue);
  delay(RATE);
}

void loop() {
  double ms_in_radians = (millis() % RATE) * PI_2 / RATE;
  double breath = (sin(ms_in_radians) + 1.0) / 2.0;
  analogWrite(RED, red * breath);
  analogWrite(GREEN, green * breath);
  analogWrite(BLUE, blue * breath);
  delay(10);
}
```

 If you don't have an RGB LED, don't worry! You can use a regular LED and just write to the one pin of the LED rather than writing to the three separate color pins. You won't need to pick a random value, either; just use 255 (the full brightness). Even if you have a multicolor LED, try rewriting the example for a single-color LED as an exercise.

You can see that although we used several functions that are not part of C itself, we did not need to manually #include anything. That is all down to the magic of the Arduino IDE. It really does make development on these tiny boards simpler.

Microcontroller I/O

What else can we do with these extras supplied by our IDE? Lots! Let's try branching out from LEDs to try some inputs and some other types of output.

Sensors and Analog Input

An easy step up from the simple sketches we've been building so far is to add a sensor. Sensors come in all types: light, sound, temperature, air quality, humidity, etc. And they're usually inexpensive (although fancier ones do come with fancier price tags). For example, the TMP36 Analog Temperature sensor (*https://oreil.ly/Bczhb*) is only $1.50 over at Adafruit. Let's drop that sensor into a simple circuit like the one shown in Figure 9-2 to see how the wiring works.

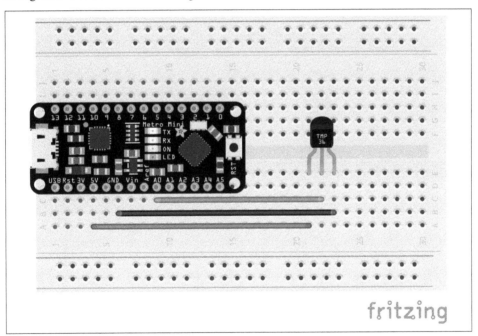

Figure 9-2. Wiring diagram for our temperature example

Pretty easy! And this is a fairly common arrangement. Sensors need power. They can either have a separate pin for power—like our TMP36—or many can draw enough current directly from the data pin you connect it to (such as a photoresistor). We use the analogRead() function to grab the current value of the sensor. Different boards and different sensors support different ranges, but 10-bit (0–1023) ranges are common. Exactly what those values mean depends on the sensor, of course. Our TMP36 ranges from –50°C (a reading of 0) to 125°C (a reading of 1023).

The Serial Monitor

While you likely won't have your Arduino project tethered to your main computer for long, while it is connected, we can take advantage of a very handy feature of most microcontrollers: the serial port. The Arduino IDE has a Serial Port Monitor you can launch, as shown in Figure 9-3. During development, this is an excellent tool for debugging and generally peeking into how things are going.

Figure 9-3. Accessing the Arduino IDE Serial Monitor

The port (selected via the Tools menu, also shown in Figure 9-3) and speed settings (selected at the bottom of the monitor window itself) will vary depending on several factors, including your OS, other devices you might have attached, and the particular

Arduino board you are using. For example, my Metro Mini on my Linux desktop communicates at 115200 baud (the classic unit of measurement for the rate of serial communication; remember modems?) on port */dev/ttyUSB0* (the filesystem path to a "device" connection) but a nifty Trinket M0 (*https://oreil.ly/eSsOI*) microcontroller uses port */dev/ttyACM0*. That same Trinket on an old Windows system I have still uses a COM port.

Is It Hot in Here?

Let's put these two new topics to use in a project. We'll use the circuit shown in Figure 9-2. You can start a new sketch or open *ch09/temp_serial/temp_serial.ino* (*https://oreil.ly/cal6o*) and follow along. The code is fairly straightforward. We set up an input pin. Then we read from that pin and print the result in the serial monitor in a loop. Let's see the code:

```
// TMP36 is a 10-bit (0 - 1023) analog sensor
// 10mV / C with 500mV offset for temps below 0
#define TMP36_PIN 0

void setup() {
  Serial.begin(115200);
}

void loop() {
  int raw = analogRead(TMP36_PIN);
  float asVolts = raw * 5.0 / 1024;  // Connected to 5V
  float asC = (asVolts - 0.5) * 100;
  Serial.print(asC);
  Serial.println(" degrees C");
  float asF = (asC * 1.8) + 32;
  Serial.print(asF);
  Serial.println(" degrees F");
  delay(5000);
}
```

Pretty spiffy! The bouncy nature of the readings is not uncommon. If we needed a steadier reading, say, to prevent a false alarm going off, there are a few electronic options we could employ, like adding resistors and capacitors. We could also read from the sensor several times and take an average. Or we could get even fancier and use statistics to toss any real outliers and then get the average. But we mostly just wanted to prove the sensor is working and that we can see the readings in the serial monitor. If you want to make sure the sensor is working, try holding it gently with your fingers—they should be warmer than room temperature, and you should see the trend of the readings going up.

For a bit of fun, try popping open the "Serial Plotter" from the Tools menu (just under the Serial Monitor). It tracks simple values printed via Serial.println() as a graph. It can even track multiple values as separate lines; just print a space in between the values on the same line.

But as I said, you likely won't have your Arduino plugged into your USB port constantly. Let's explore a better output option.

Segmented Displays

LCD and segmented LED displays come in a wealth of size and price options. You can get high-resolution LCDs the size of a postage stamp, touch-capable screens similar to those found in cell phones, or segmented LED displays for text or numeric output. I picked up a simple 4-digit LED display (a Velleman VMA425, shown in Figure 9-4) with a driver chip built in (so you don't need individual pin connections for each separate segment) for less than $7 at a local Micro Center. We can use just such a display to show our TMP36 readings (properly converted to Fahrenheit or Celsius) without resorting to the serial monitor.

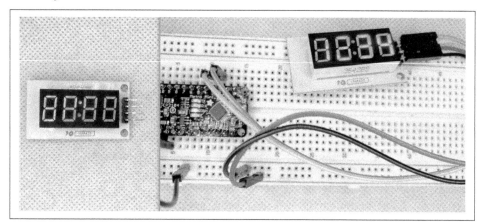

Figure 9-4. An example of a 4-digit, 7-segment display component

Unfortunately, these peripherals usually require a little help to operate. Fortunately, that help is almost always readily available in the form of a library. We'll go over libraries in much more detail in Chapter 11, but we can take a short detour now to grab what we need for our 4-digit LED display.

The driver chip I mentioned that comes with my particular display is a TM1637. There was no magic involved in finding that name—it is noted on the package and more plainly on the chip itself. Using the Arduino IDE Library Manager, I entered

"TM1637" as the search term.[5] Several results came back, and I chose a library (written by Avishay Orpaz) that looked simple and stable. After clicking the Install button, I simply included the library's lone header file and was immediately ready to put up some numbers![6]

```
#include <TM1637Display.h>
```

Doesn't get much easier than that. You will often follow this process for adding new peripherals, both sensors and other outputs. You may also decide nothing available is quite right, and roll your own code. Again, we'll look at the mechanics of creating your own libray in Chapter 11.

I shouldn't really say I was immediately ready after installing the library. I did have to wire up the display. Figure 9-5 shows the connections required. I also had to read the documentation for the library which I found by clicking the "More info" link in the Library Manager listing.

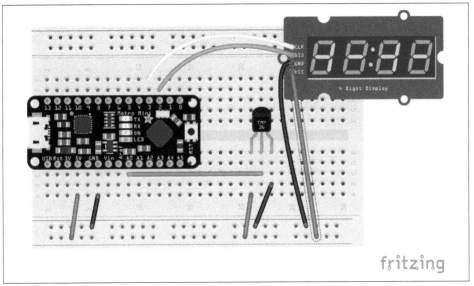

Figure 9-5. Wiring for temperatures on an LED display

Ignoring the TMP36 sensor for the moment, *ch09/display_test/display_test.ino* (*https://oreil.ly/jzXm9*) is a simple test of the 4-digit display. We'll display "1234" to prove our connections are working and that we understand the library functions from the documentation.

---

5 Other popular driver chips such as the MAX7219 will have similar search results.

6 If you are using a similar display, it has a nicely documented repo on GitHub (*https://oreil.ly/RVv2F*).

```
// Our 4-digit display uses a TM1637 chip and I2C
#include <TM1637Display.h>                          ❶

// Name our pins
#define CLK      2                                   ❷
#define DIO      3

// Create our 4-segment display object
TM1637Display display(CLK, DIO);                     ❸

void setup() {
  // Get our display ready and set a medium brightness
  display.clear();                                   ❹
  display.setBrightness(0x0f);
  display.showNumberDec(1234);
}

void loop() {                                        ❺
}
```

❶ The library I chose has one header, so include that to get going.

❷ The display needs two pins (in addition to power and ground), so name those for ease of use.

❸ Create a global `display` variable similar to how we created the NeoPixel objects.

❹ Use our `display` object with functions described in the documentation to initialize our display and put up a simple test number, 1234 in this case.

❺ Nothing changes, and the display will hold whatever number it was last sent, so we can leave the `loop()` function empty.

Hooray! If all goes well, you'll see something like Figure 9-4. If you chose a different display or library and you aren't seeing what you hoped, see if you can find other examples of using your hardware or library online. Usually someone has posted useful, minimal code examples you can easily copy and try yourself.

Buttons and Digital Input

But we're not done yet! We can add another peripheral to add a little more functionality to our temperature display sketch and expand our coding skills at the same time. Let's attach a very common input: the push button. We'll use it to toggle our display between Fahrenheit and Celsius output.

I grabbed a Tactile Button (*http://adafru.it/367*) from Adafruit; it's simple and breadboard friendly. Figure 9-6 shows the final connections for the TMP36 sensor, the 4-digit display, and our newly added button. The diagonal connections to the button are intentional. Either diagonal works; other arrangements are possible if you look at the specs for the button, but this choice guarantees we get the functionality we need.

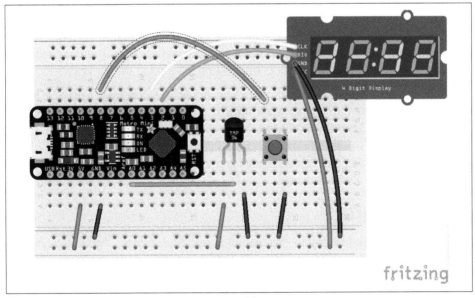

Figure 9-6. Wiring for our sensor, display, and button

To use the button, we need to set one pin to be an input and then use the digital Read() function on that pin. In particular, this button will use the INPUT_PULLUP constant. This common approach causes the default state of the pin (when the button is not pressed) to return HIGH. When the button is pressed, then, the pin will read LOW. We can watch for that LOW value and use it to trigger a change—like our F/C choice.

But watch out! Just because we're using the digitalRead() function does not mean the button is digital. It takes time to get the physical mechanism all the way down. It also takes a little time to fully release. All told, it takes a human much longer to press the button than it does for the Arduino to register a change. Consider this naive read-and-change loop snippet:

```
bool useC = false; // display temp in Celsius?

void loop() {
  // ...
  int toggle = digitalRead(BUTTON);
  if (toggle == LOW) {
    useC = !useC;
  }
  // ...
}
```

The pin will read low for tens of milliseconds during even the fastest press. Our microcontroller can read the pin and change the display much faster than we can let go of the button, causing a crazy flicker as the display rapidly bounces between our F and our C temperatures. We want to stop that flicker, so we have to be a little more clever in our code. We need to *debounce* the button. The idea of debouncing has gained traction in a lot of user interface work—it generally means making sure you don't report multiple presses (or clicks or taps or whatever) in too short a period.

I'll show you a few methods we can use to accomplish this debounce behavior. It usually involves keeping some extra state information around. For the first debounce technique, I simply keep a bool that tracks when the button state first changes. If that flag is true, we just pause for a second. (In "Just How Hot Is It?", we pause for exactly one second, in fact, but you can certainly choose a different delay.) After that gap has passed, we can read another change.

Just How Hot Is It?

So let's tie all of these new topics together and create the code for the components we wired up in Figure 9-6. We'll initialize our display in the setup. In the loop, we'll read the temperature, print out some debugging statements to the serial monitor, put the temperature on the display in the correct units, and then watch the button to see if we need to change those units. You can open *ch09/temp_display/temp_display.ino* (*https://oreil.ly/flVsn*) or type in the following code:

```
// TMP36 is a 10-bit (0 - 1023) analog sensor
// 10mV / C with 500mV offset for temps below 0
// Our 4-digit display uses a TM1637 chip and I2C
#include <TM1637Display.h>

// Name our pins
#define TMP36_PIN 0
#define CLK       2
#define DIO       3
#define BUTTON    8

// Create our 4-segment display object
TM1637Display display(CLK, DIO);

// Build the letters "F" and "C"
// Segment bits run clockwise from top (bit 1) to center (64)
uint8_t segmentF[] = { 1 | 32 | 64 | 16 };
uint8_t segmentC[] = { 1 | 32 | 16 | 8 };

// Keep track of scale
bool useC = false;

// Manage button at human time
bool debounce = false;
```

```
void setup() {
  Serial.begin(115200);
  display.clear();
  display.setBrightness(0x0f);
  pinMode(BUTTON, INPUT_PULLUP);
}

void loop() {
  int raw = analogRead(TMP36_PIN);
  float asVolts = raw * 5.0 / 1024;   // Connected to 5V
  float asC = (asVolts - 0.5) * 100;
  int wholeC = (int)(asC + 0.5);
  int wholeF = (int)((asC * 1.8) + 32 + 0.5);
  Serial.print(raw);
  Serial.print(" ");
  Serial.println(asC);
  if (useC) {
    display.showNumberDec(wholeC, false, 3, 0);
    display.setSegments(segmentC, 1, 3);
  } else {
    display.showNumberDec(wholeF, false, 3, 0);
    display.setSegments(segmentF, 1, 3);
  }
  if (debounce) {
    debounce = false;
    delay(1000);
  } else {
    for (int i =0; i < 1000; i += 10) {
      int toggle = digitalRead(BUTTON);
      if (toggle == LOW) {
        useC = !useC;
        debounce = true;
        break;
      }
      delay(10);
    }
  }
}
```

Notice I use a new function from the TM1637 library: setSegments(). This function allows you to turn on any pattern of segments you want. You can make cute animations or present a somewhat rough version of any English letter. You can see my results in Figure 9-7.

Figure 9-7. Our temperature reading on an LED display

Give this bigger example a try with your own setup. The project is in the *ch09* folder as *temp_display*. You can adjust the debounce pause or try making the "C" pattern a lowercase version. Tweaking existing projects is a great way to build up your understanding of new concepts! Speaking of new concepts, there are two more biggies I want to cover for the Arduino platform: memory management and interrupts.

Memory Management on Arduino

Memory management is much more important on small devices, so I want to highlight how memory works on a microcontroller like Arduino. Arduino has three types of memory. *Flash* memory is where our program is stored. *SRAM* is where the program operates while the Arduino has power. And finally, *EEPROM* allows you to read and write a small amount of data that will persist between power cycles. Let's look at each of these types of memory in more detail and see how we can use them in our code.

Flash (PROGMEM)

If the word "flash" sounds familiar, it probably is. This is the same type of memory found in flash (or thumb) drives. It is much slower than something like RAM, but it is generally on par with storage like hard drives. It is also persistent and does not require power to retain its information. That makes it perfect for storing our compiled sketches.

In microcontroller parlance, you may also hear a less familiar term: *PROGMEM* or "program memory." It's the same memory, but the latter term tells you a little more about what we're doing with that memory.

Even though this flash is the same technology as you find in thumb drives, we don't have write access to this memory when our program is running. Writing is reserved for the "upload" step in our IDE. The chip is put in a special mode for modification, and the new program is loaded. After the upload is complete, the chip restarts, reads the new program from flash, and off we go. We do have read access, though.

Most Arduino chips have more flash storage than you need for your compiled program. You can make use of the leftover space to reduce the amount of RAM needed to run your program. Since RAM is almost always more limited, this feature can be a real boon. You can store arrays or strings or individual values. You can use special functions to grab those stored values as you need them while your program is actively running.

Storing values in flash

To get a particular value into flash for use in your code, you can use the special `PROG MEM` modifier when declaring and initializing the variable. For example, we could store an array of 32-bit colors that would work with the RGBW NeoPixel ring from "C++ Considerations" on page 185:

```
const PROGMEM uint32_t colors[] = {
  0xCC000000, 0x00CC0000, 0x0000CC00, 0x000000CC,
  0xCC336699, 0xCC663399, 0xCC339966, 0xCC996633
};
```

At this point, the `colors` array is no longer a simple list of 32-bit values. It now contains the location of these values in flash. You need a special function to get at the contents of this array.

Reading values from flash

Those special functions are defined in the *pgmspace.h* header (*https://oreil.ly/nIk62*). In recent versions of the Arduino IDE, that header is one of the many "behind-the-scenes" elements handled for you automatically. There are several functions for reading absolutely every data type supported on Arduino. Table 9-4 lists the few functions we'll use in our projects.

Table 9-4. Program memory (flash) read functions

Name	Description
pgm_read_byte()	Read one byte
pgm_read_word()	Read one word (two bytes, like int on many microcontrollers)
pgm_read_dword()	Read one double word (four bytes, like long)
pgm_read_float()	Read four bytes as a float or double

If we wanted to get the first entry from our colors array for actual use, we could use the pgm_read_dword() function like so:

```
uint32_t firstColor = pgm_read_dword(&colors[0]);
```

This is obviously a little cumbersome. When you are running low on RAM, though, cumbersome is often a fair trade-off. 32 bytes for eight colors is not much, but what about a 256-color palette? At four bytes per color, that's an entire kilobyte. Some microcontrollers like our Metro Mini have a tiny 2K operating memory, so offloading such a palette to flash memory is a big win.

Reading strings from flash

Printing to the serial monitor is a great way to debug your program, or even just to watch what's going on as a sort of cheap status indicator. However, every one of the strings you print consumes some precious runtime memory. Moving these strings off to flash is a great way to reclaim some of that space. You simply pull the string you need out of flash just at the moment you need it. If you put it into a common, reusable buffer, that buffer is the only memory we have to make room for at runtime.

This is such a common memory-saving technique that the Arduino environment includes a special macro to simplify the round trip: F(). (Again, more on macros and #define in "Preprocessor Macros" on page 239.) F() is remarkably easy to use and provides an immediate savings. Say we have a few debugging statements like this:

```
setup() {
  Serial.begin(115200);
  Serial.println("Initializing...");
  // ...
  Serial.println("Setting pin modes...");
  // ...
  Serial.println("Ready");
}
```

There are likely other variables and such in your program, too. Verifying your code in the Arduino IDE might produce some output similar to this:

```
Sketch uses 4548 bytes (14%) of program storage space. Maximum is 32256 bytes.
Global variables use 275 bytes (13%) of dynamic memory,
leaving 1773 bytes for local variables. Maximum is 2048 bytes.
```

Great. We have plenty of room at the moment, but 1773 bytes is not much! Let's use the F() macro now to move those strings to flash memory:

```
setup() {
  Serial.begin(115200);
  Serial.println(F("Initializing..."));
  // ...
  Serial.println(F("Setting pin modes..."));
  // ...
  Serial.println(F("Ready"));
}
```

Pretty simple to incorporate, right? And now if we verify our program, we can see a small but advantageous change:

```
Sketch uses 4608 bytes (14%) of program storage space. Maximum is 32256 bytes.
Global variables use 225 bytes (10%) of dynamic memory,
leaving 1823 bytes for local variables. Maximum is 2048 bytes.
```

Our new sketch takes up a little more room in flash, but a little less room at runtime. That's exactly what we came for. Now, obviously, removing those debugging statements entirely saves space in both types of memory, but there are certainly times when you will have nice peripherals such as mini LCD displays that show text. F() can give you more room to play without much added effort.

SRAM

I've been tossing around the terms "at runtime" and "operating memory," among others. These terms refer to a type of memory called *SRAM*. Static random-access memory is the Arduino equivalent to the generic RAM term so often applied to bigger systems.[7] Flash is where our program is stored, SRAM is where our program operates. The stack and heap mentioned in Figure 6-3 are found here in SRAM while your program is running. The operating size of your program is limited by the amount of SRAM you have. Let's take a look at some implications of this limit.

Stacks and heaps

Recall the discussion of global variables and the heap from "Local Variables and the Stack" on page 131. I mentioned that you could potentially run out of memory if you had too many variables or made too many nested function calls. It is a largely theoretical discussion if you have gigabytes or even terabytes of memory like modern

---

7 Dynamic random-access memory, or *DRAM*, is the type of memory you buy in "sticks" and physically insert into your aging Windows 7 box so you can eke one more year out of it. The "dynamic" term here indicates this RAM needs to be refreshed periodically by drawing a little power—in contrast to SRAM, which does not. Both types, however, require at least *some* power and are therefore termed *volatile*, as their contents will be reset during a power cycle.

desktop systems. But 2K? What about our Metro Mini and its meager 2K of SRAM? The stack and heap—active at runtime, so not part of flash memory—must fit in this limited space as we run our Arduino sketches.

Imagine redoing the addresses from Figure 6-3 to fit in 2K. That middle is *much* smaller now. It is much easier to imagine too many function calls or too many global variables or `malloc()` allocations. If you wrote out 32 bytes per line (64 hexadecimal characters), it would take just 64 lines to represent the entire contents of SRAM on some microcontrollers. That's *one* two-sided piece of paper from a high school notepad! That means a careless loop or large array can overrun our SRAM and cause our program to crash.

For example, our recursive Fibonacci calculating function could easily fill up available memory after a few dozen calls—especially since we will still need memory for our LEDs, sensor libraries, etc. It's not forbidden to use recursion when working with microcontrollers, but it does require paying a little more attention to detail on your part.

Global variables in Arduino

Unlike desktop applications where globals (allocated on the heap) are almost always optional (if convenient), the Arduino environment makes regular use of them. The Arduino IDE hides a lot of the effort done on our behalf to create a viable, executable program. Remember that we don't write our own `main()` function, for example. As such, if we need to initialize a variable in the `setup()` function and then refer to that variable in our `loop()` function, we have to use a globally declared variable.

That fact is not terribly controversial. Many examples online, and certainly in this book, rely on globals. But given our limited space, it does require more of that attention to detail. For example, I often use `int` for any numeric variable that I know isn't going to store numbers in the billions. It's almost muscle memory to type out `int count = 0;`. Well, if I'm going to be counting successive button presses so that I can distinguish between single or double (or even triple) clicks, that count fits easily in a `byte`. Remembering to use the smallest appropriate data type is a great habit to get into.

In fact, if you get *really* pressed for memory, remember that you can read and manipulate individual bits using the operators we discussed in "Bitwise Operators" on page 96. If you had two buttons and needed to track potential triple clicks, those counts could *both* fit in one byte variable. Indeed, you could store the count of *four* buttons in that variable. That's definitely a little extreme, but again, when you need it, every byte counts. We're not on desktops anymore, Toto.

EEPROM

If you did come to Arduino from the land of desktop computing, you may also have noticed the lack of filesystem discussions. You likely weren't surprised that a physical, 3.5" hard drive was not attached to your tiny microcontroller, but the lack of long-term, read-write storage may have caught you off guard. Power cycle your Arduino, and every variable starts off back at the beginning. Many, many satisfying projects do not require any such storage, but some do. Happily, many controllers have some (limited) capacity for storing values you can manipulate in the form of electronically erasable programmable read-only memory, or *EEPROM*.

Not every microcontroller includes EEPROM. Enough don't, in fact, that this type of memory is not something the IDE expects you to use. You have to include the *EEPROM.h* header manually to store and retrieve values from this area. We only need two of the functions from this libray: get() and put(), but you can see the other functions available in the EEPROM library documentation (*https://oreil.ly/Hbgqn*).

Both functions take two arguments: an offset into EEPROM (the "address" in the documentation) and some "data," which can be a variable or struct for get(), or also a literal value for put(). Putting and getting a float, for example, would look something like this:

```
#include <EEPROM.h>

float temperature;

void setup() {
  EEPROM.get(0, temperature);
  // ... other initialization stuff
}

void loop() {
  // ... things happen, temperature changes
  EEPROM.put(0, temperature);
  // things continue to happen ...
}
```

Notice that unlike the scanf() function we have used to accept input from users, I did *not* use & with the temperature variable in the call to get(). This library does the work of assigning the value to the correct location for you. You usually read from EEPROM during setup(), so hopefully it's easy to be a little careful and remember to use simple variables and not their addresses. In the snippet above, EEPROM.get() will fill our temperature variable with the value stored in EEPROM exactly as we expect.

Using get() and put() and remembering the exact byte offset of where you stored your persistent values in EEPROM may seem tedious, and I agree that it is. In return, however, you have total control over what goes in and how you retrieve it. Just make sure that you manage your addresses correctly. If you are storing two `float` numbers and a `byte`, in that order, you need to make sure the second `float` is stored at address 4 and the `byte` at address 8. Or better yet, use `sizeof` to advance a running location variable by exactly the right amount.

It's important to know that reading and writing to EEPROM is "expensive," in that it is not a speedy operation. EEPROM also has limits on how often it can be read and changed. You aren't likely to hit those read/write limits, and the speed is fine for initializing our tiny projects, but EEPROM is definitely not a simple extension of SRAM.

Remembering Choices

All of this memory stuff sure is esoteric. I think it's time for another kitchen sink example! Let's get that nifty LED ring wired back up and add a tactile button to change its color. We'll store the selected color in EEPROM, too, so that if we shut off the Arduino and turn it back on later, the ring will light up with our most recent choice. This project uses only the ring and the button, as shown in Figure 9-8.

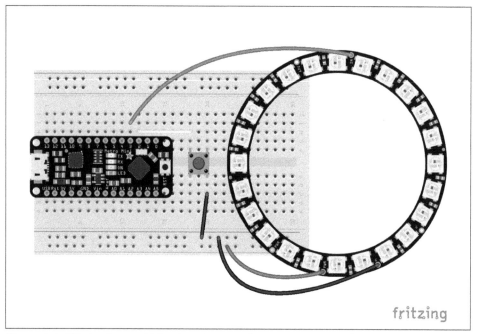

Figure 9-8. Wiring for our EEPROM demo with our LED ring and button

Along the way, we can use a new technique to debounce the button, and we'll even borrow the debounce concept to keep from writing to EEPROM too much. When you let users change things, they often take you up on the offer and change them a lot. If they press the button to change the color, we'll wait a few seconds before committing that change to EEPROM, in case they just want to quickly cycle through the colors to see their options.

If you are up for a challenge, try sketching out (get it?) a solution yourself before reviewing the code here. But that is a pretty hefty challenge. Feel free to enter in this code or compile and upload *ch09/ring_eeprom/ring_eeprom.ino* (*https://oreil.ly/yir2G*) if you'd rather just get on with the joy of changing LED colors!

```
#include <Adafruit_NeoPixel.h>
#include <EEPROM.h>

#define RING_PIN     3
#define RING_COUNT 24
#define BUTTON_PIN   2

int previousState = HIGH;
int pause = 250;
int countdown = -1;

const PROGMEM uint32_t colors[] = {
  0xCC000000, 0x00CC0000, 0x0000CC00, 0x000000CC,
  0xCC336699, 0xCC663399, 0xCC339966, 0xCC996633
};
const byte colorCount = 8;
byte colorIndex;

Adafruit_NeoPixel ring(RING_COUNT, RING_PIN, NEO_GRBW);

void setup() {
  Serial.begin(115200);
  pinMode(BUTTON_PIN, INPUT_PULLUP);
  retrieveIndex();
  ring.begin();                // Initialize our ring
  ring.setBrightness(128);  // Set a comfortable mid-level brightness
  ring.fill(pgm_read_dword(&colors[colorIndex]));
  ring.show();
}

void loop() {
  int toggle = digitalRead(BUTTON_PIN);
  if (toggle != previousState) {
    if (toggle == LOW) {
      // "falling" state, so do our work
      previousState = LOW;
      colorIndex++;
      if (colorIndex >= colorCount) {
        colorIndex = 0;
      }
      ring.fill(pgm_read_dword(&colors[colorIndex]));
      ring.show();
      countdown = 10;
```

```
      } else {
        // "rising", just record the new state
        previousState = HIGH;
      }
    }
    if (countdown > 0) {
      countdown--;
    } else if (countdown == 0) {
      // Time's up! Record the current color index to EEPROM
      countdown = -1; // stop counting down
      storeIndex();
    }
    delay(100);
  }

  void retrieveIndex() {
    Serial.print(F("RETRIEVE ... "));
    EEPROM.get(0, colorIndex);
    if (colorIndex >= colorCount) {
      Serial.println(F("ERROR, using default"));
      // Got a bad value from EEPROM, use default of 0
      colorIndex = 0;
      // And try to store this good value
      storeIndex();
    } else {
      Serial.print(colorIndex);
      Serial.println(F(" OK"));
    }
  }

  void storeIndex() {
    Serial.print(F("STORE ... "));
    Serial.print(colorIndex);
    EEPROM.put(0, colorIndex);
    Serial.println(F(" OK"));
  }
```

There are three parts of this program I specifically want to highlight. The first is the use of the previousState variable to track the state of our button. Rather than use a Boolean value to know if we are in the middle of a debounce period, I only act on the button press when I notice it changing from a HIGH state to the LOW state. It's about the same amount of work, but I wanted to show you an alternative.

The other two interesting parts are the functions at the bottom, retrieveIndex() and storeIndex(). Here you can see the use of the EEPROM functions. Storing the index is straightforward, but I added a safety check when reading the index to make sure that it is a valid value.

Interrupts

There is one last bit of cool functionality that can streamline the code you write to handle inputs like our tactile buttons. While not peculiar to Arduino, the use of *interrupts* is not something many desktop or web developers encounter anymore. Interrupts are hardware signals that can trigger software responses. Interrupts can let you know that some network data has arrived, or that a USB device was connected, or maybe a key was pressed. They get their name from the advantageous fact that they "interrupt" the normal flow of your program and transfer control somewhere else.

I say advantageous because interrupts can significantly simplify the process of worrying about asynchronous, unreliable events. Think about typing at your keyboard. One way your operating system could go about "listening" for keys to be pressed is to run a big loop and check every key, one after the other, to see if it had been pressed recently. What a tedious task. Even if we abstract things a little bit so that the operating system can ask if *any* key has been pressed, we would need to ask this question of every input device. Every hard drive, every thumb drive, the mouse, the mic, every USB port, etc., etc. That type of polling just isn't something we want to worry about. Interrupts take away that worry. When a key is pressed, a signal arrives telling your computer to go check the keyboard. It's an on-demand system.

When such a demand is made, the computer typically goes to a function you have supplied with the express intent of handling the interruption in question. You register a handler and the operating system does the management of stopping anything else that is happening and switching to that handler.

On an Arduino project, you can use interrupts for various input devices like our tactile buttons. Rather than polling the button like we've done in some of our previous projects, we can register a function for the button press. We write our loop without any mention of the button. No polling, no debounce flag or timer, nothing. The microcontroller is doing its own internal work to watch each of its pins, and when one of them changes, say the one attached to our button, an interrupt fires and we jump to our registered function.

Interrupt Service Routines

An interrupt service routine, or ISR, is really just a function. But you do want to obey a few rules and a few guidelines:

- An ISR cannot have any parameters (rule)
- An ISR should not return any values (guideline)

- Timing functions like delay() and millis() themselves use interrupts so you can't use them inside an ISR (rule)[8]

- Because you are "holding up the line" while inside your ISR, these functions should be designed to run as quickly as possible (guideline)

To register an ISR in Arduino, you use the attachInterrupt() function. That function takes three arguments:

- The interrupt to listen for: use the function digitalPinToInterrupt(pin) for this argument
- The ISR: just give the name of the function you want to use
- The mode, one of:
  — LOW: triggered when the pin is LOW
  — CHANGE: triggered when there is any change in the pin's value
  — RISING: triggered when the pin goes from LOW to HIGH
  — FALLING: triggered when the pin goes from HIGH to LOW
  — HIGH: some—but not all—boards support triggers when a pin is HIGH

If you no longer want to handle an interrupt, you can use detachInterrupt(). That function takes one argument, the same digitalPinToInterrupt(pin) as the first argument to attachInterrupt(). (This helper function correctly translates your pin number to the necessary interrupt number. It is not recommended to supply the interrupt number directly.)

Interrupt-Driven Programming

Let's dive into one more project to try harnessing an interrupt. We'll take our LED ring and light up one LED after the other to make a cycling animation. We'll use a button to change the speed of that cycle. We certainly could write this type of program without interrupts, but I think you'll like how much cleaner this project is than our example that polled the button to change the color of the LED ring. We'll actually use the exact same hardware setup as we did for that project. You can look back at Figure 9-8 if you need to re-create it.

---

8 The micros() function will work, but only for a millisecond or two. delayMicroseconds() uses a different mechanism to pause, so it actually can be used. But you really don't want to delay inside an ISR at all if you can help it.

As always, feel free to grab this sketch (*ch09/ring_interrupt/ring_interrupt.ino* (*https://oreil.ly/iZ5JJ*)), or enter it yourself. The only wiring on this project is connecting the power and ground of the NeoPixel ring and the data line to an acceptable pin on your microcontroller. You'll need to check the documentation for your board to see which pins support interrupts. For our Metro Mini (compatible with the Arduino Uno), we can use either pin 2 or pin 3:

```
#include <Adafruit_NeoPixel.h>

#define RING_PIN     3
#define RING_COUNT 24
#define BUTTON_PIN   2

int pause = 1000;                                          ❶

Adafruit_NeoPixel ring(RING_COUNT, RING_PIN, NEO_GRBW);

void nextPause() {                                         ❷
  if (pause == 250) {
    pause = 1000;
  } else {
    pause /= 2;
  }
}

void setup() {
  pinMode(BUTTON_PIN, INPUT_PULLUP);                       ❸
  attachInterrupt(digitalPinToInterrupt(BUTTON_PIN),       ❹
      nextPause, FALLING);
  ring.begin();                // Initialize our ring       ❺
  ring.setBrightness(128);     // Set a comfortable brightness
  ring.show();                 // Start with all pixels off
}

void loop() {
  for (int p = 0; p < RING_COUNT; p++) {                   ❻
    ring.clear();
    ring.setPixelColor(p, 0, 255, 0, 0);
    ring.show();
    delay(pause);
  }
}
```

❶ Set an initial pause duration of 1 second for our ring animation.

❷ Create a concise function to respond to button presses by cycling through different pause durations.

❸ Setup our button pin as an INPUT_PULLUP, just as we have before.

❹ Configure `nextPause()` to handle the event of our button being pressed.

❺ Set up our LED ring, also like we have before.

❻ Our animation loop does not have to include any button-polling logic (hooray!).

Hopefully, this feels simpler than our other projects that included buttons. Our `loop()` function is devoted solely to driving the animated pixel around the ring. And although I use the `FALLING` mode to trigger the interrupt, we could have used `RISING` just as easily for this example. Changing that mode is a great tweak to try now if you're curious about the effect.

Exercises

Now that we've seen several sketches up and running with help from the Arduino environment to make use of some interesting peripherals, here are a few small projects you can try to test your new skills. I'm including the wiring diagrams for my setups, but you are certainly welcome to arrange the components however you like and use whichever pins are appropriate for your microcontroller. The solutions are in the *ch09/exercises* (*https://oreil.ly/ezhYB*) folder.

1. *Automatic night-light.* With a photoresistor and an LED (see Figure 9-9), create a night-light that responds to a decrease in light by increasing the brightness of the LED. Try using the `map()` function to convert the sensor reading value to an appropriate LED value. (You can use a NeoPixel or a regular LED with PWM.)

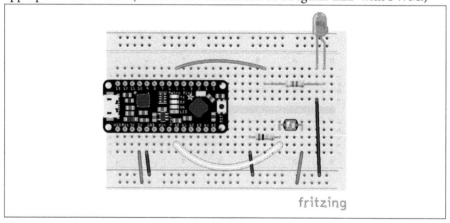

Figure 9-9. Wiring for an automatic night-light

2. *Stopwatch.* Use our 4-digit display and one button (see Figure 9-10) to create a stopwatch. When you first press the button, the stopwatch starts and tracks the elapsed time in seconds (up to 99:99 seconds). Pressing the button again will stop the count. Pressing it a third time will reset the stopwatch to 0:00.

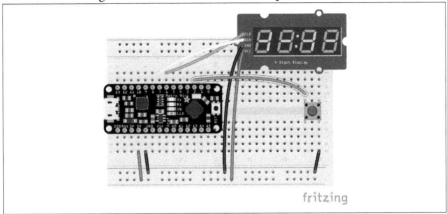

Figure 9-10. Wiring for a simple stopwatch

3. *Scoreboard.* Use four buttons and a 4-digit display (see Figure 9-11) to run a small scoreboard for two teams. The left two digits of the display will keep the score for team 1, the right two digits for team 2. Use two buttons for each team: one to increase their score and one to decrease it. Start small and build up. Get one button working. Then get one team working. Finally, get both teams working. You may need to consult the documentation for your segmented display library to make sure you can update the score for one team without clobbering the score for the other team.

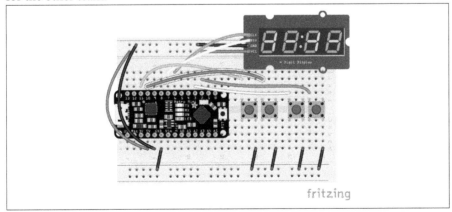

Figure 9-11. Wiring for a scoreboard

Next Steps

My goodness that was a lot of code. But I sincerely hope you enjoyed our tour of the functions and features available for programming in Arduino. We tried out several new peripherals and covered the ways Arduino programmers can work with limited memory. We also introduced the topic of interrupts (*https://oreil.ly/z4YpN*). You are wholly encouraged to feel overwhelmed! Hopefully not discouraged, though. If any of the examples remain unclear, let them sit a day or two and come back to try again.

The next chapter won't be quite so intense. In the discussion on memory, we saw that sometimes you have to be a bit clever when dealing with microcontrollers. We'll take a look at how you can optimize some patterns common in Arduino programming by concentrating on a single, simple example. The optimizations are certainly valid on desktops, too, they just might not make as much of an impact. But right now, we're still focusing on Arduino, so read on to see just how much of an impact a few small changes can have!

CHAPTER 10

Faster Code

I mentioned at the very beginning of Chapter 1 that C was designed for machines with limited resources—at least by today's standards. Microcontrollers have many of those same limitations, making C a pretty natural fit as a development language. Indeed, if you want to get the maximum possible performance out of a tiny chip, C's ability to work directly with memory addresses, as we saw in "Addresses in C" on page 127, is unparalleled, if tedious.[1]

I'm happy to say that even without diving into the depths of datasheets (seriously technical specifications produced by component and microcontroller manufacturers), you can employ several straightforward tricks to speed up your code. But do remember that sometimes good enough is, well, good enough! Try getting your code going with the patterns you know first. Does your program run? Does it do what you need? If so, the interesting options I highlight in this chapter, such as using integers rather than floating point numbers or unrolling loops, are just that: interesting. They are not really "better" and certainly not necessary. Usually. The Arduino and its cousins are definitely more limited than desktops. Sometimes your program won't run or doesn't quite do what you need. In those instances, consider bringing some of the following optimizations to bear.

---

1 Making use of this feature requires understanding the really low-level details of your chip. That understanding comes with a pretty steep learning curve that's well beyond our goals in this book. Even the SAM D21 heart of tiny controllers like Adafruit's Trinket M0 has a 1000+ page datasheet for your reading pleasure!

The Setup

Rather than toss another slew of new gadgets and configurations and wiring diagrams at you, I'm going to focus on a hardware setup similar to our first Arduino projects back in Chapter 8. We'll use one NeoPixel strip. Figure 10-1 shows the usual wiring diagram and my Metro Mini wired (and powered) up.

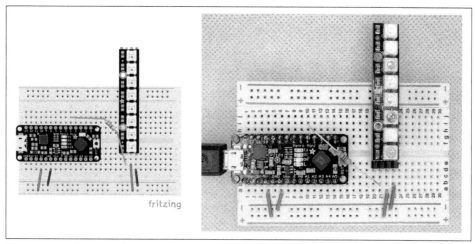

Figure 10-1. Our simple LED setup

Next, we'll steal the "breathing" logic from "Trying Out the Arduino 'Stuff'" on page 194 and apply it to each pixel in the strip. Rather than start with random colors, we'll simply assign some nice rainbowy ones. Feel free to tweak the colors, by the way. Pick a palette you will enjoy staring at; we'll be using this sketch as the basis for every optimization in the chapter.

Pull up *ch10/optimize/optimize.ino* (*https://oreil.ly/UHE04*) and try it out on your own setup. Be sure to adjust the LED_PIN and LED_COUNT values if needed.

```
#include <Adafruit_NeoPixel.h>

#define LED_PIN     4
#define LED_COUNT   8
#define RATE      5000
#define PI_2 6.283185

Adafruit_NeoPixel stick(LED_COUNT, LED_PIN, NEO_GRB);
uint32_t colors[] = {
  0xFF0000, 0x00FF00, 0x0000FF, 0x3377FF,
  0x00FFFF, 0xFF00FF, 0xFFFF00, 0xFF7733
};

void setup() {
  Serial.begin(115200);
```

```
  stick.begin();            // Initialize our LEDs
  stick.setBrightness(128); // Set a comfortable brightness
  // Show our colors for a few seconds before animating
  for (byte p = 0; p < LED_COUNT; p++) {
    stick.setPixelColor(p, colors[p]);
  }
  stick.show();
  delay(RATE);
}

void loop() {
  double ms_in_radians = (millis() % RATE) * PI_2 / RATE;
  double breath = (sin(ms_in_radians) + 1.0) / 2.0;
  for (byte p = 0; p < LED_COUNT; p++) {
    byte red   = (colors[p] & 0xFF0000) >> 16;
    byte green = (colors[p] & 0x00FF00) >> 8;
    byte blue  = colors[p] & 0x0000FF;
    red = (byte)(red * breath);
    green = (byte)(green * breath);
    blue = (byte)(blue * breath);
    stick.setPixelColor(p, red, green, blue);
  }
  stick.show();
  delay(10);
}
```

With this minimal example in place, we can look at some popular techniques for gaining performance. Many of these techniques are squarely in the trade-off realm. Many take up a little extra storage in flash memory or in SRAM in return for speeding up the work you have to do in the loop() function. Some, though, are trade-offs involving your time and energy as a programmer. But again, if your program is already working the way you want, there's not really anything overly superior in the alterations that follow. :)

Floating-Point Versus Integer Math

A lot of computer hardware press these days discusses the ever more powerful GPUs (graphics processing units, impressive chips devoted to displaying and manipulating graphics) available from various venders. But not so long ago, you could also talk about separate FPUs, or floating-point units (impressive chips devoted to performing —and speeding up—floating-point calculations).[2] Floating-point math takes power, and it took a while for computers to get generally powerful enough that such niceties could be integrated.

---

2 I had the distinct pleasure of upgrading my 8086 CPU with an *amazing* 8087 FPU coprocessor. I'll leave it to you, gentle reader, to suss out the incriminating dates of this lovely bit of nostalgia.

Happily, our computers have really grown in power (while shrinking in size) and Arduino projects do have access to good floating-point support and fancier things that use floating-point math like trigonometric functions. But doing that math still takes more horsepower than doing purely integer math. If you hang around the Arduino forums (*https://oreil.ly/xT1E6*), you'll see anecdotes about floating-point math taking twice (or more!) the time that comparable calculations take with integer operands.

 It's worth pointing out that on microcontrollers, float and double are not always 4- and 8-byte types like they usually are on desktops. On the Metro Mini (with a 16MHz ATmega328P chip), for example, both types are 4 bytes. It's unlikely this fact will cause much trouble, but on the off chance you need really high-precision floating-point numbers, you may need to look for a library to help out.

Floating-Point Math Alternatives

Many times, programmers use floating-point numbers without really considering the costs. Decimal numbers and fractions are everywhere around us: gas gauges, gas prices, tax rates, tip percentages, and on and on and on. It can make sense to use them in some cases, especially when outputting information meant to be read by humans. (For example, we converted the raw voltage readings of our TMP36 sensor from "Segmented Displays" on page 200 to floating-point degrees.)

But if we are just doing some internal work, and not showing those results to users, sometimes we can get the same results with integers. Consider these two calculations:

```
int dozen = 12;
int six = dozen * 0.5;
int half_a_dozen = dozen / 2;
```

Both six and half_a_dozen will contain the int value 6, but multiplying by 0.5 is more expensive. This example is obviously contrived, but only slightly. Let's look at our breath calculation and think about what, exactly, we are trying to do:

```
double ms_in_radians = (millis() % RATE) * PI_2 / RATE;
double breath = (sin(ms_in_radians) + 1.0) / 2.0;
// ...
red = (byte)(red * breath);
```

We are taking an ever-increasing count and turning it into a value between 0.0 and 1.0. We then multiply that value to give us a "portion" of our various colors. The net result, though, is still a byte value. We never use 140.7 units of red, we only use 140. What we're really trying to do is convert a value from the range (0 to RATE) to a value in the range (0 to 255) along a wave-like curve.

It just so happens that this task is very common for LED applications—it makes for nice fading animations, as we've seen. There is a very spiffy sine8() function in the NeoPixel library that approximates the sine calculation with uint8_t values[3] as both inputs and outputs. sine8() treats the input range of (0 to 255) as if it were the classic radian range of (0 to 2π). In turn, it outputs values between 0 and 255 as though it were the classic (–1 to 1) range of the sine wave.

That might sound too mathy, but the upshot is that we can get our brightness anima-tion by constraining our (increasing) milliseconds to the range (0 to 255) and using the sine8() function to get a cycling value between 0 and 255. We can then treat breath / 255 as a fraction with all integer parts. That allows us to apply our half_a_dozen trick. Rather than multiply by a floating-point value between 0.0 and 1.0, we multiply by breath and then divide by 255:

```
uint8_t ms = (millis() % RATE) / 20; // close enough :)
uint8_t breath = stick.sine8(ms);
// ...
red = red * breath / 255;
```

Slick! But be careful not to use parentheses around our "fraction" breath / 255. While it might read nicer and highlight the proportional value we're after, in integer math, dividing a smaller number (something between 0 and 255) by a larger number (always 255) will just give us 0, except for the very last case of 255 / 255, which does result in 1.

Integer Math Versus No Math

You know what's better than integer math? No math at all! Sometimes a little plan-ning can make a big difference. Look at how we use the colors array. We use the actual, full 32-bit values only once in setup(). Inside loop(), though, we break up those colors into their respective red, green, and blue parts. And we do that every 10 milliseconds. Yikes! So rather than store single 32-bit values, why not store individual bytes from the get-go? We could use a two-dimensional byte array if we want:

```
---
byte colors[8][3] = {
  { 0xFF, 0x00, 0x00 }, { 0x00, 0xFF, 0x00 },
  { 0x00, 0x00, 0xFF }, { 0x33, 0x77, 0xFF },
  { 0x00, 0xFF, 0xFF }, { 0xFF, 0x00, 0xFF },
  { 0xFF, 0xFF, 0x00 }, { 0xFF, 0x77, 0x33 }
};
---
```

---

3 The NeoPixel documentation (*https://oreil.ly/hMmZw*) uses the type uint8_t rather than byte, so I will follow suit for the temporary variables.

We could also store them in a single, simple array and do the tiny amount of math required to get the green and blue index values as needed:

```
- - -
byte colors[] = {
  0xFF, 0x00, 0x00,   0x00, 0xFF, 0x00,
  0x00, 0x00, 0xFF,   0x33, 0x77, 0xFF,
  0x00, 0xFF, 0xFF,   0xFF, 0x00, 0xFF,
  0xFF, 0xFF, 0x00,   0xFF, 0x77, 0x33
};
- - -
```

What's more, both options save us eight bytes of storage! Since both options require either a second index or a bit of math on the lone index, it's up to you which feels easier. Here's how we can alter both the initial show in `setup()` and the more interesting uses in `loop()` with the two-dimensional approach:

```
void setup() {
  // ...
  for (byte p = 0; p < LED_COUNT; p++) {
    stick.setPixelColor(p, colors[p][0], colors[p][1], colors[p][2]);
  }
  // ...
}

void loop() {
  // ...
  for (byte p = 0; p < LED_COUNT; p++) {
    byte red   = (byte)(colors[p][0] * breath);
    byte green = (byte)(colors[p][1] * breath);
    byte blue  = (byte)(colors[p][2] * breath);
    stick.setPixelColor(p, red, green, blue);
  }
  // ...
}
```

That definitely feels simpler. And while it isn't always true, one of the things I love about C is that looks are rarely deceiving. C can certainly work magic on small devices, but that magic is usually out in the open. So writing clean, simple code often increases both readability *and* performance.

Lookup Tables

While not quite as good as no math, performing a common calculation just once and then storing the answer for reuse is a close second. If we look at the calculations we're performing inside our `loop()` function, there are basically two: one to convert the current `millis()` value into a fraction, and then one to apply that function to our color channels (albeit separately for each channel). It would be great to get rid of those calculations.

When you have more storage space than processing power (another trade-off), a popular trick is to use *lookup tables*. You essentially run every calculation you need ahead of time, and store the answers in an array. Then when you need one of those answers, all you have to do is pluck the correct entry out of that array.

Depending on how expensive the calculation you want to store actually is, you have two options for creating your lookup table. If it's not too expensive, you can build the table up at runtime before it's needed. (For example, in an Arduino project, we can use the setup() function to do this work. Then we read from the array in the loop() function.) If the calculation is just impossibly expensive, you can do all the work "offline" and then simply transcribe the results into your program and initialize your array with a litany of literal values.

With limited memory, this type of optimization won't always make sense. Filling up a large global array might put too much of a squeeze on the rest of your program. But if the calculation is expensive enough, even reading from the slightly slower flash memory becomes feasible and you can store your lookup table there. In the latter case, of course, you have to do the offline calculation and initialize the array in PROGMEM when you declare it.

The Project So Far

Let's put our lookup table (we'll build ours in setup()) and our simpler math to work. When you do sit down to optimize one of your projects, it's a good idea to try out your ideas in small steps. This incremental approach makes it less likely you'll break anything. But when you do break something, the incremental approach should make it easier to fix—or rip out and start over if worse comes to worst. Here's *ch10/optimize2/optimize2.ino* (*https://oreil.ly/eDKmd*):

```
#include <Adafruit_NeoPixel.h>

#define LED_PIN      4
#define LED_COUNT    8
#define RATE       5000

Adafruit_NeoPixel stick(LED_COUNT, LED_PIN, NEO_GRB);
byte colors[8][3] = {                                  ❶
  { 0xFF, 0x00, 0x00 }, { 0x00, 0xFF, 0x00 },
  { 0x00, 0x00, 0xFF }, { 0x33, 0x77, 0xFF },
  { 0x00, 0xFF, 0xFF }, { 0xFF, 0x00, 0xFF },
  { 0xFF, 0xFF, 0x00 }, { 0xFF, 0x77, 0x33 }
};

uint8_t breaths[256];                                  ❷

void setup() {
  Serial.begin(115200);
  stick.begin();           // Initialize our LEDs
```

```
      stick.setBrightness(80);  // Set a comfortable brightness
      // Show our colors for a few seconds before animating
      for (byte p = 0; p < LED_COUNT; p++) {
        stick.setPixelColor(p,                                    ❸
            colors[p][0], colors[p][1], colors[p][2]);
      }
      stick.show();
      // Now initialize our sine lookup table
      for (int s = 0; s <= 255; s++) {                            ❹
        breaths[s] = stick.sine8(s);
      }
      delay(2000);
    }

    void loop() {
      uint8_t ms = (millis() % RATE) / 20;                        ❺
      uint8_t breath = breaths[ms];                               ❻
      for (byte p = 0; p < LED_COUNT; p++) {
        byte red   = colors[p][0] * breath / 255;
        byte green = colors[p][1] * breath / 255;
        byte blue  = colors[p][2] * breath / 255;
        stick.setPixelColor(p, red, green, blue);
      }
      stick.show();
      delay(10);
    }
```

❶ Break out our pixel colors into a two-dimensional array (for easier calculations in loop()).

❷ Make a global for our lookup table so we can initialize it in setup() and refer to it in loop().

❸ Use an alternate function to set the pixel colors that accepts the red, green, and blue values individually.

❹ Fill in our sine value lookup table using the handy (and speedy) sine8() function from the NeoPixel library.

❺ Simplify our translation from milliseconds to lookup index.

❻ Now put our lookup table value to use in calculating the current brightness.

You can certainly give this a try on your controller, but hopefully the behavior of your LED strip is the same. The intent is to make sure you understand the changes we made before tackling more tweaks.

Notice that I used an `int` variable for the `breaths` array initialization. Since we need to go right to the edge of what a `byte` can store (namely, we need to use 255), we can't use a byte-sized variable for the index value. The adjustment step where we increment `s` will occur one more time when `s` is 255, pushing it to 256. Except that for a `byte` variable, that push will force the variable to rollover back to 0. After that rollover, we check the loop condition. Since 0 is less than or equal to 255, we keep going. I made this mistake the first time I wrote up the initialization loop. It took me a few minutes to figure out why the `setup()` function never ended!

The Power of Powers of 2

One more math-related optimization to keep in your bag of tricks: use bitwise operations instead of multiplication and division. Multiplication is not cheap. Division is downright expensive. On microcontrollers, these operations can be *very* expensive—except when you are multiplying or dividing by 2 or a power of 2 (i.e., 4, 8, 1024, etc.). The remainder operation (%) is really a division operation as well, so it is also expensive, except where a power of 2 can be used.

We have removed a lot of expensive steps from our breathing loop, but we do still have some remainder and division operations. Let's see how powers of 2 help on these calculations.

When we multiply a color by our `breath` variable and divide by 255 to get the correct shade of that color, we're trying to make sure that the shade is somewhere in the 0 to 255 range. That fraction we create has a denominator tanalizingly close to a power of 2, namely 255 is almost 256. For example, consider our brightest red. Ideally, we would display the value 255 on our LED. The calculation we currently use looks like this:

```
red = red * breath / 255;
//  = 255 *   255  / 255;
//  = 65025 / 255;
//  = 255
```

This calculation results in 255, which is exactly what we want. But I said dividing by 256 would speed things up. I'll show you how shortly, but first let's explore an important question: is it OK to divide by 256 rather than 255? Well, 65025 / 256 is ~254.004. For an LED, that is definitely close enough. So how is dividing by 256 faster than dividing by 255?

It turns out that for computers with their binary brains, dividing by a power of two is the same thing as using the right shift operator, `>>`. That is marvelously fast compared to division. So our `red` approximation can now be calculated like this:

```
red = (red * breath) >> 8;
```

You simply shift by the "power" part of your power of 2; e.g., dividing by 2 (2^1) means shifting right by 1. Dividing by 256 (2^8) means shifting right by 8. Multiplication by a power of 2, then, works the same way; you just shift left. Need to quadruple a value? Shift it left by 2 ($2^2 == 4$). Neat! And more importantly, speedy. All the computer has to do is scoot some bits left or right. That type of work is very simple compared to the algorithms for multiplying and dividing, even though the results are the same.

But what about remainders? They are just as expensive as division since you perform the division on the way to finding the leftover amount. But if you are using % and a power of two, that can be expressed with the bitwise & operation and the correct *mask*. You'll often hear about bit "masks," which are simply numbers that keep certain bits but hide (or mask) others. To find the remainder of a division by 64 (2^6), say, you create a mask of 6 bits: 0x3f. (That turns out to be 63, or 64−1.) If we were to adjust our breathing rate to about four seconds (4096 milliseconds, or 2^{12}, to be precise), we could rewrite our millisecond conversion like this:

```
uint8_t ms = (millis() & 0x0fff) / 20;   // Bit mask with 12 bits
```

And since we really want that ms value to lie in the range of 0 to 255 so it is an appropriate index into our lookup table, we can turn that division into another shift operaion with a small adjustment to our divisor (5000 / 20 is roughly 4095 / 16):

```
uint8_t ms = (millis() & 0x0fff) >> 4;
```

Not bad. Not bad at all. We did have to fudge our breath rate, though. Remember my caveat at the top of the chapter: if it's working, it's working! If you get a satisfactory animation with all the floating-point math and nice round numbers like 5 seconds, your project is a success. But if you aren't getting the results you want, consider making adjustments to take advantage of these optimization tricks.

Loop Optimizations

We have one more clever alteration we could make to our breathing LED sketch to make it run even faster.[4] Looping sections often sacrifice a little performance for the sake of readable, reusable code. When performance is the top goal, you can steal back a little of that speed by reducing that reusability.

---

4 An important side effect of "running faster" is that you also make room for more calculations—or more complex calculations—to run in the same amount of time as your old calculations used to run. So without losing any performance, we could support longer strips of LEDs instead, or LEDs with more than just red, green, and blue channels.

Unrolling for Fun and Profit

The motivation behind this optimization is that it takes a little bit of time to manage a loop. In our loop() function, we have a for loop that sets the color for each LED on our little stick. After one LED has been updated, we have to increment the p variable and then test to see if there are more LEDs to process. Those few steps are tiny, but they are not nothing. If you are counting microseconds, this might not be time you can spare.

To get those microseconds back, you can *unroll* or *unwind* your loop. Basically, you take the body of your loop and simply copy it once for every iteration required, then hardcode the controlling variable (p in our case). I want you to try some of this optimizing as good practice, so I won't fully unwind the for loop. We can also use the >> trick to replace the division required when calculating the red/blue/green values. Updating the first couple LEDs would then look like this:

```
void loop() {
  uint8_t ms = (millis() & 0x0fff) >> 4;
  uint8_t breath = breaths[ms];

  byte red, green, blue;

  // Pixel 0
  red   = (colors[0][0] * breath) >> 8;
  green = (colors[0][1] * breath) >> 8;
  blue  = (colors[0][2] * breath) >> 8;
  stick.setPixelColor(0, red, green, blue);

  // Pixel 1
  red   = (colors[1][0] * breath) >> 8;
  green = (colors[1][1] * breath) >> 8;
  blue  = (colors[1][2] * breath) >> 8;
  stick.setPixelColor(1, red, green, blue);

  // Pixel 2
  // ...

  stick.show();
  delay(10);
}
```

As with other optimizations, there is a trade-off here: we will consume more program space with the unrolled loop. But again, we're here for performance—as long as we have the space. Just make sure you get the loop working correctly before you unroll it. Any bug hiding in an unrolled loop will require tedious copying and pasting to fix each and every expanded chunk.

Recursion Versus Iteration

There is another loop option that is not quite an optimization, but one worth mentioning. On devices with limited memory, recursive algorithms can run amok rather quickly. Happily, every recursive algorithm can also be written iteratively. Sometimes the loop approach is not intuitive or looks unwieldy, but it will work. If you are worried about recursive calls in your code, consider converting them into a loop with some extra variables to help out.

As a quick demonstration, let's look at a loop approach to finding the nth Fibonacci number (to replace the recursive algorithm we coded up back in "Recursive Functions" on page 115). We can use a for loop and three variables:

```
int find = 8; // we want the 8th Fibonacci number in this example
int antepenultimate = 0; // F(n - 2)
int penultimate = 0;     // F(n - 1)
int ultimate = 1;        // F(n)

for (int f = 1; f < find; f++) {
  antepenultimate = penultimate;
  penultimate = ultimate;
  ultimate = penultimate + antepenultimate;
}
// After the loop completes, ultimate contains the answer, 21
```

You might recall that the recursive algorithm got sluggish with larger numbers. That won't happen here. The numbers will eventually grow quite large, so you might need something like a long long to store the results, but the algorithm would continue to run quickly. So why don't we always use the iterative option? It's not obvious with the Fibonacci series, but sometimes the recursive algorithm is simply, well, simpler (occasionally *much* simpler) to understand and translate into code.

Again we have a trade-off: complexity versus performance. In this case, though, the trade-off may be a no-brainer. If you can't finish performing a calculation, using a potentially more complex algorithm that *can* complete the calculation will win.

String Versus char[]

The String class that you can use with the Arduino IDE for storing and processing text is another candidate for optimization. Our simple LED project didn't really use any text, but if you tackle any projects with text output, say on a mini LCD screen or over a WiFi connection, you may be tempted to use String as it has some convenient features. If you are running out of room, though, consider using (and reusing) boring old char[] variables.

Many examples you'll find online make use of String precisely because of those convenient extras like converting numbers to text in a given base, or functions like toLowerCase(), or using the + operator to concatenate String objects together. (You can read about all of these extras in the String documentation (*https://oreil.ly/ 8SZ50*).) The examples with String read well, and the text involved is often incidental to the project.

But if you are doing something more serious with text like driving an LED or LCD display, or shipping JSON blobs to a web service (we'll do something similar in "IoT and Arduino" on page 268), the convenience of all those String objects flying around can start to eat into your SRAM. Using an array of characters that you control can keep that memory consumption to a minimum. At the very least, you'll be aware of exactly how much room is required to accomplish your goals.

Don't forget that you can store text in flash for on-demand use as we saw in "Flash (PROGMEM)" on page 206. Sometimes that F() macro is all you need. But relying on flash will slow your program down a little bit and you can't programmatically alter those messages you store in flash. The control you get with char[] can be a win all around; the trade-off here is your time and energy.

Our Final Offer

Even for such a simple project, there were a surprising number of optimizations available. Here's our final version of the project, *ch10/optimize3/optimize3.ino* (*https:// oreil.ly/J8Myy*):

```
#include <Adafruit_NeoPixel.h>

#define LED_PIN     4
#define LED_COUNT   8

Adafruit_NeoPixel stick(LED_COUNT, LED_PIN, NEO_GRB);
byte colors[8][3] = {
  { 0xFF, 0x00, 0x00 }, { 0x00, 0xFF, 0x00 },
  { 0x00, 0x00, 0xFF }, { 0x33, 0x77, 0xFF },
  { 0x00, 0xFF, 0xFF }, { 0xFF, 0x00, 0xFF },
  { 0xFF, 0xFF, 0x00 }, { 0xFF, 0x77, 0x33 }
};

uint8_t breaths[256];

void setup() {
  Serial.begin(115200);
  stick.begin();            // Initialize our LEDs
  stick.setBrightness(80);  // Set a comfortable brightness
  // Show our colors for a few seconds before animating
  for (byte p = 0; p < LED_COUNT; p++) {
    stick.setPixelColor(p, colors[p][0], colors[p][1], colors[p][2]);
  }
  stick.show();
```

```
  // Now initialize our sine lookup table
  for (int s = 0; s <= 255; s++) {
    breaths[s] = stick.sine8(s);
  }
  delay(2000);
}

void loop() {
  uint8_t ms = (millis() & 0x0fff) >> 4;
  uint8_t breath = breaths[ms];
  for (byte p = 0; p < LED_COUNT; p++) {
    byte red   = (colors[p][0] * breath) >> 8;
    byte green = (colors[p][1] * breath) >> 8;
    byte blue  = (colors[p][2] * breath) >> 8;
    stick.setPixelColor(p, red, green, blue);
  }
  stick.show();
  delay(10);
}
```

The only change from our previous version is the use of integer math and bitwise operations in our loop() function. We convert the current millisecond count to an index we can use with our sine lookup table and simplify the current shade calculation for each of our red, green, and blue values. All told, this is quite the set of improvements! The extra efficiency leaves room to do other things. Now we could handle more LEDs or work on fancier animations. Or we could include some sensors and integrate their readings into our output. All in 2K of RAM. Your programmer ancestors would be proud. :)

But I shouldn't forget the practice I mentioned. If you want to try your own bit of optimizing, unroll the for loop like we started to do in "Unrolling for Fun and Profit" on page 231 and make sure the project still behaves as expected.

Next Steps

We've seen quite an array of optimization tricks in this chapter. There are other, more esoteric tricks, but they require more knowledge of the specific hardware you plan to use. I don't have any specific exercises this time, but I hope you'll revisit this chapter after you get some of your own Arduino projects off the ground.

If you end up with any useful functions that you optimize and tune to perfection, you can put them in a custom library for reuse with future projects. You can even publish them for others to use! Either way, Arduino makes making libraries relatively easy. Let's see how it's done in the next chapter.

CHAPTER 11

Custom Libraries

We've already seen how to include the headers of useful libraries that come with the Arduino IDE as well as how to add third-party libraries for some of the more interesting peripherals and sensors. But as you build up your catalog of microcontroller projects, you're likely to create some code that you reuse. I regularly employ the maxim that there are only three numbers in the universe: 0, 1, and many. If you find a chunk of code you use a second time, you're in that "many" category and it is probably time to consider making your own library.

That statement may seem dramatic. It certainly sounds grandiose. Happily, it is a fairly straightforward process and really does make reuse a snap down the road.

I do want to admit that the project in this chapter is bigger than our past projects in every sense. If remote-control robotic cars don't spike your interest, feel free to skip the bulk of this chapter. I would still recommend reading "Multifile Projects" on page 244 and "Creating the Library" on page 253 to get a sense of the steps involved in writing a library for your own use within the Arduino IDE. You can safely skip this chapter in favor of exploring an IoT project in Chapter 12.

Creating Your Own Library

To get started on a custom library, you'll need some code to reuse. The best way to find reusable code is to create some usable code first. We can kick off a normal project and then extract the parts that seem likely to work well in other projects.

For this project, we'll create a motorized car that can be driven with simple forward, backward, left, and right buttons. Once that is all working, we can break out the various "drive" functions into a separate file to highlight how the Arduino IDE works with multiple files. And finally, with a little multifile experience in your back pocket, we'll make the leap to radio control and see how to encapsulate that communication in a library that can be shared between our car and a separate navigation project.

Figure 11-1 shows the setup we're going to use. I bought these parts from Adafruit, but you can assemble a similar car from other parts just as easily. (See Appendix B for the exact part numbers I used.) The physical car is reasonably simple, but definitely requires some assembly. I had to make a trip to my local hardware store for a few of the small machine screws, but the prefabricated chassis from Adafruit sure made things simpler. The chassis has perfect holes and sockets to guide the attachment of both the rear motors and the loose caster on the front. I just rested a breadboard and battery on top, but there are ample spots to mount these with clips, screws, or zip ties.

Figure 11-1. Our robot car

Figure 11-2 shows the wiring of our microcontroller, navigation joystick, and the DRV8833 motor driver breakout board. There are a lot more connections on this project, but hopefully not so many that you are overwhelmed.

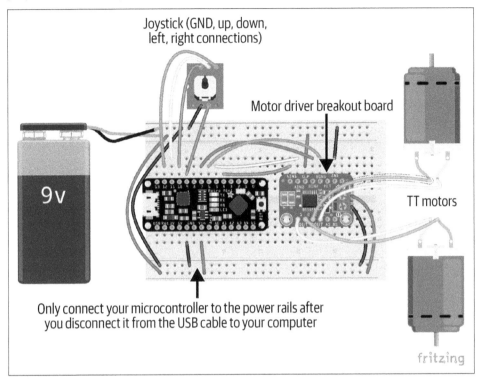

Figure 11-2. Wiring for the robot car

Robotics in general is a big interest of mine, but the mechanical elements are (way) out of my field of expertise. The extra learning required to pull off this project my first time around was challenging but fun—at least more fun than frustrating. I've never worked with motors before, so getting them mounted, powered, and properly connected so I could control them through software certainly required a little trial and error and no small amount of exasperated utterances. But if this particular project does not hold much interest for you, feel free to just follow along with the deconstruction of our code and see how to pull those parts back together in a library. But I will say that the first time you make a wheel spin by pressing a button, you feel like you can conquer the world. :)

If looking at the diagram in Figure 11-2 gives you the heebie-jeebies, you can look for robotic car kits that come with all the necessary parts as well as detailed assembly instructions. The kits usually have their own coding instructions, too. Feel free to get the kit running "as is" and get comfortable with the electronics first. Then come back here to work through my code examples and apply them (probably with a few modifications that will reinforce the work we're doing here) to your fully functioning car.

Preprocessor Directives

We've seen a couple of preprocessor directives already: #include and #define are both handled by the preprocessor. And the name "preprocessor" probably gives you a hint about its role in compiling your code. These directives are processed before your code is compiled.

The #include directive is used to bring in code defined in a separate file. After inclusion, it looks to the compiler as if you had typed in that external file as part of your own code.

The #define directive, as we've been using it, puts a human-friendly name on some literal. We can then use the name in our code rather than remembering the correct literal every time. And if we ever need to change that value, say, move an LED connection to a different pin on our controller, we only need to change it once. As with #include, the preprocessor replaces each instance of a #define name with its literal as though you had typed the literal directly.

For our car, let's use #define for the pins on our navigation joystick as we have with other connected peripherals:

```
#define LEFT_BTN   12
#define RIGHT_BTN  9
#define FWD_BTN    10
#define BKWD_BTN   11
```

I should point out that you can use #define with values other than numbers. Perhaps you have a standard error message or text response. Those can be defined, too:

```
#define GOOD_STATUS  "OK"
#define BAD_STATUS   "ERROR"
#define NO_STATUS    "UNKNOWN"
```

Knowing how #define works with the preprocessor also explains why we don't put a semicolon at the end. We don't want the semicolon showing up in our code, after all.

Preprocessor Macros

You can take #define a step further as well. Not only does it handle strings, it can handle small pieces of logic, almost like a function. These snippets are often referred to as *macros* to distinguish them from actual functions. A macro (or macroinstruction) transforms some bit of input to a corresponding bit of output, typically via substitutions. Macros are not function calls. Macros are not pushed onto or popped off of the stack.

Macros are great when you have a repeated bit of code that just doesn't rise to the level of needing a function. They are also great when you want your snippet to remain data-type agnostic. For example, consider a simple macro to determine the minimum of two values. Here's the definition and an example of how to use it:

```
#define MIN (x,y) x < y ? x : y

int main() {
  int smaller1 = MIN(9, 5);
  float smaller2 = MIN(1.414, 3.1415);
  // ...
}
```

To create the macro, we use #define and a name, like before, but then we supply a variable (or variables) in parentheses. Whatever arguments you pass to the macro replace the variables in the macro's snippet. That snippet, in turn, replaces the spot where it was called. It's as if you had typed the following:

```
int main() {
  int smaller1 = 9 < 5 ? 9 : 5;
  float smaller2 = 1.414 < 3.1415 ? 1.414 : 3.1415;
}
```

That simple replacement process can be powerful. But do be careful. Because the replacement is so simple, you can create problems if you pass complex expressions to your macro. If, say, your expression uses an operator of lower precedence than one used in your macro, the intended outcome can be wrong or even uncompilable. You can avoid some of these problems with judicious use of parentheses, like this:

```
#define MIN (x,y) (x) < (y) ? (x) : (y)
```

Even then you can create some odd code by passing just the right (er, wrong) expressions. The GNU documentation on C and the C preprocessor even has an entire section devoted to macro pitfalls (*https://oreil.ly/aKdZT*).

We don't need any macros just yet, but they're common enough that I want you to recognize them if you find them in the wild. The C preprocessor is actually quite an interesting entity in its own right. It's a great target for some independent research after you finish this book!

Custom Type Definitions

Beyond constants and macros, libraries often make use of another feature of C: the typedef operator. You can use typedef to assign an alias to some other type. That might sound unnecessary, and it technically is, but there are several cases where it is very convenient and leads to more readable, maintainable code.

We saw the use of some of these typedef aliases in Chapter 10. The byte, uint8_t, and uint32_t specifiers were all created with typedef. If the Arduino environment didn't provide those for you, you could create them yourself like so:

```
typedef unsigned char byte;
typedef unsigned char uint8_t;
typedef unsigned long int uint32_t;
```

The "_t" suffix is popular for these aliases. It's an easy way to highlight the fact that the name is an alias built with typedef.

You can also use typedef with the struct keyword to make more palatable names for your custom, rich data types. For example, we could have used typedef in "Defining Structures" on page 141 and defined our transaction like this:

```
typedef struct transaction {
  double amount;
  int day, month, year;
} transaction_t;

// Transaction variables can now be declared like this:
transaction_t bill;
transaction_t deposit;
```

This feature is not something strictly necessary for our simple library, but many libraries do use typedef to provide names for types that make more sense in the context of the library or that are simply easier to work with. Let's go ahead and define a type for any variables that might store one of our direction constants:

```
typedef signed char direction_t;
```

We'll stick with the signed version of char since we might find uses for negative values down the road. Negative numbers make great error codes if you are otherwise only expecting positive numbers, for example. Now let's use our new type to create some typed constants:

```
const direction_t STOP   = 0;
const direction_t LEFT   = 1;
const direction_t RIGHT  = 2;
```

```
const direction_t FORWARD  = 3;
const direction_t BACKWARD = 4;
```

Recall the discussion of `const` versus `#define` in "Constants: const versus #define" on page 191. This is one of those spots where we aren't really doing anything that demands one approach or the other, but the `const` approach does add some inherent documentation to our code that could be useful to other readers. And I should say that 90% of the time the first "other reader" that sees your code is you, but you after a few weeks or months away from the project. Hints about your intentions like the `direction_t` type can be very useful in jogging your own memory.

Our Car Project

Let's get going! This will be our "version one" project with some extra abstraction that should help as we break up this project into reusable pieces. (You can take a look at version 0 (*https://oreil.ly/Mr2ED*) if you want to start with a simple proof of functionality.) As you work with your own project, you may not have the motors wired up exactly as I do. Your navigation input (buttons or a joystick) might be connected a little differently. Test out your setup and don't be afraid of changing which pins get set HIGH or LOW in the various driving functions. Happily, that can all be tweaked here in software. The end goal is simply to get your car to roll forward when you push the joystick up.

Here's version 1 of our car build. As always, you can type this up yourself or just open *ch11/car1/car1.ino* (*https://oreil.ly/8kqQL*):

```
// Define the pins we're using for the joystick and the motor
#define LEFT_BTN   12
#define RIGHT_BTN  9
#define FWD_BTN    10
#define BKWD_BTN   11

#define AIN1 4
#define AIN2 5
#define BIN1 6
#define BIN2 7

// Define our direction type
typedef char direction_t;

// Define our direction constants
const direction_t STOP     = 0;
const direction_t LEFT     = 1;
const direction_t RIGHT    = 2;
const direction_t FORWARD  = 3;
const direction_t BACKWARD = 4;

void setup() {
  // Tell our board we want to write to the built-in LED
```

```
  pinMode(LED_BUILTIN, OUTPUT);

  // Accept input from the joystick pins
  pinMode(LEFT_BTN, INPUT_PULLUP);
  pinMode(RIGHT_BTN, INPUT_PULLUP);
  pinMode(FWD_BTN, INPUT_PULLUP);
  pinMode(BKWD_BTN, INPUT_PULLUP);

  // Send output to the motor pins
  pinMode(AIN1, OUTPUT);
  pinMode(AIN2, OUTPUT);
  pinMode(BIN1, OUTPUT);
  pinMode(BIN2, OUTPUT);

  // And make sure our LED is off
  digitalWrite(LED_BUILTIN, LOW);
}

void allstop() {
  digitalWrite(AIN1, LOW);
  digitalWrite(AIN2, LOW);
  digitalWrite(BIN1, LOW);
  digitalWrite(BIN2, LOW);
}

void forward() {
  digitalWrite(AIN1, LOW);
  digitalWrite(AIN2, HIGH);
  digitalWrite(BIN1, HIGH);
  digitalWrite(BIN2, LOW);
}

void backward() {
  digitalWrite(AIN1, HIGH);
  digitalWrite(AIN2, LOW);
  digitalWrite(BIN1, LOW);
  digitalWrite(BIN2, HIGH);
}

void left() {
  digitalWrite(AIN1, HIGH);
  digitalWrite(AIN2, LOW);
  digitalWrite(BIN1, LOW);
  digitalWrite(BIN2, LOW);
}

void right() {
  digitalWrite(AIN1, LOW);
  digitalWrite(AIN2, LOW);
  digitalWrite(BIN1, LOW);
  digitalWrite(BIN2, HIGH);
}
```

```
direction_t readDirection() {
  if (digitalRead(FWD_BTN) == LOW) {
    return FORWARD;
  }
  if (digitalRead(BKWD_BTN) == LOW) {
    return BACKWARD;
  }
  if (digitalRead(LEFT_BTN) == LOW) {
    return LEFT;
  }
  if (digitalRead(RIGHT_BTN) == LOW) {
    return RIGHT;
  }
  // No buttons were pressed, so return STOP
  return STOP;
}

void loop() {
  direction_t dir = readDirection();
  if (dir > 0) { // Driving!
    digitalWrite(LED_BUILTIN, HIGH);
    switch (dir) {
      case FORWARD:
        forward();
        break;
      case BACKWARD:
        backward();
        break;
      case LEFT:
        left();
        break;
      case RIGHT:
        right();
        break;
    }
  } else {
    // Stopping, or eventually we could handle errors, too
    digitalWrite(LED_BUILTIN, LOW);
    allstop();
  }
}
```

Feel free to take a break from the book at this point and just have some fun. :) Can you drive both forward and backward? When you move the joystick left or right, does the car turn the way you want? Can you parallel park between two stuffed animal obstacles? It might feel a little awkward following your car around with the tethered joystick, but we'll fix that shortly.

Multifile Projects

Welcome back! Hope you managed to safely parallel park your new roadster. With a working program as our baseline, let's break it up into some reusable parts.

C, as a language, does not really worry about where your code lives. As long as *gcc* can find all of the source files, header files, and libraries you mention in your code, it will produce usable output. Creating multifile projects for the Arduino IDE is a little different, however. The IDE manages some integration steps that would normally be left to you on the desktop. Since we're concentrating on microcontrollers at this point, we'll stick to what needs to be done in the Arduino IDE. If you are curious about building larger projects outside of Arduino, I'll again recommend Prinz and Crawford's *C in a Nutshell*.

We'll start by converting our current project into a multifile project with no change in functionality. Then we'll extend our robot car to support remote radio control and see how powerful shared code can be.

In our small car example, we have several functions devoted to making the car move. Those related functions are perfect for separating into their own file. They all serve a similiar purpose. Their related purpose is not necessary for creating separate files, but it's a popular means of organizing the pieces of a larger project. A small number of files, each with a small number of functions, can be easier to maintain and debug than a huge file with lots of functions. But if you break up functions randomly, it will be difficult to remember which files contain which functions.

The Arduino IDE gives us a few options for breaking up our projects: we can add new *.ino* files, we can include custom header files, or we can create and then import a custom library. The rest of this chapter looks at all three of these mechanisms.

Code (.ino) Files

To start, let's save this project under a new name so that we have a backup in case something goes awry and we want to refer back to a working project. From the "File" menu in the Arduino IDE, select the "Save As..." option. I chose the highly creative and original name *car2*. You are free to be as creative or even more so if the muse strikes.

Now let's take all five of our driving functions and move them to their own file. To add a new file, use the downward pointing triangle button on the right-hand side near the top. That button opens a small menu, as shown in Figure 11-3. Select "New Tab" from that menu.

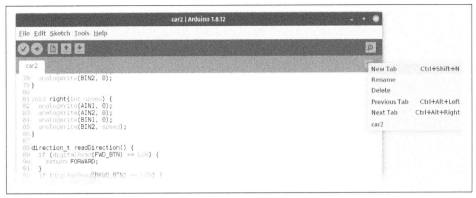

Figure 11-3. Creating a new tab in the Arduino IDE

Next, you'll be prompted to name the tab, as shown in Figure 11-4. Enter the name **drive.ino** in the field and then click the OK button.

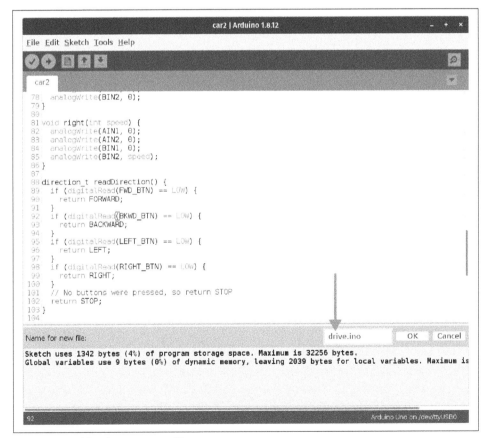

Figure 11-4. Naming our new file

You should now have a new tab named "drive" (with no suffix showing). Go ahead and cut the five driving functions (including `allstop()`) from the "car2" tab and then paste them into our new "drive" tab. That tab will end up with the following code (*ch11/car2/drive.ino (https://oreil.ly/pRodD)*):

```
void allstop() {
  digitalWrite(AIN1, LOW);
  digitalWrite(AIN2, LOW);
  digitalWrite(BIN1, LOW);
  digitalWrite(BIN2, LOW);
}

void forward() {
  digitalWrite(AIN1, LOW);
  digitalWrite(AIN2, HIGH);
  digitalWrite(BIN1, HIGH);
  digitalWrite(BIN2, LOW);
}

void backward() {
  digitalWrite(AIN1, HIGH);
  digitalWrite(AIN2, LOW);
  digitalWrite(BIN1, LOW);
  digitalWrite(BIN2, HIGH);
}

void left() {
  digitalWrite(AIN1, LOW);
  digitalWrite(AIN2, HIGH);
  digitalWrite(BIN1, LOW);
  digitalWrite(BIN2, LOW);
}

void right() {
  digitalWrite(AIN1, LOW);
  digitalWrite(AIN2, LOW);
  digitalWrite(BIN1, HIGH);
  digitalWrite(BIN2, LOW);
}
```

That's actually all the work required to separate these pieces of code! You now have your first multifile Arduino project. Click the Verify (checkmark) button to make sure your project still compiles in its new, two-file configuration. Everything should still work. You can even upload this to your controller and still drive your car.

If the project does not verify or upload, check to make sure you didn't drop a curly brace or perhaps grab an extra line from the original file. You should also make sure the name you picked for your newly separated file ends with that *.ino* extension.

The Arduino IDE performs a little magic for us with *.ino* files. Our main project file (*car2.ino* in the *car2* folder, in this case) is prepared first. Any other *.ino* files will then be included in alphabetical order. You may have noticed that our *drive.ino* file has no `#include` statements. And yet, we clearly use the pin constants defined in our main file. As far as the compiler is concerned, there is only one large *.ino* file to compile, so successive *.ino* files see all of the functions, `#defines`, and global variables from the files that came before. At this time, there is no way to change the order of the separate *.ino* files; they are always incorporated alphabetically.

Header Files

So how can all these separate files work together so seamlessly? The IDE adds one more piece of magic before loading these separate files. It creates a header file with *forward declarations* of all of the functions and global variables in your *.ino* file. Forward declarations are brief descriptions of what your function is named, what parameters it has, and what type of value it will return. They allow separate files to use a function without needing to have its full implementation. Each header, in turn, is automatically included in your main project file.

You can see the effect of this in our simple two-tab project. The *drive.ino* file does not need to include any extra information to make use of our `#define` pin entries. And the code in our main *car2.ino* file can call the functions defined in *drive.ino* without worrying about the ordering or specific location of the functions. In the end, both files fit together perfectly to complete our project.

You can also create your own header files. This can be nice for housekeeping. For example, if you have many `#define` statements, you could place them in their own header. Or if you want a low-tech means of sharing some directives between projects, you can make a copy of a header and put it in another project. It is largely up to you what makes the most sense for your own projects. Many successful makers out there have dozens or hundreds of projects each with one single *.ino* file. I just want to make sure you know how to split things into more manageable pieces if that one big file starts to overwhelm you.

In service of that goal, let's break up our main project just a little more. Let's try the trick of putting some of our `#define` directives in their own header file. We'll move the eight pin constants. Create a new tab as before, and name it **pins.h** when prompted. The new tab should show the full name of the file, *pins.h*, to help distinguish it from *.ino* files that hide the extension.

Cut the eight `#define` lines and the relevant comments from *car2* and paste them into *pins.h*. The result should look like *ch11/car2/pins.h* (*https://oreil.ly/pwQM6*):

```
// Define the pins we're using for the joystick and the motor

#ifndef PINS_H
#define PINS_H

#define LEFT_BTN  12
#define RIGHT_BTN 9
#define FWD_BTN   10
#define BKWD_BTN  11

#define AIN1 4
#define AIN2 5
#define BIN1 6
#define BIN2 7

#endif /* PINS_H */
```

Preventing Duplicate Includes

The first and last lines in *pins.h* might look a little strange. `#ifndef` and `#endif` are more preprocessor directives. `#ifndef` checks to see if a given name is "Not DEFined," and `#endif` is the end of that block, much like a closing curly brace ends a block statement in C. (There is also a `#ifdef` directive to test if a particular term is defined.)

Combined with the empty `#define PINS_H` line, these directives form an *include guard*. They prevent this header file from being included multiple times. Or more precisely, they prevent the contents of the header from being processed multiple times. This makes it safe to include a header, even if some other header may have already included the same header.

You'll likely see these `#ifdef` and `#ifndef` statements in many headers. They are a handy tool for environments that have to accommodate different values for different situations. In the Arduino IDE, for example, when you select a new development board, a series of these defined/not-defined tests makes sure that constants like `LED_BUILTIN` have the correct pin assigned for the board you chose.

Now we just need to add an include statement to our *car2* tab at the top of our file:

```
#include "pins.h"
```

You can check your work against my version 2 (*https://oreil.ly/EWAV9*). Your project should still verify (and upload) just as before. Feel free to give it a try and make sure you can still drive your car.

Pay close attention to the double quotes around our *pins.h* header name. Previous #include statements used angle brackets (<>: less than, greater than). The distinction is intentional. The angle brackets tell the compiler to look for the header in the standard include path. Typically, that means you are bringing in a header from a known library.

The quotes tell the compiler the file to be included is in the same folder as the file doing the including. Typically, that means you are bringing in a header file you wrote specifically for this project.

Again, divvying up a project is not a requirement or something you always do with large files, but it can be helpful. It allows you to concentrate on one part of your code without accidentally changing another part. If you collaborate with other programmers, working on separate files can also make it easier to combine your efforts at the end. In the end, though, it really is up to you and what you feel comfortable with.

Importing Custom Libraries

Beyond multiple *.ino* and *.h* files, though, you can also build your own Arduino IDE library. If you have code that you want to use in multiple projects or perhaps share with others via public code sites like GitHub, a library is a great choice.

Happily, creating a custom library doesn't require too much effort. You need at least one *.cpp* file and a matching header (*.h*) file. You can have more files, if needed, as well as a few niceties we'll discuss in the next section.

Facilitating Communication

Our robot car is spiffy, but following it around with a tethered joystick is clunky. A *radio-controlled* robot car would be even spiffier! We can do that, and using a library to manage that radio communication is a great way to guarantee we don't cross any signals—literally. We can use a library to make sure multiple parties have access to common definitions (say, the value for driving "forward"). We can also put the rules of a protocol into a library's functions. It's a bit like making sure everyone is speaking the same language.

Libraries can supply more than the vocabulary of this hypothetical language. They can also enforce the rules of conversation. Who speaks first? Who speaks next? Is a response required? Can there be more than one listener? You answer questions like these with the functions you write in your library. As long as two (or more) projects use the same library, the details you encoded in the library's functions will make sure everyone plays nicely together.

Let's create a library to send and receive radio signals. We'll create two separate projects that both use this library. We'll start by replacing the joystick that is currently wired to our car with a radio component. Then we'll create a controller project that pairs our newly liberated joystick with a similar radio. This does mean we need two microcontrollers, by the way. I'll use another Metro Mini, but they don't have to be identical. If you have some other controller lying around that is compatible with our radio and can use our library, any combination of controllers should work.

Retrofitting Our Car

Let's swap out the joystick for a radio transceiver. I'm using the nicely packaged RFM69HCW (*https://oreil.ly/JhUn8*) high-power breakout from Adafruit. It's about $10 and is reasonably straightforward to connect. Plus, it comes with some nice features like encrypted transmissions that can only be decrypted by a similar chip with the same encryption key (that you provide in code). Figure 11-5 shows the wiring diagram for our microcontroller, the motor driver, and our radio. I had to relocate several of the DRV8833 connections as the RFM69HCW requires the use of specific pins on our Metro Mini microcontroller (more on that in "Our radio-control library header" on page 255).

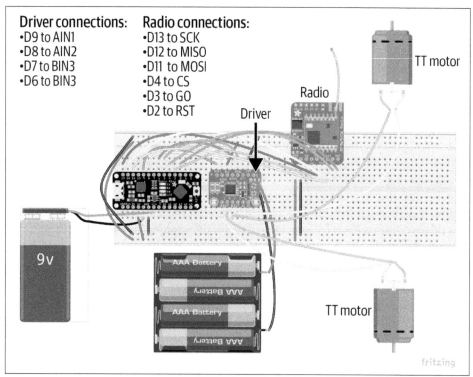

Driver connections:
- D9 to AIN1
- D8 to AIN2
- D7 to BIN3
- D6 to BIN3

Radio connections:
- D13 to SCK
- D12 to MISO
- D11 to MOSI
- D4 to CS
- D3 to GO
- D2 to RST

Figure 11-5. Wiring for the robot car with radio transceiver

Of course the power and ground pins should be connected as well. I used a 9V for the microcontroller (which in turn supplies power to the radio) and a separate power supply for the DRV8833. The lonely green wire attached to the top of the RFM69HCW is just a three-inch piece of wire serving as the simplest possible antenna.[1]

Figure 11-6 shows the assembled components, all ready to roll with no wires attached!

Figure 11-6. Our wire-free robot car

---

1 There are certainly fancier options (*https://oreil.ly/AEvxE*) available if you are so inclined or want to communicate over longer distances.

Well, no wires to a joystick, that is. The breadboard is rather lousy with wires. This *is* a bigger project than we've tackled so far. If a radio-controlled car isn't up your alley, feel free to skip to the next chapter. But before you go, check out "Creating the Library" on page 253 on creating the library code and its header file.

I'm using two separate power supplies to keep the motors separate from the micro-controller and the radio. If you have more experience powering Arduino projects and want to use a different configuration, go right ahead! The important part is that we have our radio ready to receive driving instructions.

Creating a Controller

We also need a new project to take input from our joystick and send that information out over the radio. Figure 11-7 shows the wiring. Only one battery is required for the controller; the radio can be safely powered from the 5V pin of our microcontroller.

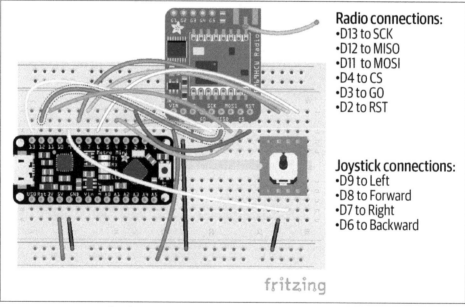

Radio connections:
- D13 to SCK
- D12 to MISO
- D11 to MOSI
- D4 to CS
- D3 to GO
- D2 to RST

Joystick connections:
- D9 to Left
- D8 to Forward
- D7 to Right
- D6 to Backward

Figure 11-7. Wiring for the radio controller

I powered the controller with a USB power pack plugged into the Metro Mini. Figure 11-8 shows the final result.

Figure 11-8. Our wire-free controller

Not the most glamorous of gadgets, but it does send radio signals! At least, it will once we add a little code.

Creating the Library

The code for both our car and our controller will require our radio library, so let's start there. We'll be creating one header file and one *.cpp* file to accommodate the C++-centric nature of the Arduino IDE. The actual code will still be (mostly) vanilla C, it just needs to live in a file with that *.cpp* extension.

How you go about writing this code is really up to you. You can write everything in one file and then separate out the parts that go into the header (much like we did earlier in this chapter). You can also use the header as a sort of outline or plan. Fill out the header with your constants and names of your functions, then go create the *.cpp* file to implement those functions. Regardless of which path sounds better to you, we need to put the files in a specific place before the IDE will recognize them.

The libraries folder

We place all of the files for our library inside one folder that goes in the *libraries* folder wherever your Arduino sketches live. On my Linux box, that's the *Arduino* folder in my home directory. If you're not sure where that folder is on your system, you can check the preferences in the Arduino IDE. From the File menu, select the Preferences option. You should see a dialog similar to Figure 11-9. Notice the "Sketchbook location" toward the top. That's where the *libraries* folder needs to go. If there isn't one there already, go ahead and create that now.

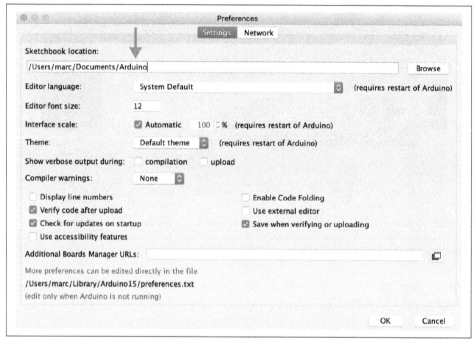

Figure 11-9. The Sketchbook location preference setting

It's actually useful that we're looking at this folder now, since we need to manually install the library for our radio breakout. It will go in this same folder. I'm using the radio library (*https://oreil.ly/YLphd*) written by the folks at Adafruit.[2] Download the ZIP archive from the green "Code" drop-down button. Unzip that file and rename the resulting folder **RadioHead**. Place this *RadioHead* folder in the *libraries* folder, and that's it.

---

2 *Forked* would be a better verb than *written*. The Adafruit library is based on the AirSpayce RadioHead (*https://oreil.ly/nP82M*) library written by Mike McCauley.

Well, that's it for the radio library. We still need to make a folder for our own, yet to be written, library. Inside the *libraries* folder, create a new folder and pick a name for your custom library. Since this is a radio control library for a *robot car*, and the title of this book ends in those two letters, I chose to name mine *SmalleRC*. You are under no pressure to use such delightful, nerdy puns for your library names, by the way. This is where the "custom" adjective comes in. Customize your library however you like!

Our radio-control library header

Inside your new library folder, then, let's create our files. I'll use the second approach and start with the header file, *SmalleRC.h* (*https://oreil.ly/koHtr*).

We'll load the headers we need for our radio work as well as the *Arduino.h* header in case we rely on any Arduino-specific functions in our library code. We'll define several constants and then provide some function prototypes:

```
#ifndef SMALLERC_H              ❶
#define SMALLERC_H

#include "Arduino.h"            ❷
#include <SPI.h>                ❸
#include <RH_RF69.h>            ❹

#define RF69_FREQ 915.0         ❺
#define RFM69_CS     4
#define RFM69_INT    3
#define RFM69_RST    2
#define LED         13

#define rc_INIT_SUCCESS  1      ❻
#define rc_INIT_FAILED  -1
#define rc_FREQ_FAILED  -2

// Define our direction type
typedef signed char direction_t;   ❼

// Define our directions
const direction_t rc_STOP     = 0;
const direction_t rc_LEFT     = 1;
const direction_t rc_RIGHT    = 2;
const direction_t rc_FORWARD  = 3;
const direction_t rc_BACKWARD = 4;

char rc_start();                ❽
void rc_send(int d);
int  rc_receive();

#endif /* SMALLERC_H */
```

❶ We'll use a header guard like we did with *pins.h*.

❷ Our library code may need some of the Arduino-specific types or functions, so we include this header. It is automatically included in our main project by the IDE, which is why we haven't seen this `#include` before.

❸ The SPI (Serial Peripheral Interface (*https://oreil.ly/eZmyO*)) header allows us to perform complex communication (i.e., something other than `HIGH` and `LOW` or single values) with a peripheral using only a few wires. We'll use this type of connection with our radio breakout board. Our microcontroller has very specific pins for SPI, so we don't have to specify which ones to use. Figure 11-7 shows the correct connections to make.

❹ We'll need the RH_RF69 library we just installed to talk to the radio.

❺ While SPI takes care of most communication needs, these `define` entries fill in some details needed by the RH_RF69 library to operate our radio, including the frequency to use (RF69_FREQ; use 433 MHz in Europe and 868 or 915 MHz in the Americas) and which pins handle the interrupts and resets.

❻ We'll define a few of our own constants to help coordinate the initialization of our radio. We'll distinguish failures in a way that can help us debug any issues.

❼ We can put our `typedef` here so that everyone importing this library has access to the `direction_t` type alias. We'll also include our directions.

❽ These are the forward declarations (also called function prototypes) for our library. We'll need to write the complete functions in our *.cpp* file, and those functions will have the same names and parameters as the ones declared here.

That's quite a lot of detail in one header file! But that's what header files are for. In the absence of any other documentation, reading a header file should tell you just about everything you need to know to use a library.

 I'm cheating a bit with this header. For an Arduino library that you intend to share with others, you wouldn't normally dictate the pins to use in connecting peripherals. We have the ability to make this header match up with our physical project, but other users might not have the same controller or the same free pins. See "Sharing online" on page 264 for some tips on digging deeper into shareable library creation. For libraries meant solely for your own projects, though, you're allowed a shortcut or two.

Our radio-control library code

To complete our library, then, we need to write some code and implement the functions that were prototyped in our header file. This code is not very complex, but it does have several novel parts related to enabling and communicating with our radio. You can type it in yourself or pull up *SmalleRC.cpp* (*https://oreil.ly/pc5v4*) in your editor:

```
#include "SmalleRC.h"                              ❶

RH_RF69 rf69(RFM69_CS, RFM69_INT);                 ❷

char rc_start() {                                  ❸
  pinMode(LED, OUTPUT);
  pinMode(RFM69_RST, OUTPUT);
  digitalWrite(RFM69_RST, LOW);

  // manual reset
  digitalWrite(RFM69_RST, HIGH);
  delay(10);
  digitalWrite(RFM69_RST, LOW);
  delay(10);

  if (!rf69.init()) {
    return rc_INIT_FAILED;
  }

  if (!rf69.setFrequency(RF69_FREQ)) {
    return rc_FREQ_FAILED;
  }

  // range from 14-20 for power
  // 2nd arg must be true for 69HCW
  rf69.setTxPower(17, true);

  // The encryption key is up to you, but must be
  // the same for both the car and the controller
  uint8_t key[] = {                                ❹
    0x01, 0x02, 0x03, 0x04, 0x05, 0x06, 0x07, 0x08,
    0x01, 0x02, 0x03, 0x04, 0x05, 0x06, 0x07, 0x08
  };
  rf69.setEncryptionKey(key);

  pinMode(LED, OUTPUT);
  return rc_INIT_SUCCESS;
}

void rc_send(direction_t d) {                      ❺
  uint8_t packet[1] = { d };
  rf69.send(packet, 1);
  rf69.waitPacketSent();
}
```

```
direction_t rc_receive() {                              ❻
  uint8_t buf[RH_RF69_MAX_MESSAGE_LEN];
  uint8_t len = sizeof(buf);
  if (rf69.recv(buf, &len)) {
    if (len == 0) {
      return -1;
    }
    buf[len] = 0;
    return (direction_t)buf[0];
  }
  return STOP;
}
```

❶ Include our recently built header file with all the pins, directions, and radio configuration information.

❷ Create a radio control object similar to the NeoPixel objects in previous projects.

❸ Initialize the radio. This code is based on the examples included with the library we installed. See "Sharing online" on page 264 for a few more details on examples and other library documentation.

❹ Part of the radio initialization is setting an encryption key that will make sure only other radios using the same key can communicate with us. These values are exactly those from the example. Feel free to change them, just make sure the key is 16 bytes.

❺ A simple function to broadcast a direction. The radio library expects a packet of uint8_t values, so we create a one-element array to match. The library can send longer messages, of course, but we only need to send this single value.

❻ The receiving function to read any directions coming from the controller. Again, the radio library can handle longer messages, but we only need the first byte, which should contain our direction. If there's no message at all, return -1 to let the caller know nothing was ready. Otherwise, return the direction we received or STOP as a default.

With our custom library in place, we can look at writing the actual projects for the car and the controller. But we sure whizzed through this code! If you're curious about radio communication, I encourage you to play with the examples (*https://oreil.ly/ 7YRVZ*) from the radio library to get a better feel for what possibilities and limits exist.

Updating the Car Project

Now we need to write the code for the car. (Feel free to review the physical setup of the car and breakouts in "Retrofitting Our Car" on page 250.) Essentially, we are going to replace the logic for polling the joystick with a call to check for data from the radio. We'll pause for a few milliseconds to avoid starting and stopping the motors too quickly. Otherwise, we'll run a pretty tight loop so that the car feels responsive to our remote controller.

I based this version (*car3* (*https://oreil.ly/Dk0JC*)) on the *car2* project, which had the separate *pins.h* and *drive.ino* files. We no longer need the pins for the joystick in this project, so the header file is a bit shorter:

```
#ifndef PINS_H
#define PINS_H

#define AIN1 9
#define AIN2 8
#define BIN1 6
#define BIN2 7

#endif /* PINS_H */
```

The driving functions are completely unchanged so I'll leave those out, but you can review the code ("Code (.ino) Files" on page 244) if you want. The code for the main *car3.ino* (*https://oreil.ly/JcLJl*) file should feel familiar, but obviously we need to include the header file of our new radio library:

```
#include "pins.h"
#include "SmalleRC.h"

void setup() {
  Serial.begin(115200);
  // Send output to the motor pins
  pinMode(AIN1, OUTPUT);
  pinMode(AIN2, OUTPUT);
  pinMode(BIN1, OUTPUT);
  pinMode(BIN2, OUTPUT);

  if (rc_start() != rc_INIT_SUCCESS) {
    Serial.println("Failed to initialize radio.");
  }
}

void loop() {
  direction_t dir = rc_receive();
  if (dir > 0) { // Driving!
    switch (dir) {
      case rc_FORWARD:
        forward();
        break;
```

```
    case rc_BACKWARD:
      backward();
      break;
    case rc_LEFT:
      left();
      break;
    case rc_RIGHT:
      right();
      break;
  }
  delay(20);
} else {
  // Stopping, or eventually we could handle errors, too
  allstop();
  }
}
```

Notice that I'm using the new navigation constants (like rc_LEFT) defined in the *SmalleRC.h* file. But that's really all the code we need now to drive our car! This is one of the many benefits from separating out chunks of common code. By building on that shared code, you can more quickly create some very interesting projects.

There's no good way to test this new *car3* project just yet, but go ahead and upload it to your microcontroller. If nothing else, you can use the Serial Monitor tool to ensure that there were no errors in starting up the radio to receive. I went with the "no news is good news" approach to errors in the setup() function, but feel free to alter that a bit to produce a success message if you like.

 Now that the Arduino IDE knows about our *SmalleRC* library, you can actually edit the source files of that library in place and then reverify or reupload the project. If you do have some trouble starting the radio, for example, add some debugging calls to Serial.println() in *SmalleRC.cpp*. Once you have the problem isolated and solved, you can remove the debugging statements and upload once more.

Getting It Under Control

Next up is getting the controller programmed. (Again, look back at "Creating a Controller" on page 252 if you still need to build the physical remote control.) Here we take the joystick polling and instead of sending the results to the motors, we broadcast any directional information over our radio. This is a pretty small project thanks to the library, so I left it in a single *ch11/controller/controller.ino* (*https://oreil.ly/rSPTh*) file:

```
#include "SmalleRC.h"

#define LEFT_BTN   9
#define RIGHT_BTN  7
#define FWD_BTN    8
#define BKWD_BTN   6

void setup() {
  Serial.begin(115200);
  // Accept input from the joystick pins
  pinMode(LEFT_BTN, INPUT_PULLUP);
  pinMode(RIGHT_BTN, INPUT_PULLUP);
  pinMode(FWD_BTN, INPUT_PULLUP);
  pinMode(BKWD_BTN, INPUT_PULLUP);

  if (rc_start() != rc_INIT_SUCCESS) {
    Serial.println("Failed to initialize radio.");
  }
}

direction_t readDirection() {
  if (digitalRead(FWD_BTN) == LOW) {
    return rc_FORWARD;
  }
  if (digitalRead(BKWD_BTN) == LOW) {
    return rc_BACKWARD;
  }
  if (digitalRead(LEFT_BTN) == LOW) {
    return rc_LEFT;
  }
  if (digitalRead(RIGHT_BTN) == LOW) {
    return rc_RIGHT;
  }
  // No buttons were pressed, so return STOP
  return rc_STOP;
}

void loop() {
  direction_t dir = readDirection();
  rc_send(dir);
  delay(10);
}
```

We could have put the logic of the readDirection() function right inside our loop() function, but I like how concise loop() is with this small abstraction.

Try verifying this new project and if you hit any snags, add a few more Serial.println() statements. And remember, you can also add those to your library code if needed.

For projects like this, where so much work is done in libraries (not just our custom one, but also libraries like RF_RH69) println() calls may not help with every problem. Bugs in downloaded libraries do happen, but they're pretty rare. I find many problems are caused by me getting some of the wiring wrong. So if things still aren't working, try double-checking your connections between the microcontroller and the various peripherals.

Go Driving!

No code. No diagrams. No instructions. Just another point in this chapter where I wholly encourage you to go play. :) Try powering up both projects and see what happens when you move the joystick. There are definitely things that could go wrong! If the wiring isn't quite right, for example, the car might move, but not in the direction you meant. (I accidentally swapped the right-side motor input pins when moving the project to a full-size breadboard, for example. The right wheel turned, but in the wrong direction.) Or if we have the wrong pins connected to the joystick, we might not send any signal at all.

If the car doesn't budge, it's time yet again to break out your debugging skills. You can have both projects connected to your computer at the same time, by the way. They will simply be on different serial ports. (Remember, you can set which port you use for your microcontroller through the Tools menu in the Arduino IDE.) You can use Serial.println() statements to make sure your inputs, sends, receives, and drives are all doing what you expect them to do. Just watch out for success! When you do get things working, it's surprisingly easy to drive your car right off the desk and leave a string of electronics dangling from your USB cable. Or, you know, so I'm told.

Documentation and Distribution

Once your library is working and you've had enough fun zipping around your room, it's time to think about adding a little documentation to your project. Documentation is great. Not just for other programmers who might use your library, either. If you step away from a project even just for a few days, any documentation you wrote can be surprisingly useful for helping you get your own mind back up to speed.

Keywords

One very simple piece of documentation that you can add for use with the Arduino IDE is a single text file called *keywords.txt*. For a custom library, it should contain two columns, separated by a tab. The first column contains functions, constants, and data types defined in your library. The second column should contain one entry from Table 11-1 indicating the category of the name in the first column.

Table 11-1. Keyword categories for documenting Arduino libraries

Category Name	Purpose	Appearance
KEYWORD1	data types	orange, bold
KEYWORD2	functions	orange, plain
LITERAL1	constants	blue, plain

While limited, these few categories can still help programmers who rely on the IDE cues for things like whether or not they spelled a function name correctly.

For our library, then, we could create the following entries (again, separated by a tab) in our own *keywords.txt* (*https://oreil.ly/o3KjH*) file:

```
rc_INIT_SUCCESS LITERAL1
rc_INIT_FAILED  LITERAL1
rc_FREQ_FAILED  LITERAL1

direction_t KEYWORD1

rc_STOP LITERAL1
rc_LEFT LITERAL1
rc_RIGHT    LITERAL1
rc_FORWARD  LITERAL1
rc_BACKWARD LITERAL1

rc_start    KEYWORD2
rc_send KEYWORD2
rc_receive  KEYWORD2
```

Basically, that list is everything we defined in our *SmalleRC.h* file minus the few constants that were used only by the radio library. If you restart your IDE at this point, the functions and other names listed in the file will share the same syntax highlighting that the core language uses! Very cool.

Be sure to use real tab characters to separate the columns in *keywords.txt*. Spaces will not work. Many editors (like VS Code, for example) have a reasonable setting that turns all tabs into the appropriate number of spaces when the file is saved. There are many reasons that quiet change can be useful in source files, but we don't want it here.

If you can't temporarily disable this feature in your editor of choice, *keywords.txt* really is just a text file. You can create or edit it using any text editor, including very simple ones like Notepad in Windows 10 or TextEdit in macOS.

Including examples

Including a few example projects with your library is another great addition that doesn't require too much effort. You simply create an *examples* folder in the folder with your library code and *keywords.txt* file. Inside *examples*, then, you can place a few project folders. (Use the entire folder, not just the *.ino* file inside.)

Example projects should be short and sweet. Don't include unnecessary features that don't make use of the library if at all possible. You want a new user to see the important parts of your library and how they fit within a sketch. If your library is fairly rich, don't be afraid of providing several smaller examples that each focus on a particular aspect of the library.

Of course, you will find the other end of that "smaller, focused" spectrum in the wild. Sometimes a single example contains a demonstration of every single feature in a library. While these expansive examples do highlight the use of a library, they can make it more difficult for an outsider to extract details. If you're only trying to learn about one or two of the functions in a library, big examples can be overwhelming.

But any example is better than no examples! If you only have the energy for the single, comprehensive approach, include it. If you host it somewhere public like GitHub, you might even invite other users to contribute some focused examples from their own projects.

Sharing online

If you do get serious about sharing your code, you'll want to check out the official Library Guide (*https://oreil.ly/hB0rX*) online, as well as the excellent Library Specification (*https://oreil.ly/uifGf*) document. There are a few more things you can add to your library folder if you want it to feel polished. You can even get your library to work with the Library Manager in the IDE. A quick heads-up, though: these docs (reasonably) use C++. C++ has many more facilities for sharing the appropriate parts of your code while hiding the implementation details. There are definitely bits of syntax that will be new to you, but hopefully nothing too overwhelming.

As a first step toward publishing your library, check out the FAQ (*https://oreil.ly/3y4IT*) direct from the Arduino team.

Next Steps

Even if you never publish a library, we have seen how to manage larger projects with several tricks including preprocessor macros, type aliasing, and using multiple tabs in the Arduino IDE. We also covered creating simple libraries that you can manually install on your system to share between your own projects.

It's useful to remember that the tab and library stuff is peculiar to the Arduino IDE. Other IDEs or environments may have their own quirks, but you can almost always find a way to use multiple files when needed. The main goal is to keep you productive with whatever tools you choose.

I mentioned that you might want to know a little C++ if you publish any libraries. C++ in general is an excellent topic to explore after this book. In the next chapter, we'll look at a more advanced project as a stepping-stone out into the wider world. I'll also suggest a few other topics worth considering as you continue to expand your C and Arduino skills.

CHAPTER 12

Next Next Steps

First off, congratulations for making it this far! We have toured a pretty impressive breadth of the C programming language and the Arduino microcontroller ecosystem. Remember that first "Hello, World" program or that first blinking LED? You know a lot more about both worlds now, and I hope you're eager to continue expanding your skills.

In this final chapter, we'll look at one last project that connects your Arduino skills to the Internet of Things. The world of IoT is growing daily and will provide plenty of opportunities to try out new things, but we'll also cover a few other topics you might look into next.

Intermediate and Advanced Topics

There are so many paths you can take from here. The array of sensors and displays available these days is truly astonishing. Go exploring! You'll find your own inspirations and projects to tackle, which will lead to more exploring and more inspiration. My most enjoyable adventures have come from specific project ideas. I wanted an animated LED hourglass for part of a Halloween costume, so I found a capable, wearable microcontroller and some dense LED strips.[1] I had such fun with the LEDs on that project that I decided to create some weatherproof lighting for my backyard. With WiFi available to makers like us on small budgets, I could even let guests pick

---

[1] Again from Adafruit, I used the Gemma M0 (*https://oreil.ly/ZQ5JB*) and carved up one of their 144 LED/ meter (*https://oreil.ly/HlJGk*) RGBW strips to sew the hourglass onto a shirt. I powered the whole thing with a USB battery pack (*https://oreil.ly/2fpE0*) and barely dented the charge after more than four hours of continuous operation.

the colors and other effects. The success of the WiFi feature in turn propelled me to create a miniature weather station to feed my inner meteorologist.

The key to success for all those projects was picking a fairly focused goal. For example, in the next section we'll dip our toes into the world of IoT with a simple project that takes a temperature reading from the TMP36 components we've used already and reports it to a cloud service over WiFi. If you really want to cement the new knowledge and skills you've gained through the projects and examples in this book, pick your own mini project and make it a reality!

IoT and Arduino

It wouldn't do to have a chapter with no code, so let's look at one last project that introduces some really fun avenues you can explore on the way to creating your own gadgets. The Internet of Things is exploding, and Arduino is perfectly suited for playing in that space. Let's look at a simplified version of my weather station project. We'll use a WiFi-capable microcontroller to report sensor data to a cloud API.

The circuit for this project is fairly simple. We need a WiFi-capable microcontroller or a WiFi breakout that you can connect to your controller like we did with the RF breakout in "Importing Custom Libraries" on page 249. I chose the HUZZAH32 Feather (*https://oreil.ly/aySPa*) from Adafruit. It has some impressive specs like more than 500KB of SRAM and 4MB of flash in addition to the integrated WiFi support. The sensor is the same TMP36 we used in "Sensors and Analog Input" on page 197. I also added an OLED display so I could watch the output without being tied to a computer to access the Serial Monitor, but this display is definitely optional. Figure 12-1 shows the wiring diagram and my actual "station" up and running on a breadboard.

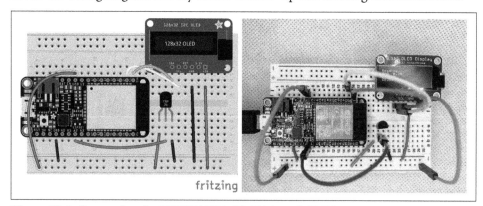

Figure 12-1. Connecting the HUZZAH32, TMP36, and OLED

The OLED uses a library provided by Adafruit that you can import through the Manage Libraries dialog of the IDE. Enter **SSD1306** in the search field and look for the "Adafruit SSD1306" library. It should be close to the top.

We also need to pick a cloud service provider and find a library for communicating with them. I use Adafruit.io (*https://io.adafruit.com*) for these types of projects, but any IoT cloud service will likely work. AWS, Google, and Azure all have IoT solutions, for example.

For Adafruit.io, we can use the Library Manager to find our communication library. Search for "adafruit io arduino" and then scroll down a bit to find the actual library called "Adafruit IO Arduino." Installing this library requires quite a few dependencies, such as the HTTP and message queue libraries, but the Library Manager will handle that for you automatically and prompt you to install those dependencies. You might have some of the listed dependencies like the NeoPixel library already, but the Library Manager isn't quite smart enough to show only the missing ones. When you do install the dependencies, though, only those that are missing will be added.

I won't go through the details of signing up, but once you have an account with your chosen provider, you'll almost certainly need a few credentials to configure the library. Adafruit.io, for example, requires a unique username and access key. Let's put this cloud service information in a separate *config.h* (*https://oreil.ly/t6UO6*) file where we can also include our WiFi details:

```
#include "AdafruitIO_WiFi.h"

#define IO_USERNAME   "userNameGoesHere"
#define IO_KEY        "ioKeyGoesHere"
#define WIFI_SSID     "HomeWifi"
#define WIFI_PASS     "password"
```

Happily, that library also contains a more generic WiFi library as a dependency. That double duty is nice for us—we don't have to go through separate steps to configure both the WiFi and our access to the cloud. But we do still have to do a little bit of setup work to make sure we can communicate with the cloud. We'll add that code in with the stuff necessary to use our nifty OLED display in the setup() function. As always, feel free to type this in yourself, or grab *ch12/temp_web/temp_web.ino* (*https://oreil.ly/muYAu*):

```
#include <SPI.h>                              ❶
#include <Wire.h>
#include <Adafruit_GFX.h>
#include <Adafruit_SSD1306.h>

// Use credentials from config.h to set up our feed
#include "config.h"                           ❷
AdafruitIO_WiFi io(IO_USERNAME, IO_KEY, WIFI_SSID, WIFI_PASS);
AdafruitIO_Feed *smallerc = io.feed("smallerc");

// Set up our OLED
#define SCREEN_WIDTH 128 // OLED width, in pixels
#define SCREEN_HEIGHT 32 // OLED height, in pixels
#define OLED_RESET    4 // Reset pin #
```

```
#define SCREEN_ADDRESS 0x3C // 128x32 screen
Adafruit_SSD1306 display(SCREEN_WIDTH, SCREEN_HEIGHT,    ❸
    &Wire, OLED_RESET);
char statusline[22] = "Starting...";

// A few things for keeping an average temperature reading
#define ADJUST 3.33 /* my office reads about 3 degrees C cold */
float total = 0.0;
int   count = 0;

void setup() {
  Serial.begin(115200);
  // SSD1306_SWITCHCAPVCC = generate voltage from 3.3V internally
  if(!display.begin(SSD1306_SWITCHCAPVCC, SCREEN_ADDRESS)) {
    Serial.println(F("SSD1306 allocation failed"));    ❹
    for(;;); // Don't proceed, loop forever
  }

  // Show Adafruit splash screen initialized by the display library
  display.display();

  // Now set up the connection to adafruit.io
  Serial.print("Connecting to Adafruit IO");
  io.connect();                                        ❺
  // wait for a connection
  while(io.status() < AIO_CONNECTED) {
    Serial.print(".");
    delay(500);
  }

  // we are connected
  Serial.println();
  Serial.println(io.statusText());

  // Set up our display for simple (if small) text
  display.clearDisplay();
  display.setTextSize(1);       // Normal 1:1 pixel scale
  display.setTextColor(SSD1306_WHITE); // Draw white text
  display.setCursor(0, 0);      // Start at top-left corner
  display.cp437(true);          // Use 'Code Page 437' font
  display.println(statusline);  // Show our starting status
  display.display();            // Update the actual display
}

void loop() {
  // put your main code here, to run repeatedly:
  int reading = analogRead(A2);                        ❻
  float voltage = reading / 1024.0;
  if (count == 0) {
    total = voltage;
  } else {
    total += voltage;
```

```
  }
  count++;
  float avg = total / count;
  float tempC = (avg - 0.5) * 100;
  float tempF = tempC * 1.8 + 32;
  if (count % 100 == 0) {
    // Update our display every 10 seconds                ❼
    display.clearDisplay();
    display.setCursor(0, 0);
    display.println(statusline);
    display.print(reading);
    display.print("  ");
    display.println(voltage);
    display.print(tempC);
    display.println("\370 C");
    display.print(tempF);
    display.println("\370 F");
    display.display();
    strcpy(statusline, "Reading...");
  }
  if (count % 600 == 0) {
    // Update our IoT feed every minute
    smallerc->save(tempF);                                ❽
    strcpy(statusline, "Feed updated");
  }
  delay(100);
}
```

❶ Include the various header files needed to communicate with the libraries that draw on our OLED.

❷ With the credentials from *config.h*, create an I/O object (`io`) and establish a connection to the Adafruit IO service, then specify which feed we will update.

❸ Instantiate our `display` object using constants and referencing the `Wire` library.

❹ Attempt to connect to the display. If that fails, print an error message and do not continue. If you do get stuck here, it's likely a problem in your wiring. Double-check the connections and make sure your display also has power.

❺ Make sure we can use the feed from ❷. Wait (potentially forever) until it's ready. If you can't connect, you might try using your credentials in a browser to verify the combination of user and key works. You can also test out your WiFi connection with a separate project. Under the File menu in the IDE, look for the Examples submenu, find your board, and pick something simple like *HTTPClient*.

❻ Read the current analog value from our TMP36 sensor and update the average, running temperature.

❼ Update our display with some nice text on the temperature and the current cloud status. The API for this display is similar to the functions we use with `Serial`.

❽ Once a minute, report the simple temperature in Fahrenheit to our feed. The next time through `loop()`, we'll note the update in our status line on the OLED.

You can certainly turn controllers like the HUZZAH32 into their own web servers and just get readings directly in your browser, but services like Adafuit.io make it easy to get fancier reports, such as the small graph of temperatures over a few minutes shown in Figure 12-2. These services typically support connecting to yet more services as well. For example, If This Then That (IFTTT) (*https://ifttt.com*) allows you to use events reported to Adafruit.io to trigger actions like sending an email or turning on smart home devices.

Figure 12-2. Graph of our reported temperatures

This little project is just the briefest of introductions to the Internet of Things. Heck, just the fun combinations possible through IFTTT could fill their own book. IoT books and blog posts abound, covering everything from user interface design for small devices to enterprise mesh configurations. This is a fun, dynamic area, and you certainly have the skills to dive in if you're curious to learn more.

Arduino Source Code

There are so many neat Arduino projects out there and so many of their authors are doing it for the joy of creating. They put their hardware specs and source code online and actively participate in the Arduino forums (*https://forum.arduino.cc*). I heartily encourage you to read some of that source code. You have the skills to understand the code in those projects now, and seeing how other programmers tackle problems can help you learn new tricks.

You can also access the source code (*https://oreil.ly/ekC2v*) behind the many boards supported out of the gate by the Arduino IDE. The various ArduinoCore packages cover the C and C++ content that goes into the Arduino "language" we discussed in "The Arduino Environment" on page 189. It'll be dense reading, to be sure, but you might be surprised how much of the basics you can pick up.

Other Microcontrollers

Of course, Arduino isn't the only microcontroller game in town. Mitchel Davis has a really enjoyable series (*https://oreil.ly/iN1Fj*) on YouTube documenting his journey from programming on Arduino to more limited controllers like the STM8. His examples are often in C, and you can see some of the more arcane topics we covered like bit-wise operators on full display.

Going the other direction toward more powerful controllers, the Raspberry Pi (*https://raspberrypi.org*) platform deserves a mention as well. These tiny computers are full-fledged desktop systems capable of running a complete Linux distribution—including running all of the developer tools like *gcc*. What's more, Pis come with the same kinds of GPIO (general purpose I/O) connections as the microcontrollers we've worked with in this book. You can use the same types of sensors and outputs and write C programs to drive them. And you get to compile those programs right on the hardware where the peripherals are attached! You can take some of the really clever projects, such as the MagicMirror (*https://oreil.ly/p4emq*), and add motion detectors so the mirror lights up only when someone is nearby to make use of it, making it even more magical.

If nothing else, I hope this book has given you the confidence to try tackling these types of projects. It's a gratifying world that lends itself to mastery. Unlike enterprise engineering projects that literally span the globe, you can concentrate on really learning the details of something like the Metro Mini controller from so many of our examples. You don't need eight different toolchains to get that LED blinking. You don't need a dozen programmers to debug a photoresistor night-light. As one of the reviewers for this book, Alex Faber, put it, there's no cruft to get in the way of the craft. I couldn't agree more.

Industry C/C++

You also aren't limited to tinkering with C at home. Arthur C. Clarke's many futures (*2001: A Space Odyssey, 2010: Odyssey Two*) are now our past, but computers and artificial intelligence figure quite prominently in our present. If you are interested in pursuing C programming as a career, search any tech job site and you will find hundreds of jobs for C programmers from entry level positions to senior architects. You can intern with a Linux kernel group or help program embedded controllers. You can get a job working on tiny toy drones or program sensors that keep the world's largest factories running.

Legacy code maintenance still requires good C programmers and pays well enough for said programmers to build a nice financial legacy for their progeny. Gaming systems need really, *really* fast code for both the game engines and the consoles they run on.

Supercomputers and microcontrollers both make use of C in a variety of environments. While it might be more obvious that microcontrollers need efficient code, massive supercomputers want every possible cycle of CPU (or, these days, GPU) time to go toward completing their calculations. C excels at providing that level of control, and companies know they need programmers who excel at making their expensive machines go fast. Just about any field you can think of these days is computerized, and anywhere they are pushing the limits of hardware (the tiniest, the deepest, the coldest, the fastest, etc.), you can find C programmers helping push those boundaries.

Back to the Future

Many languages have cropped up since C was first developed in the 1970s. Many more languages will undoubtedly appear in the years and decades to come. C remains so relevant precisely because of that extra control and speed it provides. Many more "advanced" languages like Java retain the ability to load native libraries written in C with the same kinds of header files we wrote for Arduino. Go can also call C functions. Working on embedded systems with Rust, but that one component only has C support? Rust can pull in C as well.

Just about everywhere you go in the computer programming world these days, you will find C. From its ubiquitous control statements to integration via native libraries, knowing C connects you to so much more of this world than you probably imagined. All I can say in closing is that I hope you keep imagining. Imagine new projects. Imagine new libraries. And then get that imagination running on hardware. C is a great tool for reifying those digital dreams. After working through this book, I hope you feel confident using it.

Hardware and Software

I try to point out any specific hardware parts or software packages where I first use them, but I also want to give you a quick list of the various components for easy reference. I wasn't paid for mentioning any products nor do the various owners and manufacturers endorse my book. The glowing opinions I express here are entirely my own. :)

Getting the Code

The C examples and Arduino Sketches are all available online at *https://github.com/l0y/smallerc*. Most examples have links to their particular files, but you can also download the archive using the drop-down shown in Figure A-1.

For the C examples, there's not really anything else to do. You can open any of the examples in your editor of choice. You can make and save your changes, then compile the examples right there in the same folder.

For the various sketches, you may want to drag each sketch folder over to your Arduino Sketchbook location as you work on it. (This location is set in the Arduino IDE preferences, as shown in Figure 11-9 from "The libraries folder" on page 254.) This will make sure you have access to any libraries you may have installed. It also means you can look in the "usual spot" for these projects after you're done with the book.

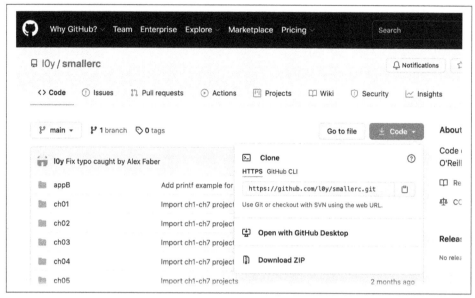

Figure A-1. Downloading the examples archive from GitHub

Getting the Hardware: Adafruit

A lot of the physical gear I use throughout the examples in this book comes from Adafruit. They have an amazing selection of controllers and components, along with some of the most fun, complete, nerdy tutorials you can find on the web. I do most of my shopping directly at their site (*https://adafruit.com*), but you can also find many of their parts through Amazon (*https://oreil.ly/CyB1X*) and Digi-Key (*https://digi key.com*). Table A-1 lists the microcontrollers I used in the many Arduino projects. Table A-2 lists the peripherals and components I used by chapter. Where I used a component in multiple projects, I went ahead and listed it in every chapter it appeared.

Table A-1. Microcontrollers and prototyping

Microcontroller	Specs
Metro Mini (*https://oreil.ly/KxFf0*) (2x)	ATmega328, 32KB flash, 2KB SRAM
Trinket M0 (*https://oreil.ly/R2fui*)	32-bit ATSAMD21E18, 256KB flash, 32KB SRAM
HUZZAH32 Feather (*https://oreil.ly/p5Ldy*)	Tensilica LX6, WROOM32, HT40 WiFi, 4MB flash, 520KB SRAM, Bluetooth
Prototyping Gear	
Full-size Breadboard (*https://oreil.ly/sZo2h*)	Standard breadboard with power rails
Half-size Breadboard (*https://oreil.ly/bfpYJ*)	Compact breadboard with power rails
Connector Wires (*https://oreil.ly/RoHW1*)	Bundle with various lengths and molex tips

Table A-2. Peripherals and components

Component	Specs
Chapter 8	
100Ω Resistor (*https://oreil.ly/YOgc7*)	Carbon fiber through-hole
470Ω Resistor (*https://oreil.ly/wwVrn*)	Carbon fiber through-hole
Blue LEDs (*https://oreil.ly/xJqOL*)	3mm diameter, ~3.0V Forward Voltage
NeoPixel Flora (*https://oreil.ly/dyCpE*)	Individual RGB NeoPixel LED
NeoPixel Stick (*https://oreil.ly/8zpaZ*)	8 RGB NeoPixel LEDs, stick mounted
NeoPixel Ring (*https://oreil.ly/Mwoph*)	24 RGB NeoPixel LEDs, ring mounted
Chapter 9	
RGB LED (*https://oreil.ly/eOTBv*)	5mm, common cathode
470Ω Resistor (*https://oreil.ly/8jyjo*)	Carbon fiber through-hole
TMP36 Temperature Sensor (*https://oreil.ly/JQFud*)	Analog, range -50 to 125 C
Four-Digit Display (*https://oreil.ly/RO5P5*)	Red, MAX7219 driver (alternative to VMA425)
Tactile Button (*http://adafru.it/367*)	Simple push-button
NeoPixel Ring (*https://oreil.ly/8GOWh*)	24 RGB NeoPixel LEDs, ring mounted
Chapter 10	
NeoPixel Stick (*https://oreil.ly/mPpVW*)	8 RGB NeoPixel LEDs, stick mounted
Chapter 11	
RFM69HCW Transceiver (*https://adafru.it/3070*) (2x)	900MHz (Americas)
Navigation Switch (*https://adafru.it/504*)	Through-hole, 5-way
Rubber Nubbin Cap (*https://adafru.it/4697*)	Fits navigation joystick
TT Motor Wheel (*https://adafru.it/3766*) (2x)	Orange spokes, clear tire
TT Motor Gearbox (*https://adafru.it/3777*) (2x)	200 RPM, 3 - 6VDC
Motor Driver Breakout (*https://adafru.it/3297*)	DRV8833 chip
Chassis for TT Motors (*https://adafru.it/3796*)	Aluminum, purple
Chapter 12	
OLED Display (*https://adafru.it/4440*)	0.91", 128x32 pixel, I2C
TMP36 Temperature Sensor (*https://adafru.it/165*)	Analog, range -50 to 125 C

In general, I tried to stick with breadboard projects that are easy to set up and alter. If you build something stable and want to reflect that stability by getting off the breadboard, I highly recommend the Adafruit Guide to Excellent Soldering (*https://oreil.ly/vytmN*). They give you some great advice on both the hardware and techniques that pro hobbyists use to create more permanent projects. I will add one bit of emphasis to their otherwise fantastic guide: in the section on soldering irons, the "Best Irons" really are the best. They are definitely more expensive, so won't be for everyone, but if you can afford it, irons like the Hakko FX-888D (*https://https://adafru.it/1204*) elevate the tedium of soldering header pins to a meditative art.

VS Code

I do my non-Arduino coding with Visual Studio Code (*https://oreil.ly/C6v3D*) from Microsoft. And while it is written by Microsoft, VS Code also works on Linux and macOS. It's highly configurable and has a vibrant extension ecosystem for just about every possible programming language and web development framework. The "C/C++" extension is great for working with C, if nothing else.

Arduino IDE

Throughout this book, I relied on the Arduino IDE (*https://oreil.ly/7vXun*) for compiling and uploading the microcontroller projects. The Arduino IDE is cross-platform and has excellent support for a wide range of microcontrollers from many different vendors.

The Arduino site also has a useful Language Reference (*https://oreil.ly/VH8RZ*) and several tutorials (*https://oreil.ly/OWYJy*) covering everything from simple "getting started" topics to more advanced hacking techniques for really diving into the Arduino platform.

 I should point out that for folks who really enjoy the VS Code environment, there is growing enthusiasm for PlatformIO (*https://platformio.org*). Per their About page: "PlatformIO is a cross-platform, cross-architecture, multiple framework, professional tool for embedded systems engineers and for software developers who write applications for embedded products."

It has a standalone option, but it also has a mature VS Code extension. You can find out more details on their VS Code Integration (*https://oreil.ly/3ZH3G*) page.

Fritzing

You may have noticed the cute circuitry-as-font word "fritzing" in our wiring diagrams. If you build any projects that you decide to share with others, you can create these types of diagrams yourself. The good folks at Fritzing (*https://fritzing.org*) created the software I used. The design application is cross-platform, and many third parties have created a truly remarkable number of visually appealing contributions to the libraries of controllers and components. It's also delightfully intuitive, especially if you've had any experience with other design and layout tools, such as OmniGraffle (*https://oreil.ly/zODll*) or Inkscape (*https://inkscape.org*). They do request a (very!) modest fee, and I find it worth every penny if you can afford it.

You can find a wealth of fritzing-friendly components online as well. Their forum contains some great, high-quality contributions such as the 4-digit, 7-segment display used in Figure 9-5, contributed by Desnot4000. You can also import SVG files to create custom components if needed.

If you really get going with your own electronics projects, Fritzing's software can also be used to produce custom circuit boards. Your hobby has never looked so professional! Dedicated to making hardware open and accessible to more and more folks, I could not be more impressed with this group and their wider user community.

GNU Compiler Collection

Last but most definitely not least, I used the GNU C compiler (as does the Arduino IDE) from the impossibly useful GNU Compiler Collection (*https://gcc.gnu.org*). As you probably noticed in "Tools Required" on page 2, it can take a little effort to get these tools installed on some platforms, but the breadth and quality of these compilers is unparalleled. Combined with their open source ethos, it really is hard to beat GNU software anywhere it's available.

printf() Format Specifier Details

The formats supported by the `printf()` function almost comprise their own language. While not an exhaustive list, this appendix details all of the options I use throughout this book. I also describe how the options work with the different types of output, even if I do not use a given combination. As with so much of programming, it is useful to try stuff out yourself to see how the pieces fit together.

The code examples include a simple C program that goes through the more popular combinations of flags, widths, precisions, and types. You can compile and run *popular_formats.c* as is, or you can edit it to tweak some of the lines and test your own combinations.

If you want to know even more about the things you can specify in `printf()`, including nonstandard and implementation-specific options, I recommend the Wikipedia page devoted to just this topic (*https://oreil.ly/Adirl*).

Specifier Syntax

The specifier as I use it throughout this book contains three optional elements and one required type arranged like so:

```
% flag(s) width . precision type
```

Again, the flag (or flags), width, and precision are not required.

Specifier Types

How `printf()` interprets a given value to print depends on the type specifier you use. The value 65, for example, would print as the letter "A" with %c (characters) but as "41" with %x (hexadecimal integers). Table B-1 summarizes the types we have used throughout this book, although it is not an exhaustive list.

Table B-1. Format specifier types for `printf()`

Specifier	Type(s)	Description
%c	char	Print out a single character
%d	char, int, short, long	Print signed integer values in decimal (base 10)
%f	float, double	Print floating point values
%i	char, int, short	Print integer values in base 10 (same as %d for output)
%o	int, short, long	Print integer values in octal (base 8)
%p	address	Print pointers (as hexadecimal address)
%s	char[]	Print a string (array of char) as text
%u	unsigned (char, int, short)	Print unsigned integer values in decimal
%x	char, int, short, long	Print integer values in hexadecimal (base 16)

The %i and %u integer types can use length modifiers. l or ll (e.g., %li or %llu) tell `printf()` to expect long or long long length arguments. For floating point types, L can be used (e.g., %Ld) to indicate a long double argument.

Specifier Flags

Each type you specify can be modified with one or more flags. Table B-2 lists the specifier flags. Not all flags have an effect on every type, and all flags are optional.

Table B-2. Format specifier flags for `printf()`

Specifier	Description
-	Left-align output within its field
+	Force plus sign (+) prefix on positive numeric values
(space)	Force space prefix on positive numeric values (as opposed to no prefix at all)
0	Pad left of numeric values with 0s (if they do not fill a field where width is specified)
#	Print a prefix (0, 0x, or 0X) when used with o, x, or X types

You see these flags used more often when you have numeric, columnar output, although flags like the "-" can be used on strings as well.

Width and Precision

For any specifier, you can supply a minimum width for the output field. (The minimum qualifier means that no truncation occurs for values that are larger than the given width.) The default is to align output to the right, but that can be changed with the - flag noted in Table B-2.

You can also supply a precision, which can affect the maximum width for output. For floating point types, it dictates the number of digits to the right of the decimal separator. For strings, it truncates over-long values. It is ignored for integer types.

Common Formats

To see some of the more common or popular formats in action, take a look at *appB/popular_formats.c* (*https://oreil.ly/R2vNI*). It's just a big batch of printf() calls, but it contains a wide variety of examples using different format specifiers. I won't bother with the source listing here, but the output makes for a quick reference:

```
appB$ gcc popular_formats.c
appB$ ./a.out
char Examples
  Simple char:            %c      |y|
  In a 9-char field:      %9c     |        y|
  Left, 9-char field:     %-9c    |y        |
  The percent sign:       %%      |%|


int Examples
  Simple int:             %i      |76|
  Simple decimal int:     %d      |76|
  Simple octal int:       %o      |114|
  Prefixed octal int:     %#o     |0114|
  Simple hexadecimal int: %x      |4c|
  Uppercase hexadecimal:  %X      |4C|
  Prefixed hexadecimal:   %#x     |0x4c|
  Prefixed uppercase:     %#X     |0X4C|
  In a 9-column field:    %9i     |       76|
  Left, 9-column field:   %-9i    |76       |
  Zeros, 9-column field:  %09i    |000000076|
  With plus prefix:       %+i     |+76|
    negative value:               |-12|
  With space prefix:      % i     | 76|
    negative value:               |-12|
  Huge number:            %llu    |28054511505742|
  (Ignored) precision:    %1.1d   |76|


float Examples
  Simple float:           %f      |216.289993|
  2 decimal places:       %.2f    |216.29|
  1 decimal place:        %.1f    |216.3|
  No decimal places:      %.0f    |216|
  In a 12-column field:   %12f    |  216.289993|
  2 decimals, 12 columns: %12.2f  |      216.29|
  Left, 12-column field:  %-12.2f |216.29      |
```

```
string (char[]) Examples
   Simple string:          %s       |Ada Lovelace|
   In a 20-column field:   %20s     |        Ada Lovelace|
   Left, 20-column field:  %-20s    |Ada Lovelace        |
   6-column field:         %6s      |Ada Lovelace|
   6-columns, truncated:   %6.6s    |Ada Lo|


And last but not least, a blank line (\n):
```

The Wikipedia page on the printf format string (*https://oreil.ly/xvtiC*) has a comprehensive overview of the options available.

Index

Symbols

B

backslash (\), as escape character, 28-29
base cases, 115
base64 encoding, 97-101
binary numbers, comparison with other bases, 92-93
binary operators, 39
bits, byte conversion, 97-101
bitwise operators, 96-97
    optimization with, 229-230
blocks of code, 16, 52
boards (see Arduino microcontrollers)
body of code, 16
bool (variable type), 192
Boole, George, 47
Boolean values
    comparison operators, 48-49
    described, 47-48
    in if statements, 52
    logical operators, 49-51
branching, 47
    else statement, 54-57
    if statement, 52-58
    nesting in, 72-75
    switch statement, 58-63
break statement, 59, 74
buffer overflows, 86
buttons
    interrupts example, 216-218
    setup, 202-204
    temperature output example, 204-206
byte (variable type), 192, 229
bytes, bit conversion, 97-101

C

C in a Nutshell (Prinz and Crawford), 48
C programming language
    compatibility with other languages, 274
    downloading examples, 275
    jobs using, 274
    requirements for, 2-3
        in Linux, 12-14
        in macOS, 9-12
        in Windows, 3-8
    standards, 1
    strengths and weaknesses, 2
The C Programming Language (Kernighan and Ritchie), 1, 140
C standard library, 150

ctype.h, 160
math.h, 157-159
stdio.h, 150
stdlib.h, 150-154
string.h, 154-157
time.h, 159-160
C++
    considerations in Arduino programming, 185-186
    objects
        creating, 182
        LED lights, 183-185
    sketches and, 179-181
calling
    functions, 104-105
        nested calls, 114-115
        recursive calls, 115-118
    methods (C++), 182
capacity of arrays, length versus, 83-84
car example project
    hardware setup, 235-238
    initial software setup, 241-243
    preprocessor directives, 238
    preprocessor macros, 239
    radio control
        controller setup, 252-253, 260-261
        creating library, 253-258
        purpose of, 249-250
        retrofitting car for, 250-252
        updating car, 259-260
    type definitions, 240-241
careers using C, 274
carriage returns, 26
case statement, 59
casting (types), 42-44
ceil() function, 158
chaining else if statements, 55-57
changing array elements, 86
char (variable type), 25, 27-29, 30
    (see also characters)
characters
    accessing in strings, 88-89
    arrays of (see strings)
    ctype.h, 160
    encoding, 28
    special, 28-29
classes (C++), 179
CLion, 3
comparison operators, 48-49

About the Author

Marc Loy caught the programming bug after learning 6808 Assembly to program his school's HERO 1 in the 1980s. He developed and delivered training classes on Java, Unix internals, and networking at Sun Microsystems back in the day and has continued training a (much) wider audience ever since. He now spends his days consulting and writing on technical and media topics. He has also caught the maker bug and is exploring the fast-growing world of embedded electronics and wearables.

Colophon

The animal on the cover of *Smaller C* is an Atlantic wild canary (*Serinus canaria*). This bird, also known as the island or common canary, can be found in a variety of habitats on the Canary Islands (after which these birds are named), the Azores, and Madeira.

The Atlantic canary can range from 3.9 to 4.7 inches in length and weighs about a half an ounce on average. In the wild, these birds are mostly yellow-green in color with brown streaks along their backs, but a number of differently colored varieties have been bred in captivity. Males and females have similar coloring, although the plumage of female Atlantic canaries tends to be more grayish in color. Juvenile Atlantic canaries are mostly brown.

While they are typically found in open areas dotted with small trees, the Atlantic canary occurs in a variety of habitats, including artificial habitats such as parks and gardens. This social bird feeds in flocks and often builds its cup-shaped nests in groups, well-hidden near the ends or forks in tree branches. Given its wide (and growing) distribution, the conservation status of this bird is Least Concern. Many of the animals on O'Reilly covers are endangered; all of them are important to the world.

The cover illustration is by Karen Montgomery, based on a black and white engraving from Rev. J.G. Wood's *Animate Creation*. The cover fonts are Gilroy Semibold and Guardian Sans. The text font is Adobe Minion Pro; the heading font is Adobe Myriad Condensed; and the code font is Dalton Maag's Ubuntu Mono.

Lightning Source UK Ltd.
Milton Keynes UK
UKHW032225120721
387053UK00006B/20

9 781098 100339